MAD's
Al Jaffee
SWEATS OUT
ANOTHER BOOK

WARNER BOOKS

A Warner Communications Company

WARNER BOOKS EDITION

For information address:
E.C. Publications, Inc.
485 Madison Avenue
New York, N.Y. 10022

This Warner Books Edition is published by
arrangement with E.C. Publications, Inc.

**Warner Books, Inc.
666 Fifth Avenue
New York, N.Y. 10103**

A Warner Communications Company

Printed in the United States of America

First Printing: August, 1988

10 9 8 7 6 5 4 3 2 1

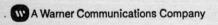

CONTENTS

DEDICATION

TO WHOM IT MAY CONCERN

EENIE, MEENIE, GENIE

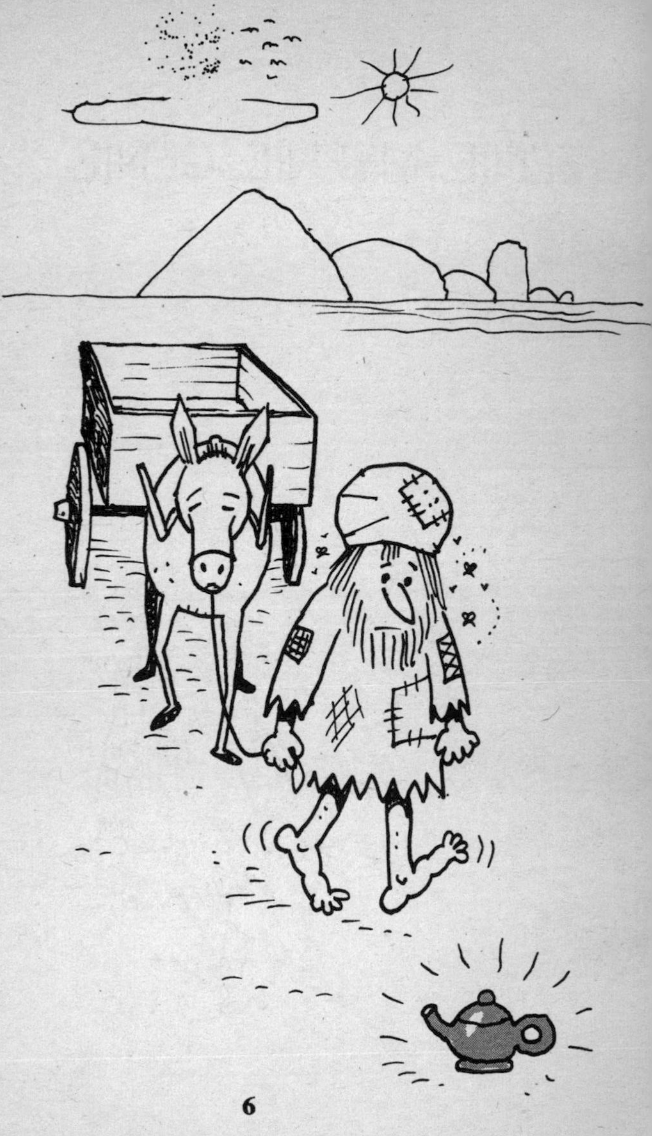

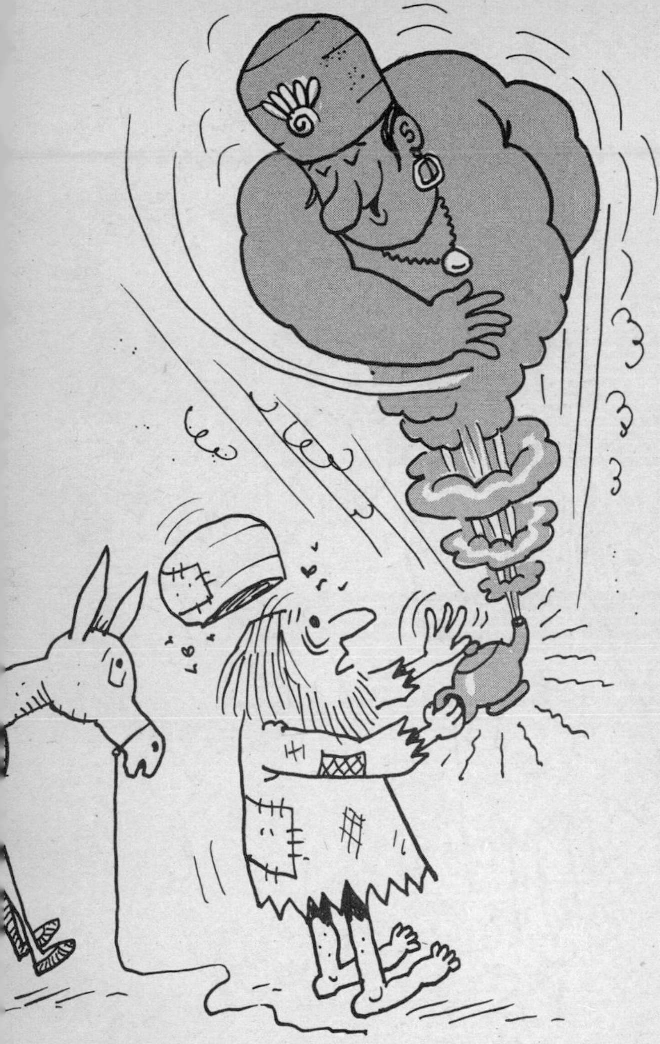

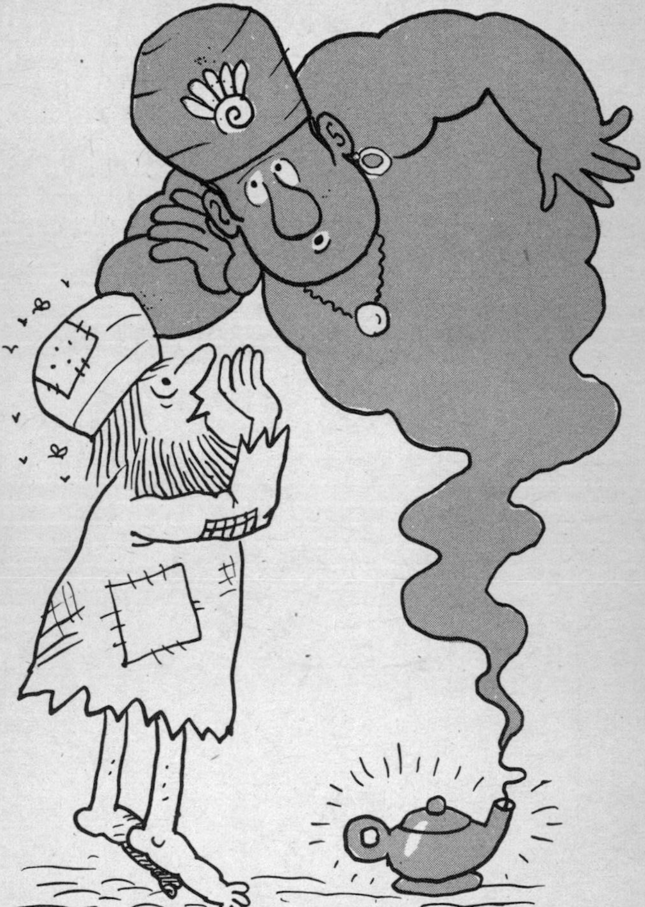

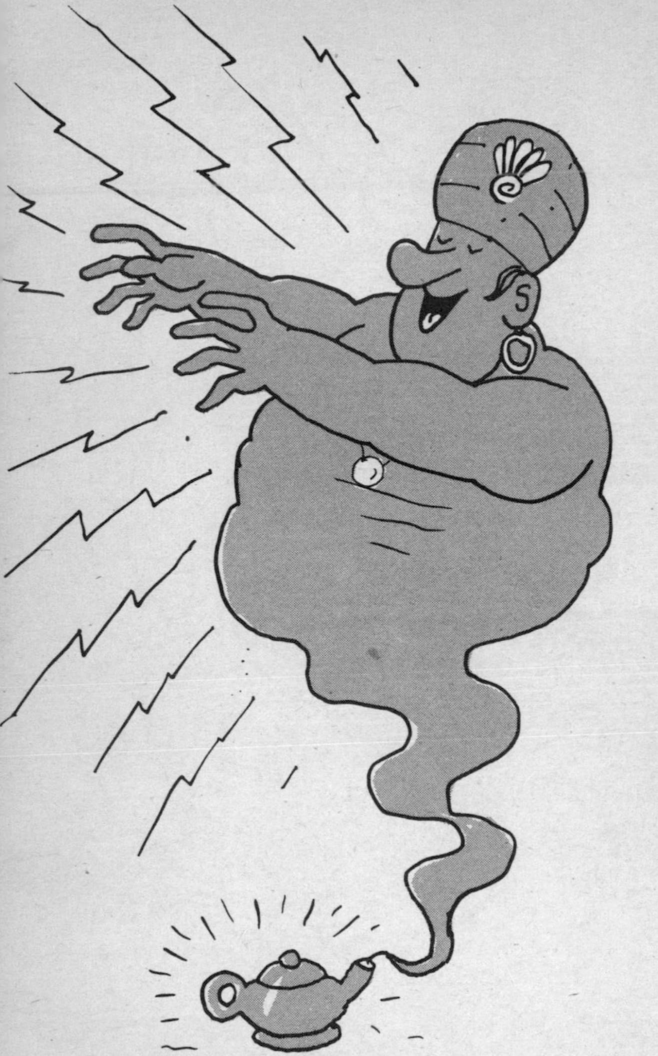
MORE

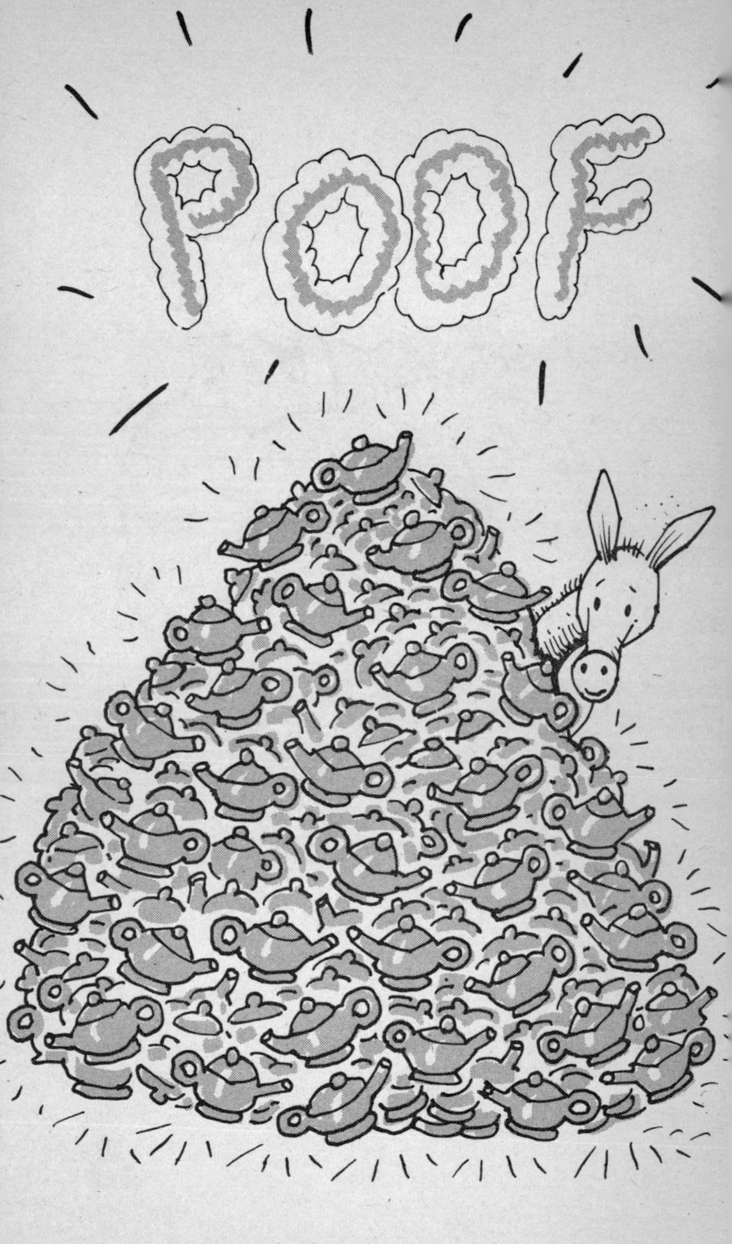
POOF

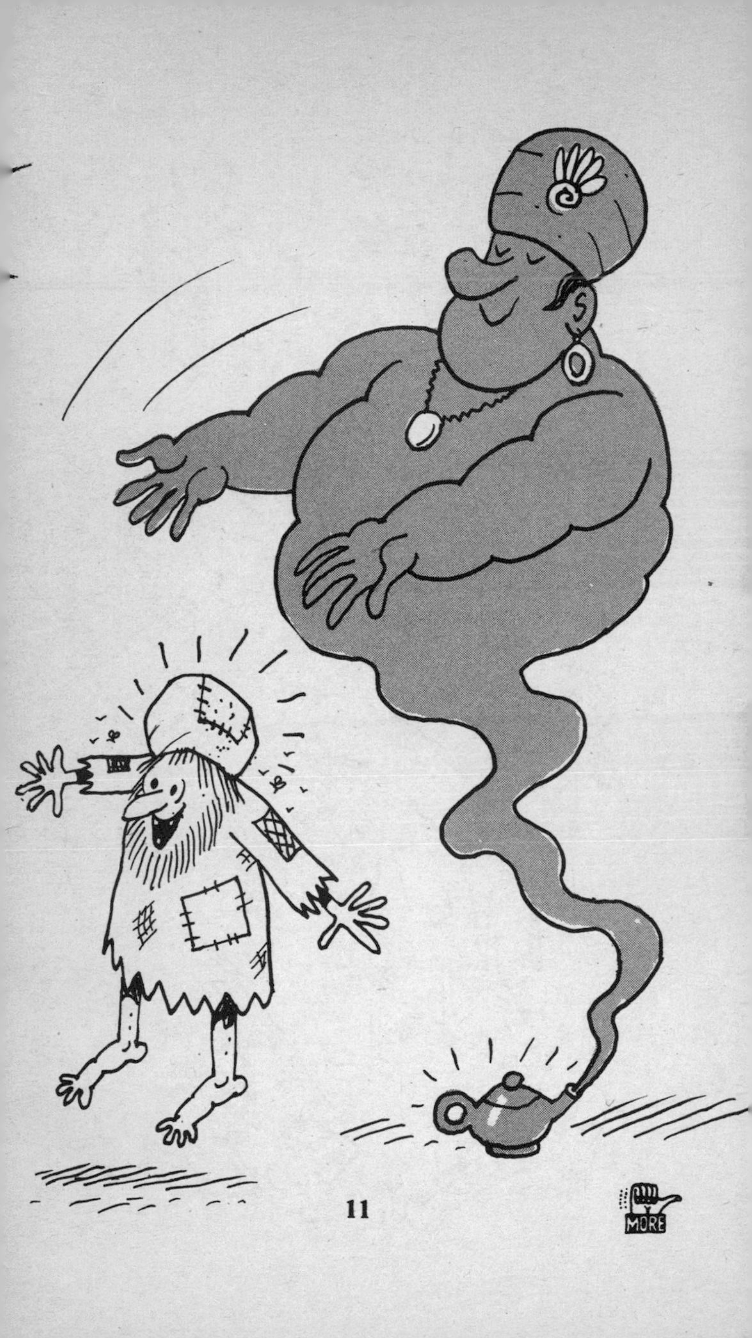
MORE

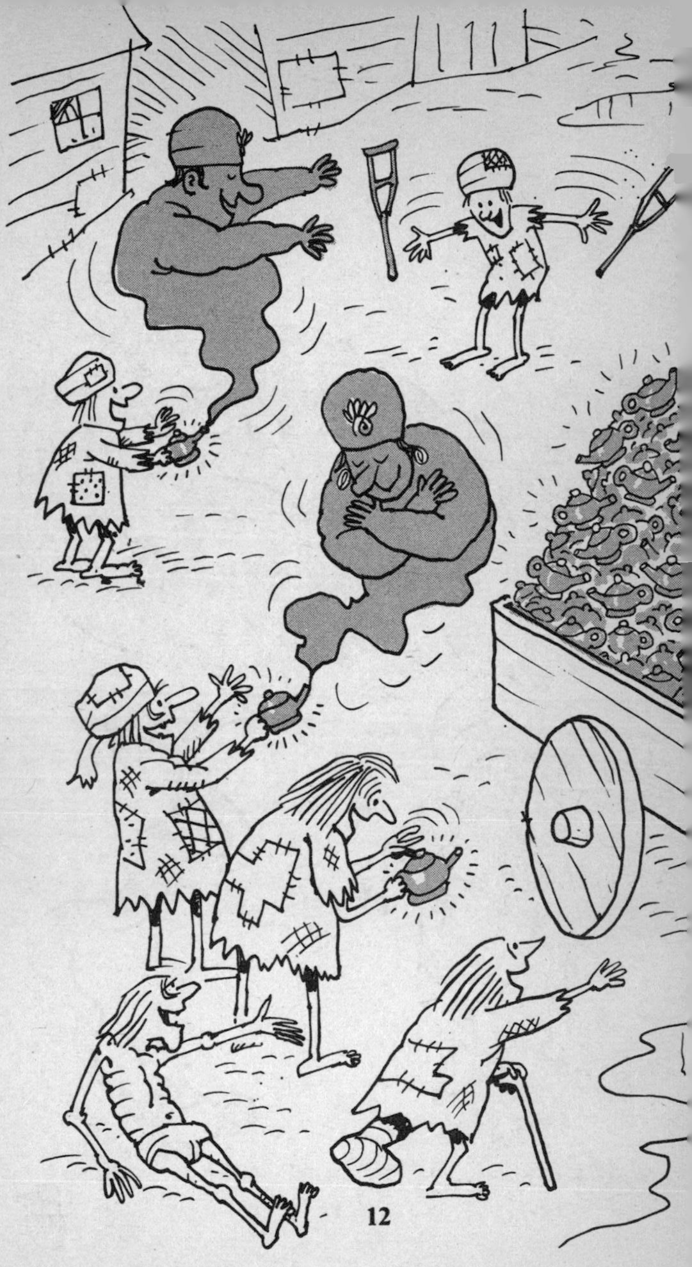

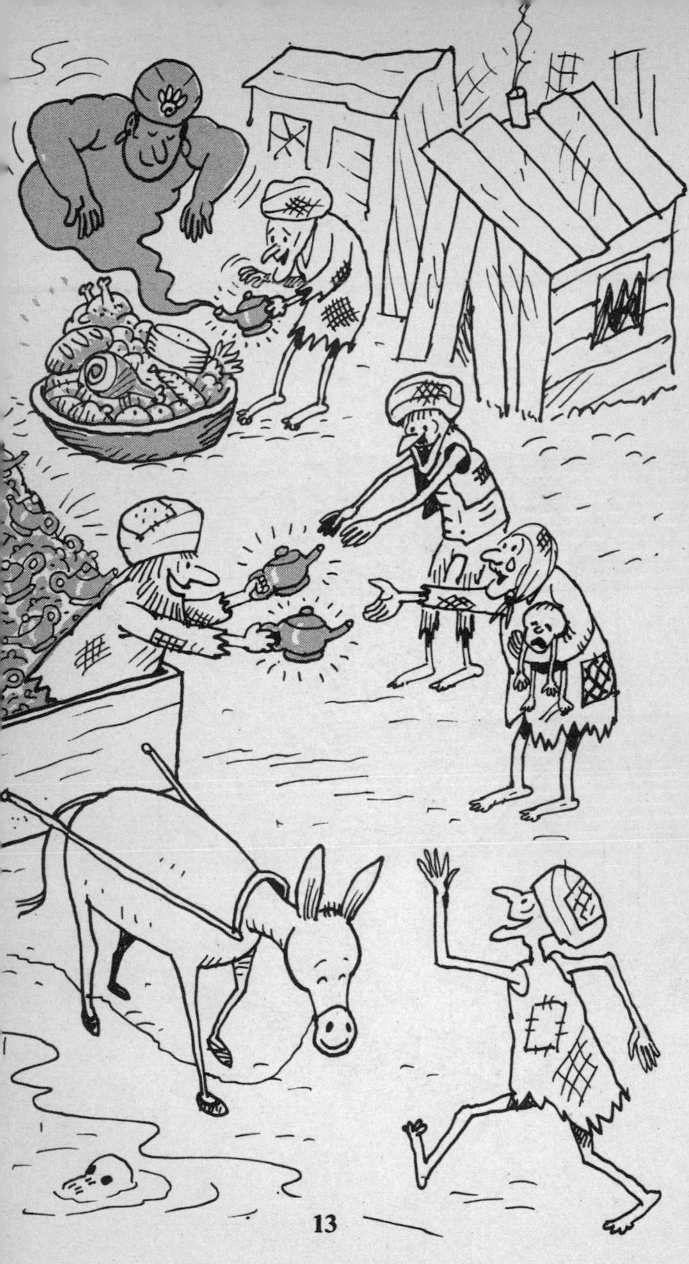

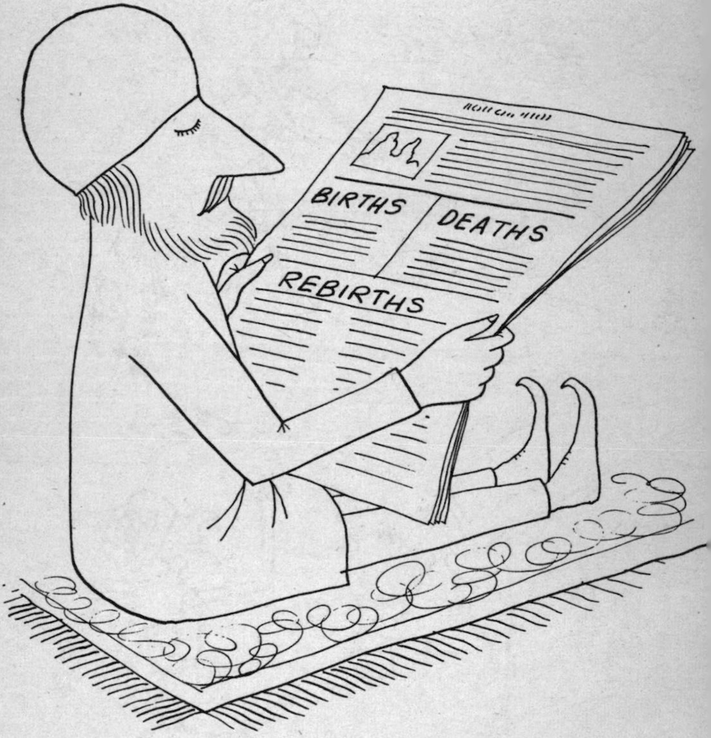
BIRTHS
DEATHS
REBIRTHS

VASE DAZE

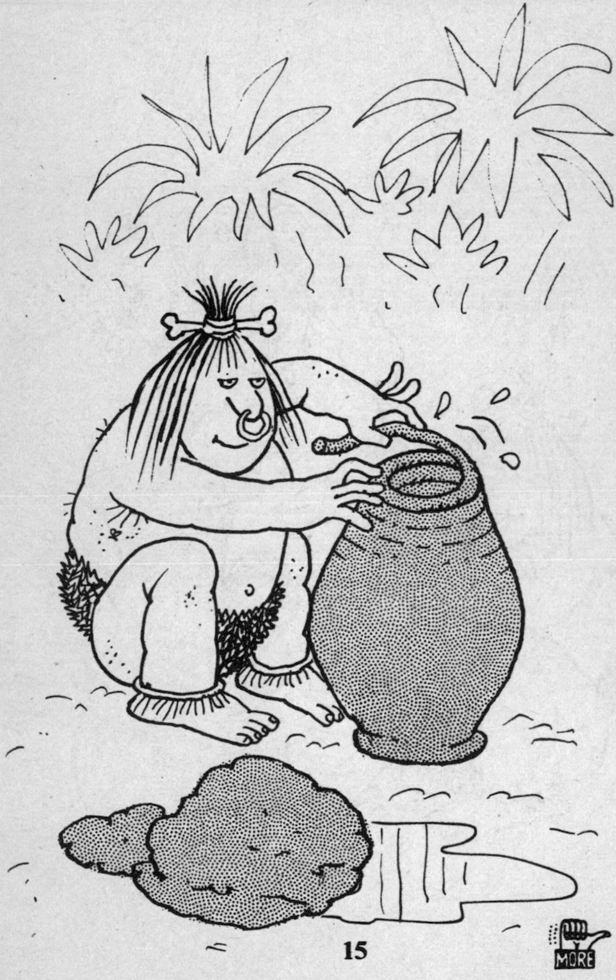

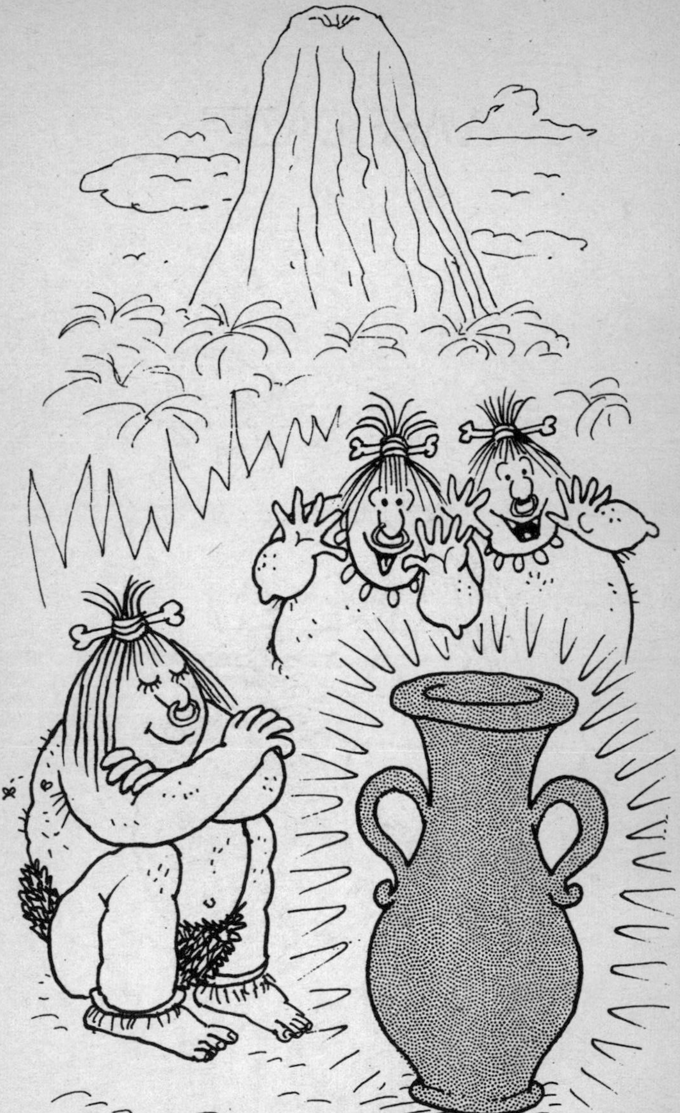

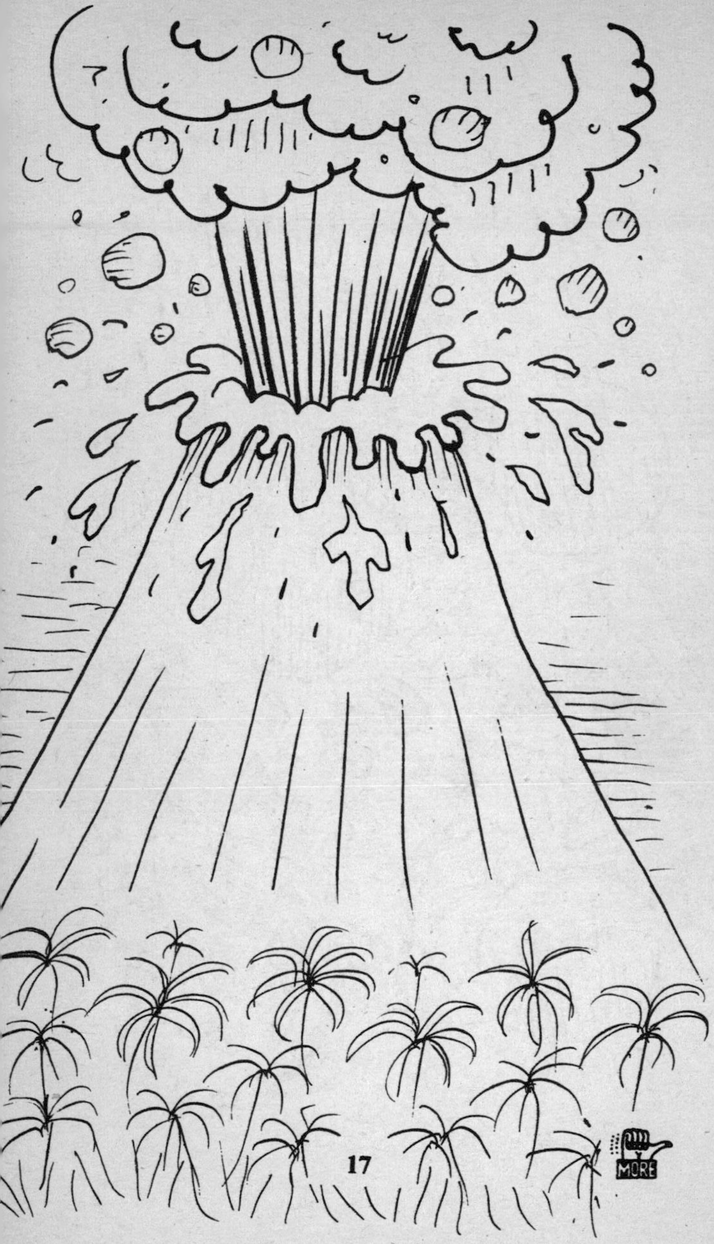

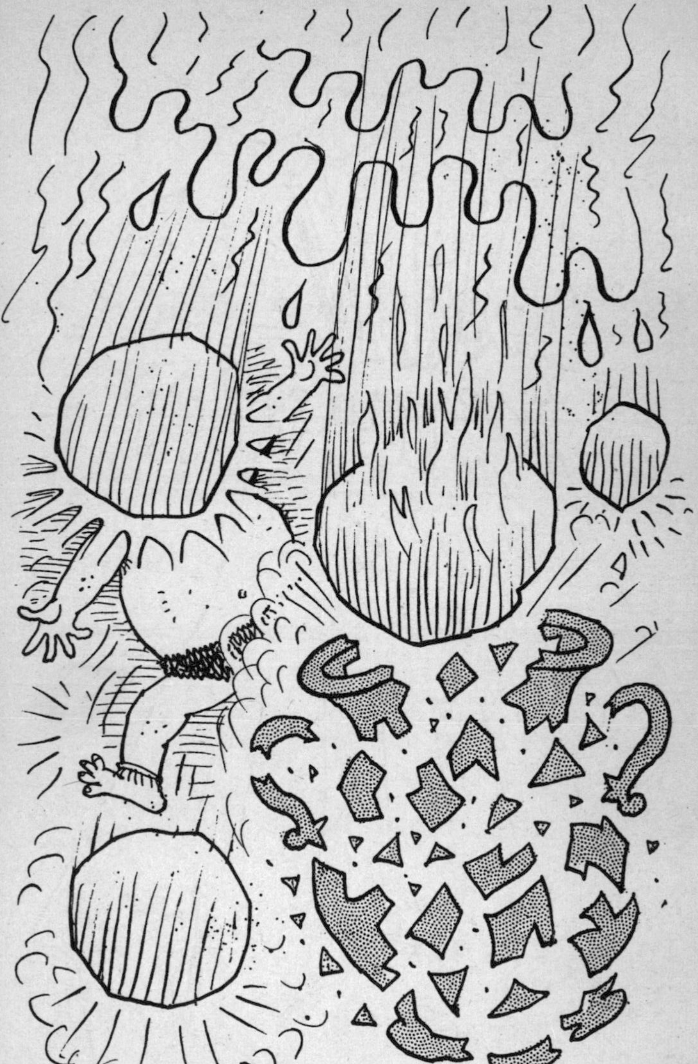

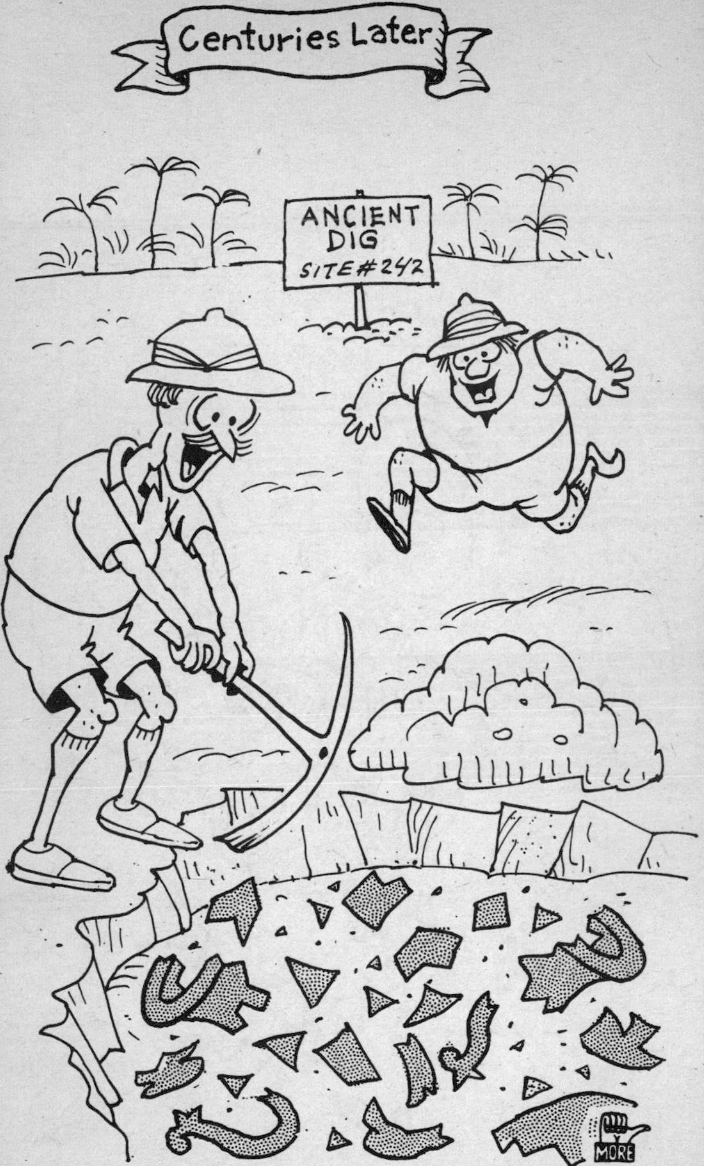
Centuries Later
ANCIENT DIG SITE #242
MORE

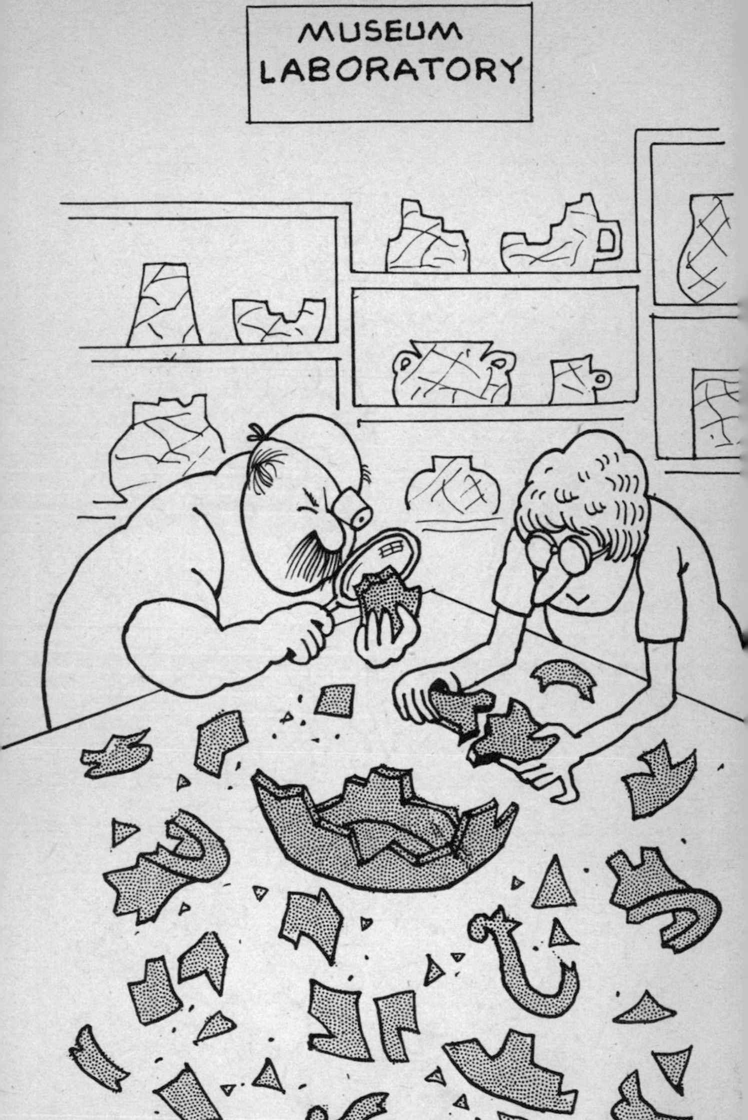
MUSEUM
LABORATORY

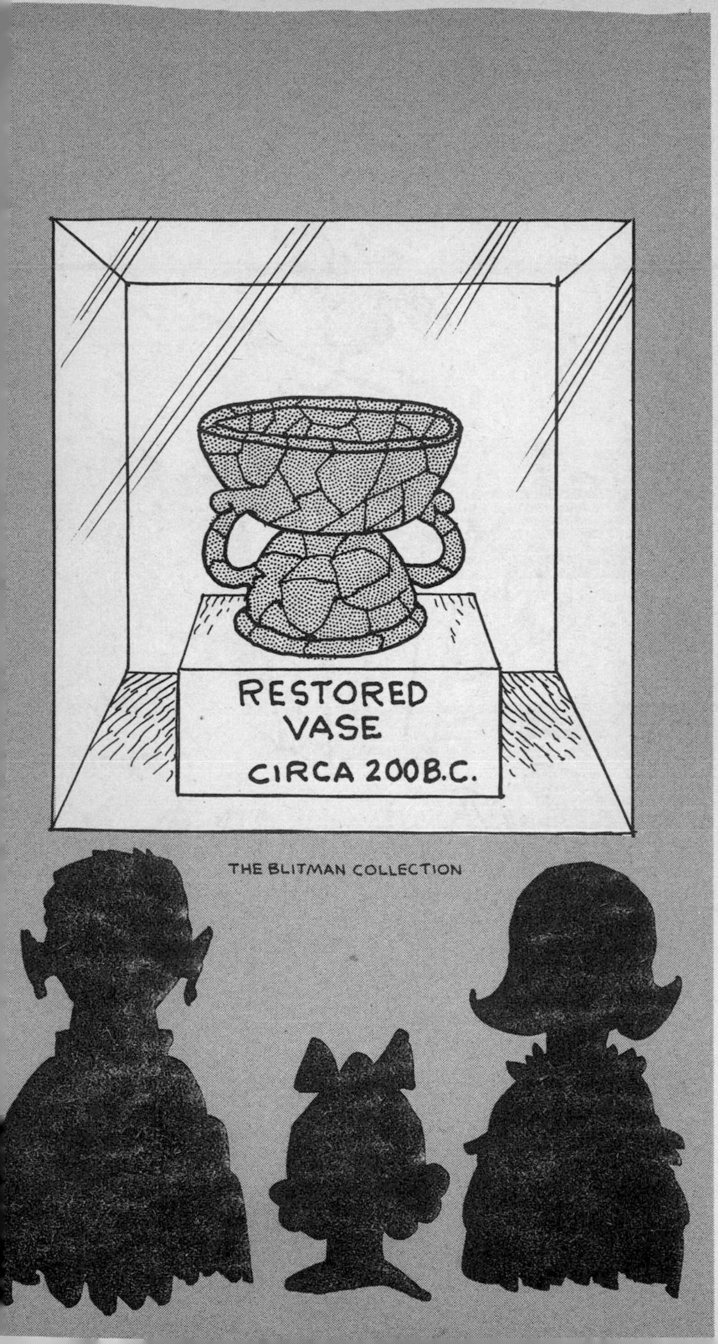
RESTORED
VASE
CIRCA 200 B.C.
THE BLITMAN COLLECTION

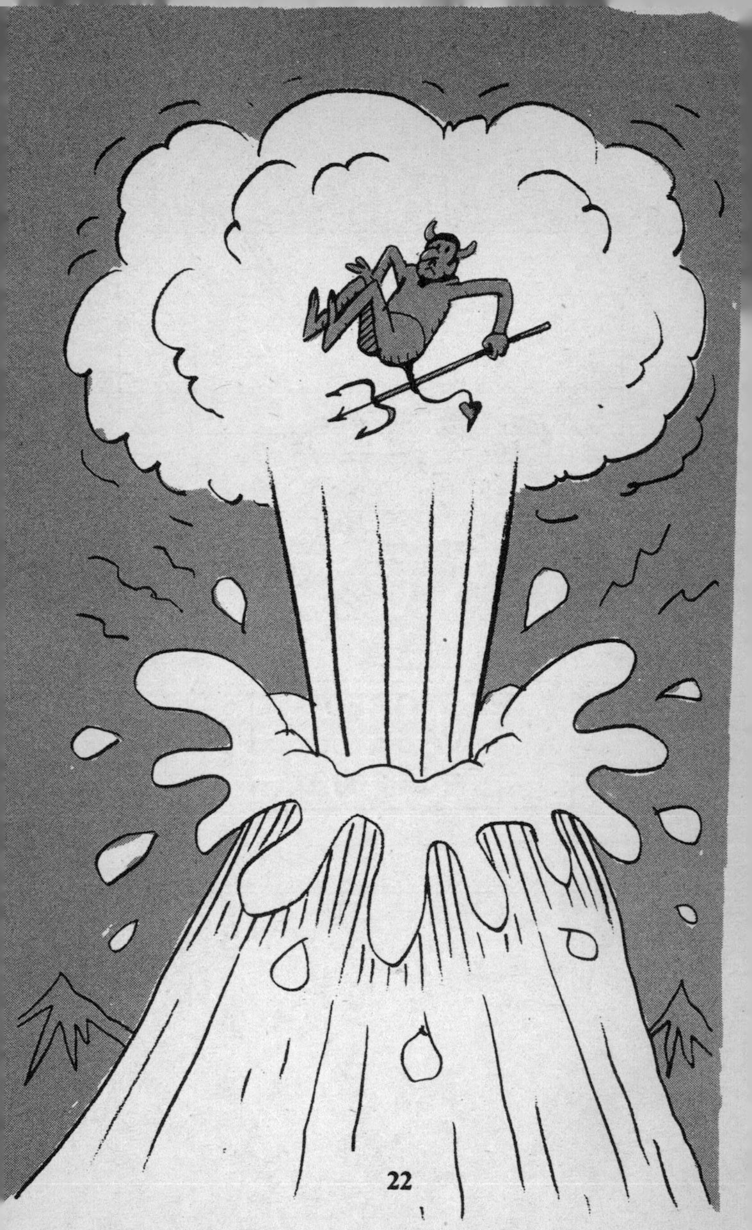

COMICAL CHEMICAL

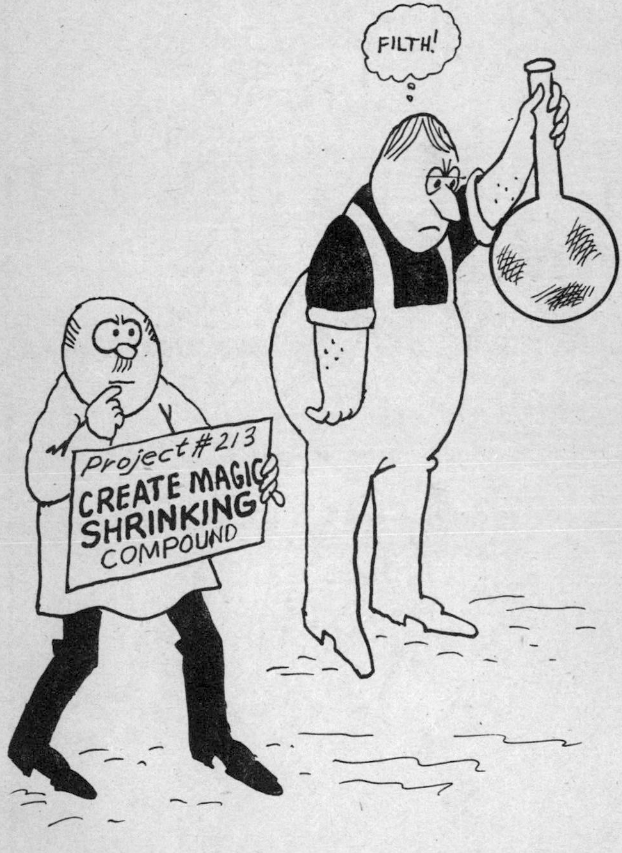
FILTH!
Project #213
CREATE MAGIC SHRINKING COMPOUND

MORE

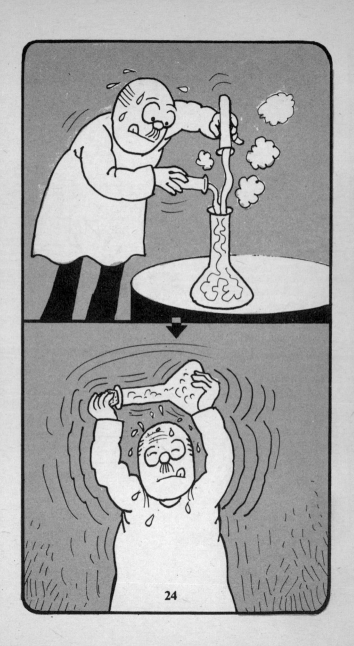

24

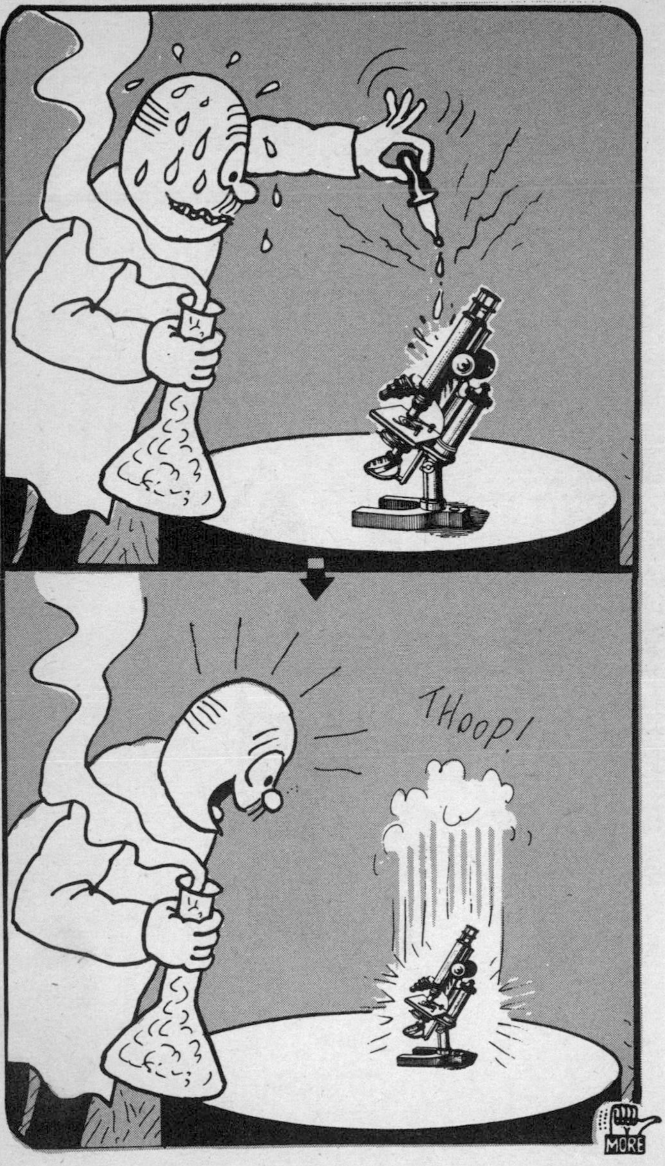
THOOP!
MORE

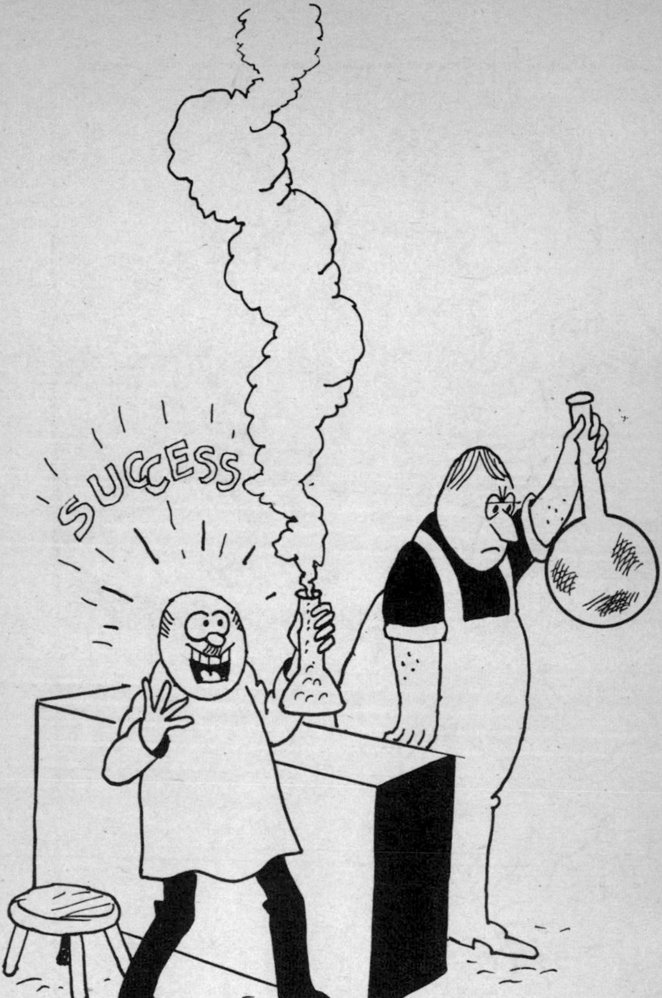
SUCCESS

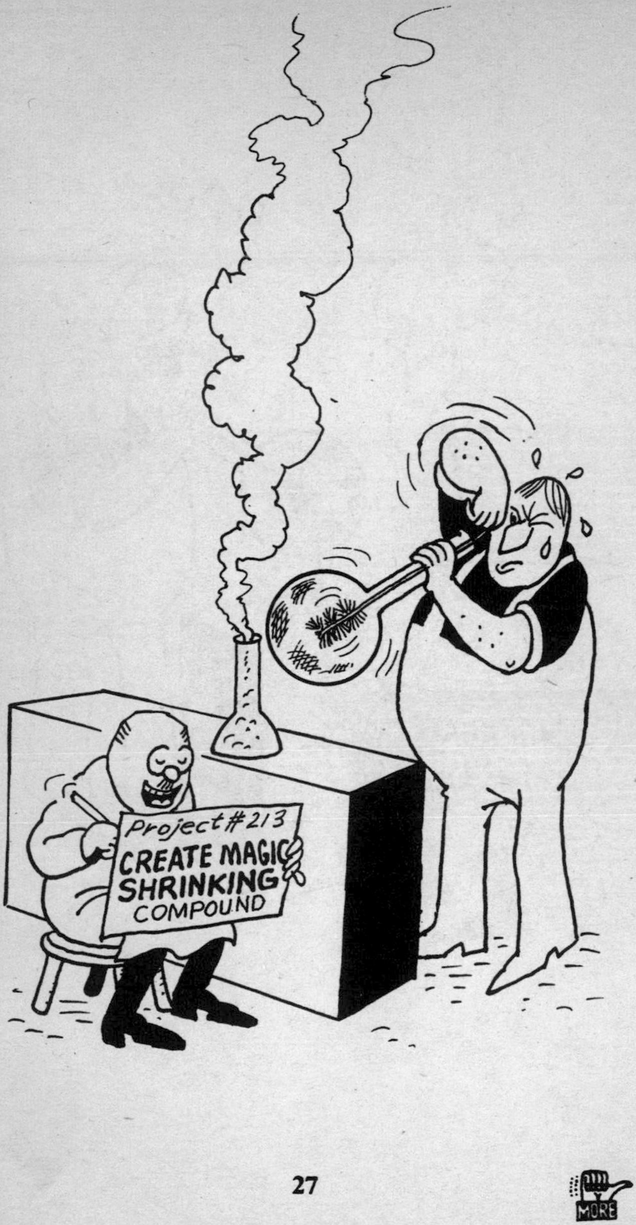
Project #213
CREATE MAGIC
SHRINKING
COMPOUND

MORE

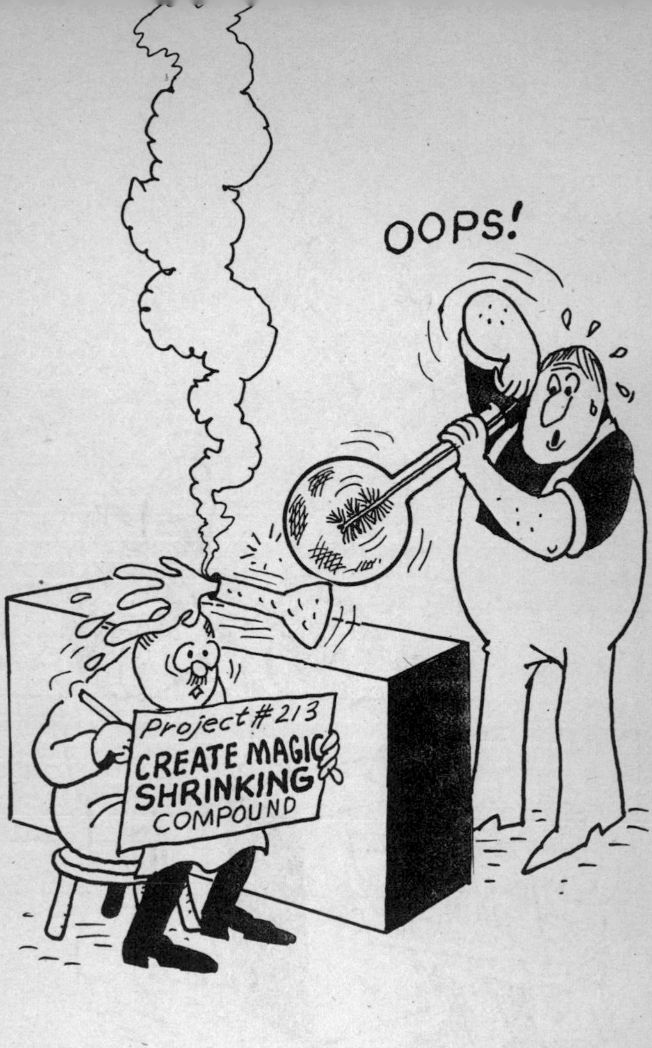
OOPS!
Project #213
CREATE MAGIC
SHRINKING
COMPOUND

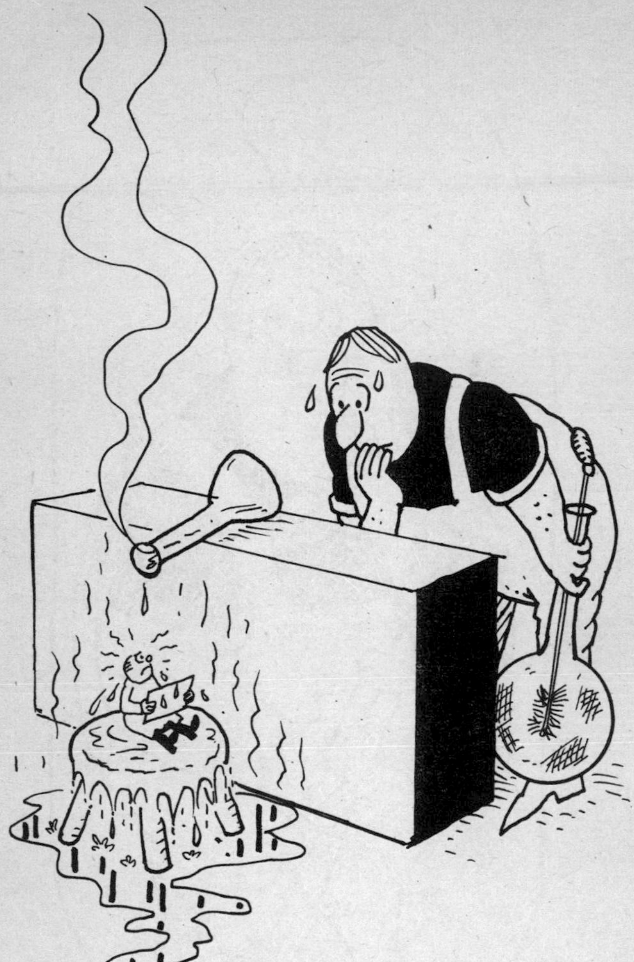

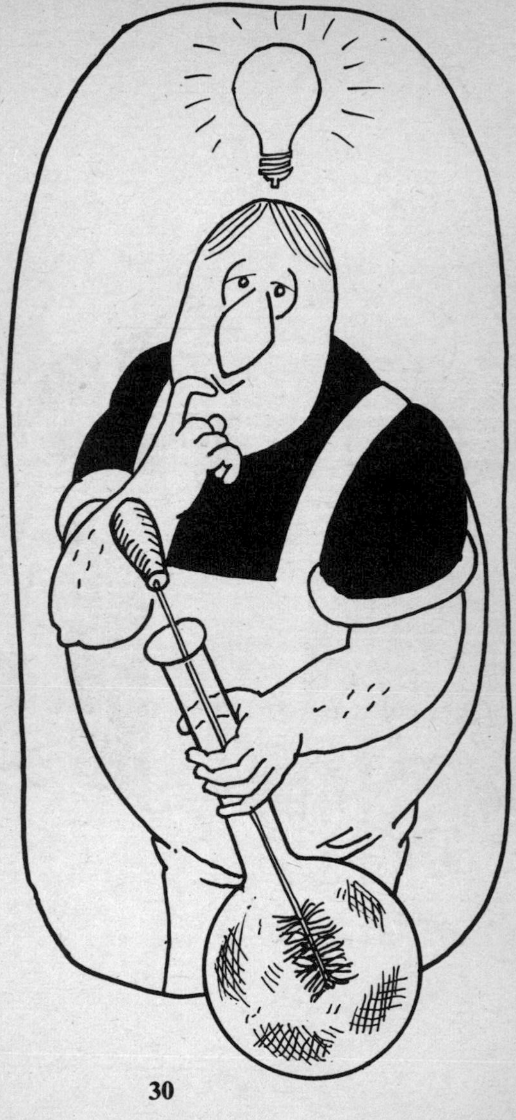

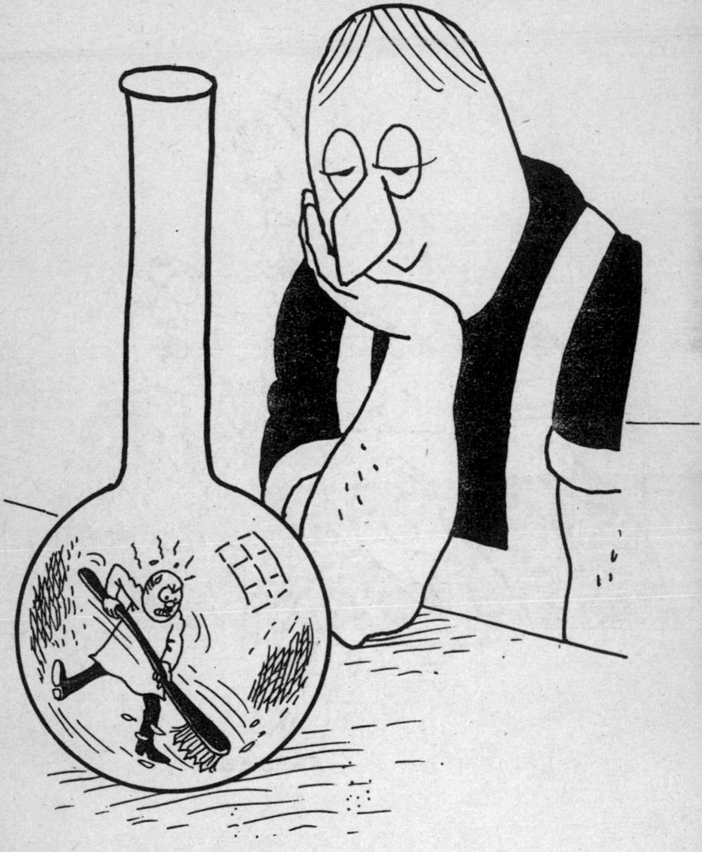

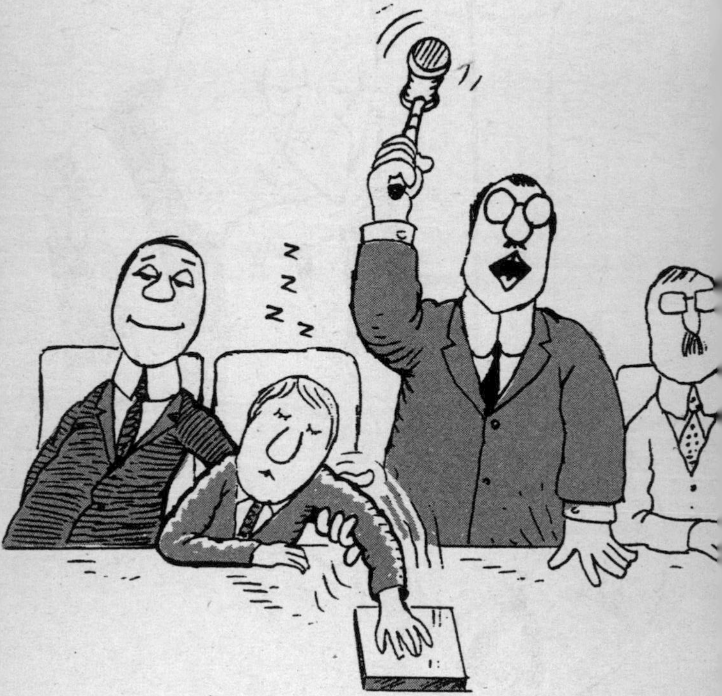
Z
Z
Z
Z

TILE TALES

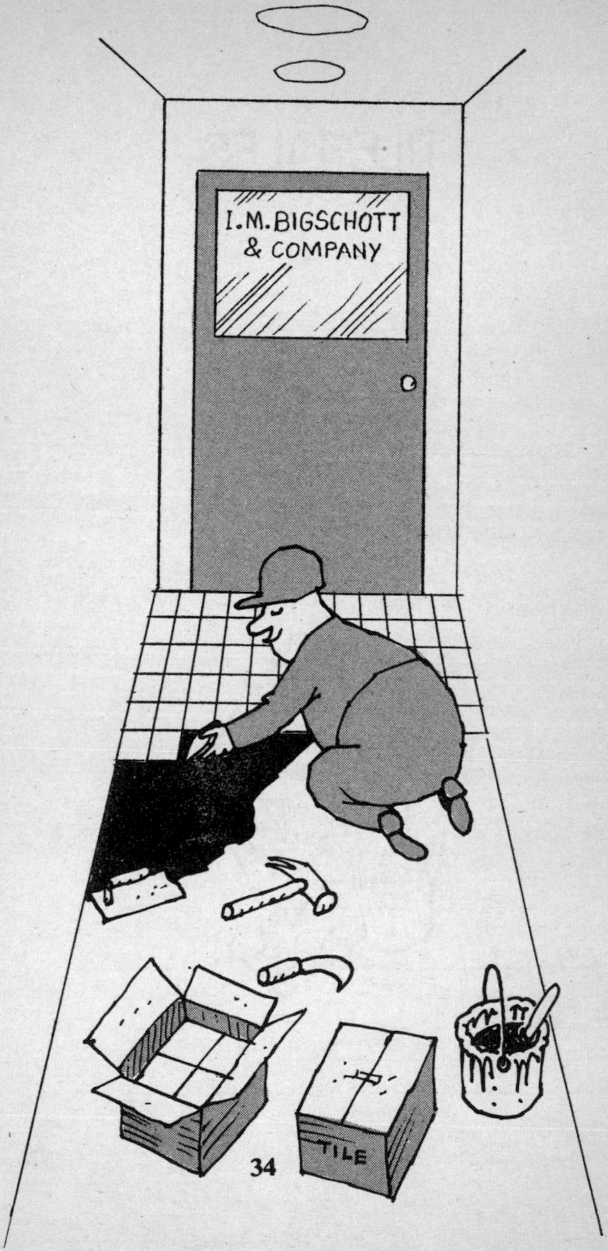
I.M. BIGSCHOTT
& COMPANY
TILE

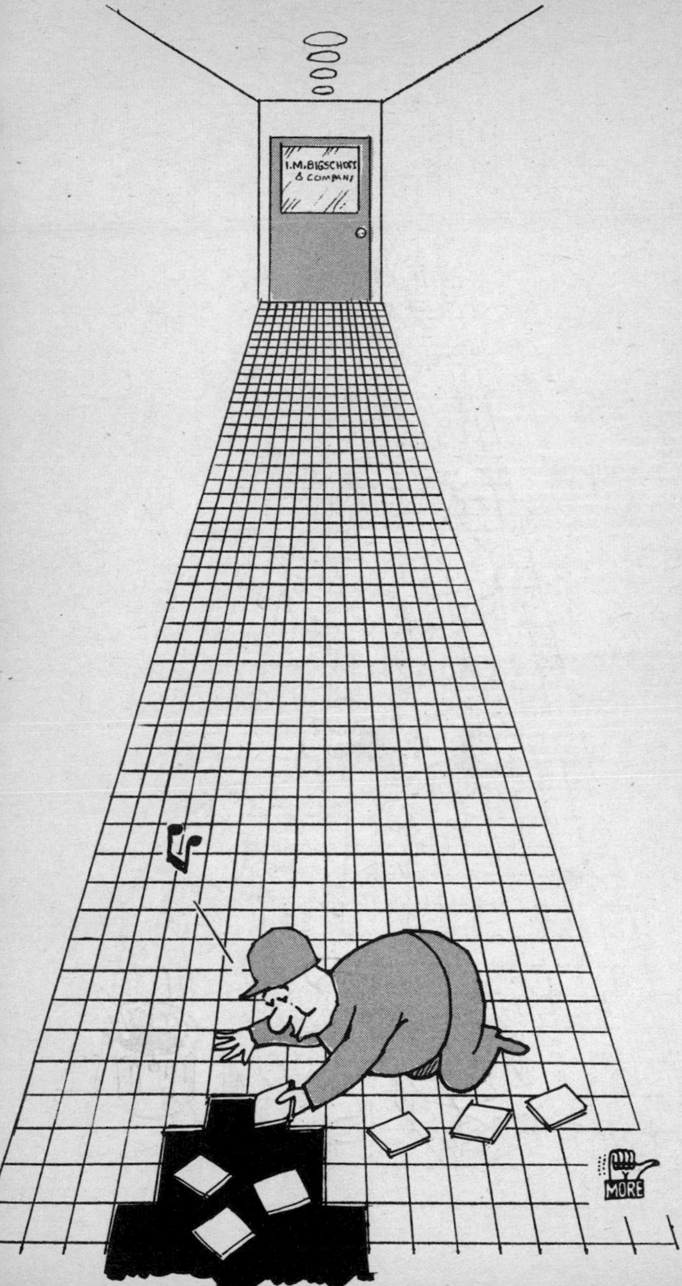
I.M. BIGSCHOTS
& COMPANY
MORE

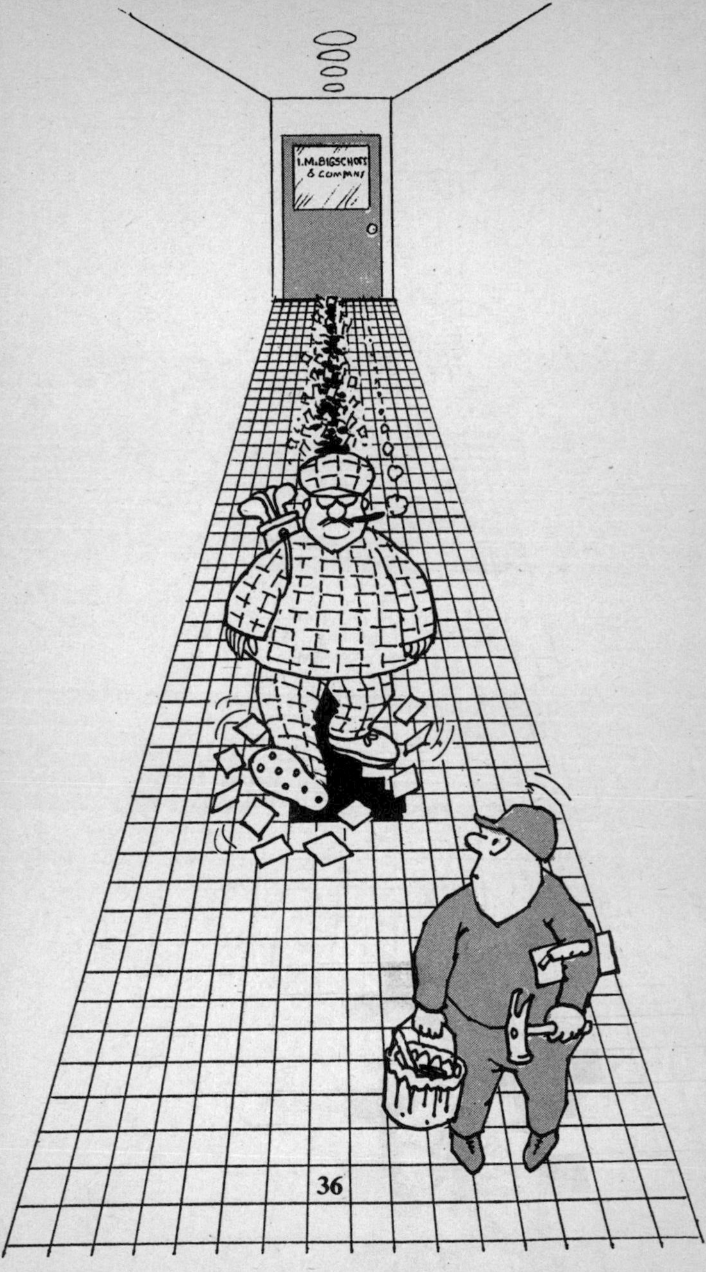
I.M.BIGSCHOTS
& COMPANY

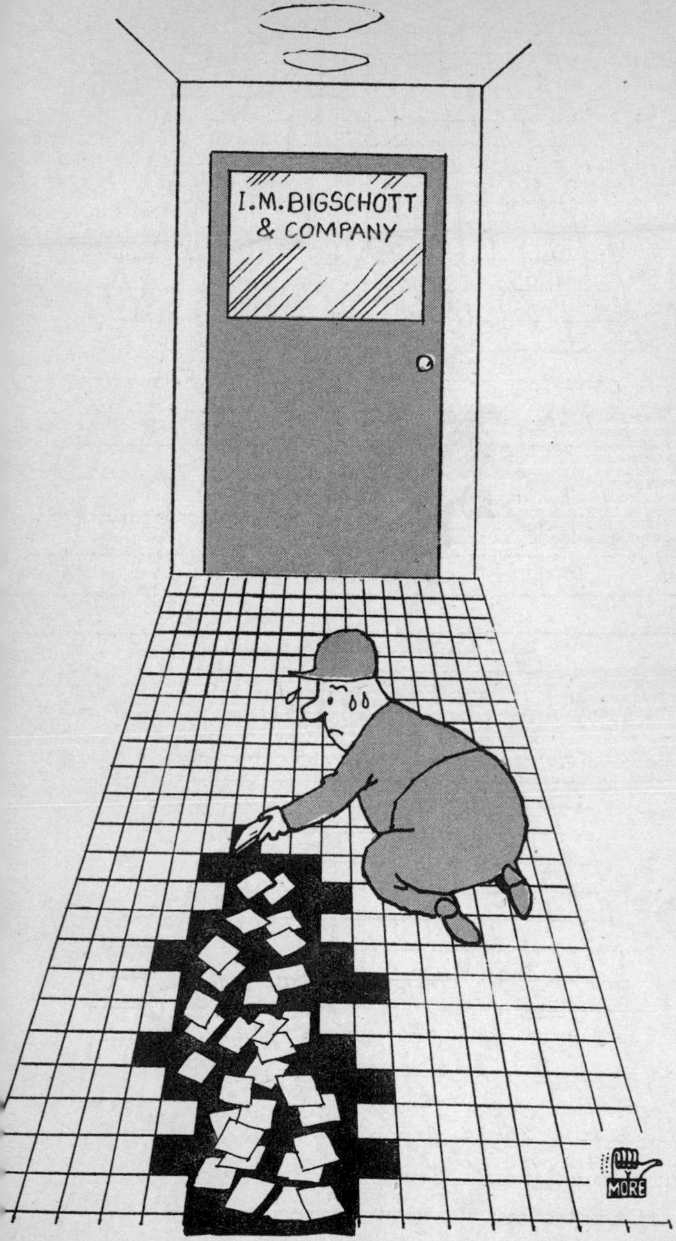
I.M. BIGSCHOTT
& COMPANY
MORE

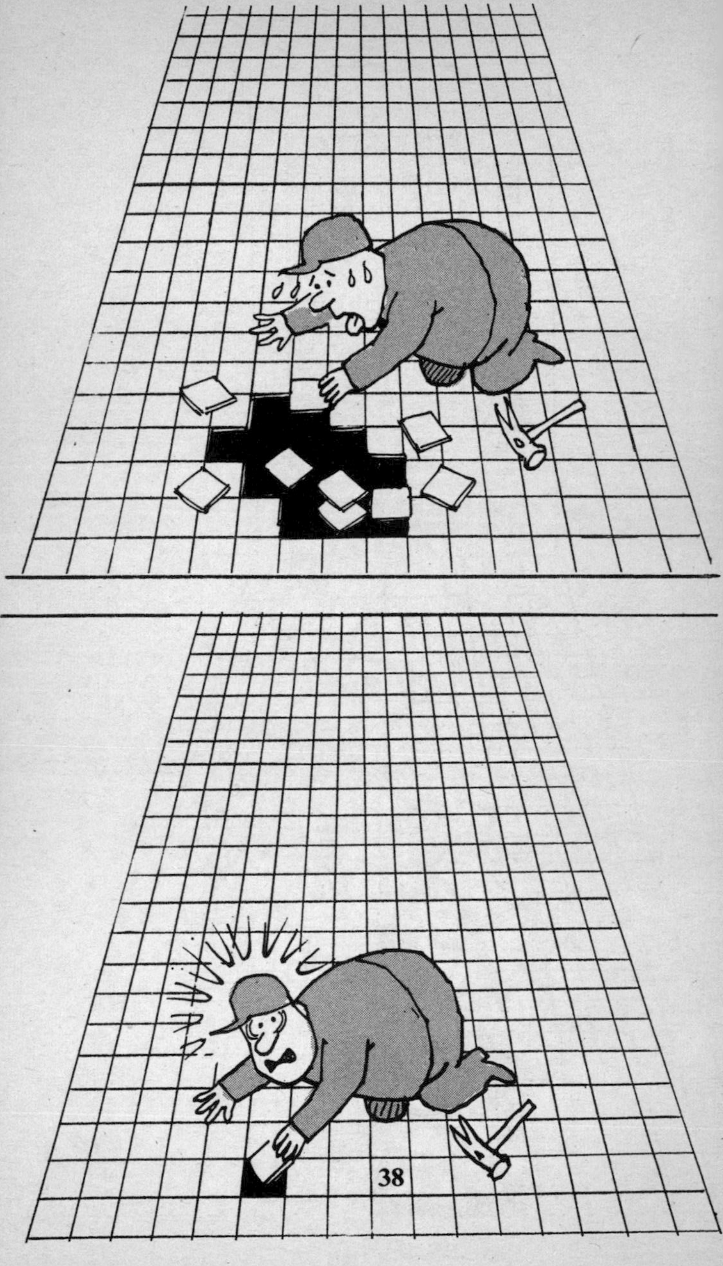

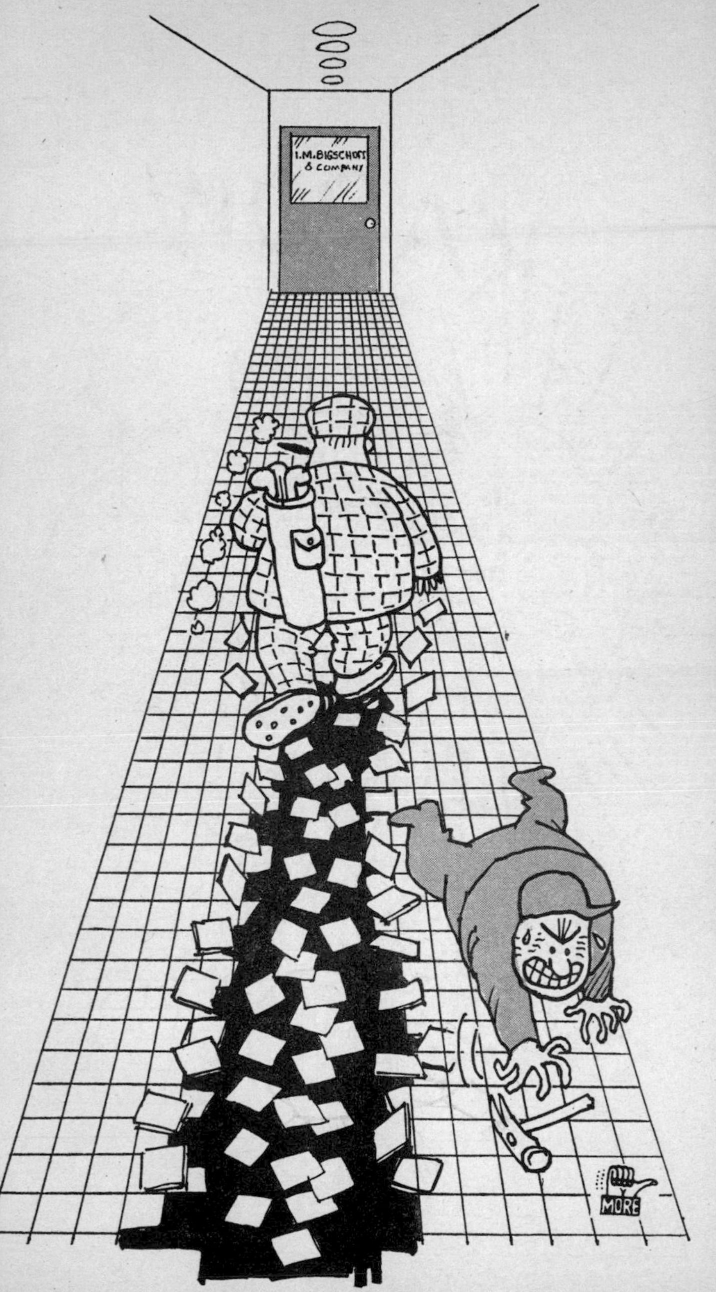
I.M. BIGSCHOTT
& COMPANY
MORE

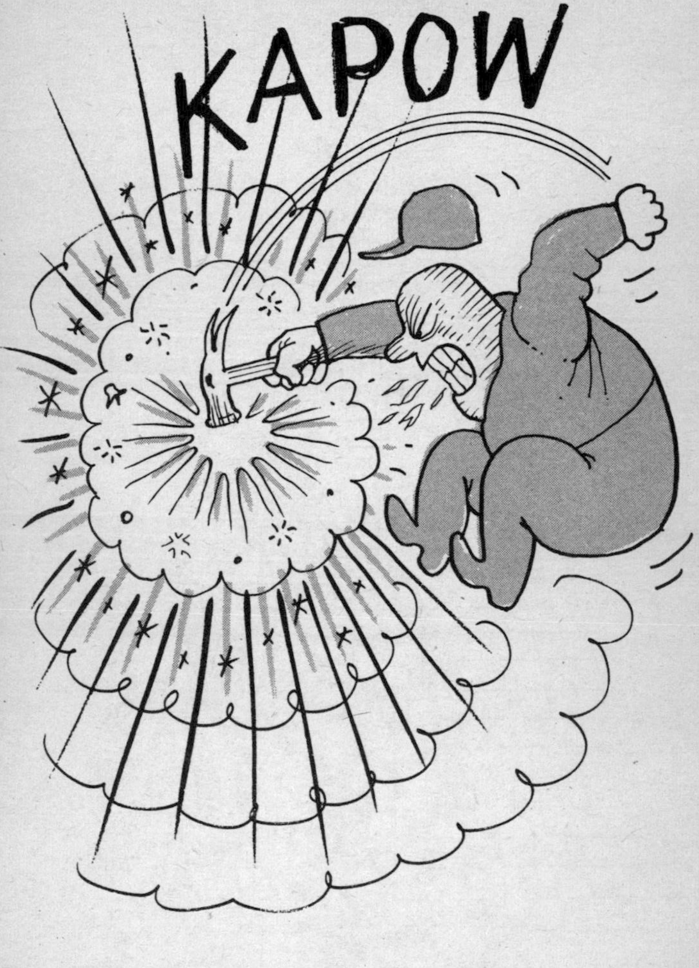
KAPOW

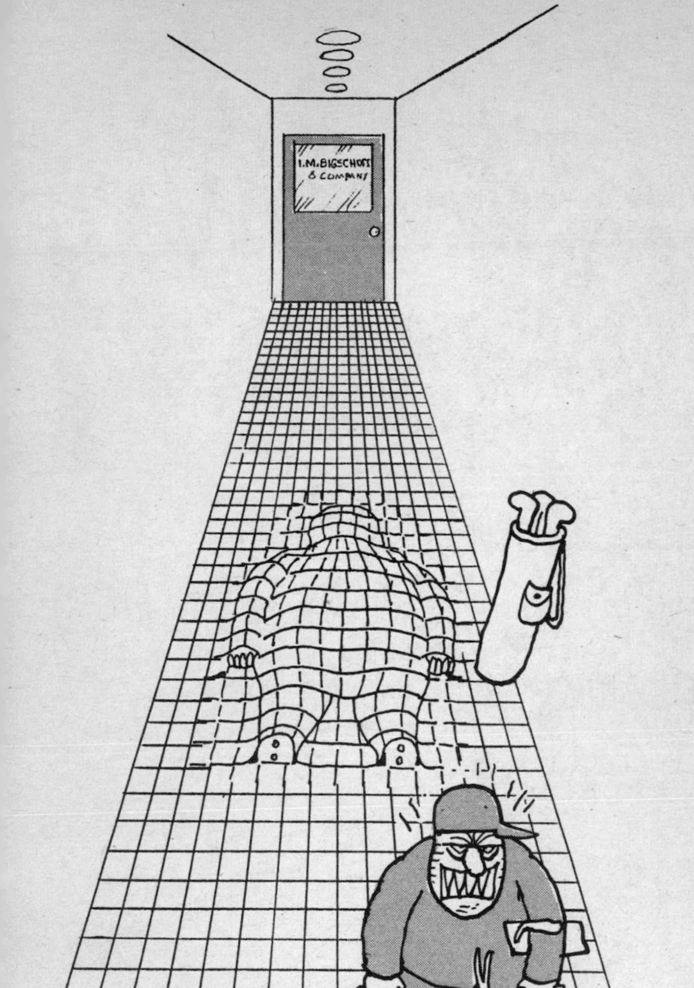
I.M. BIGSCHOT
& COMPANY

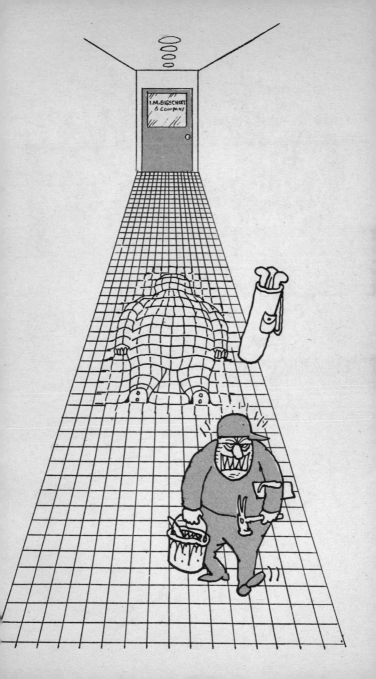

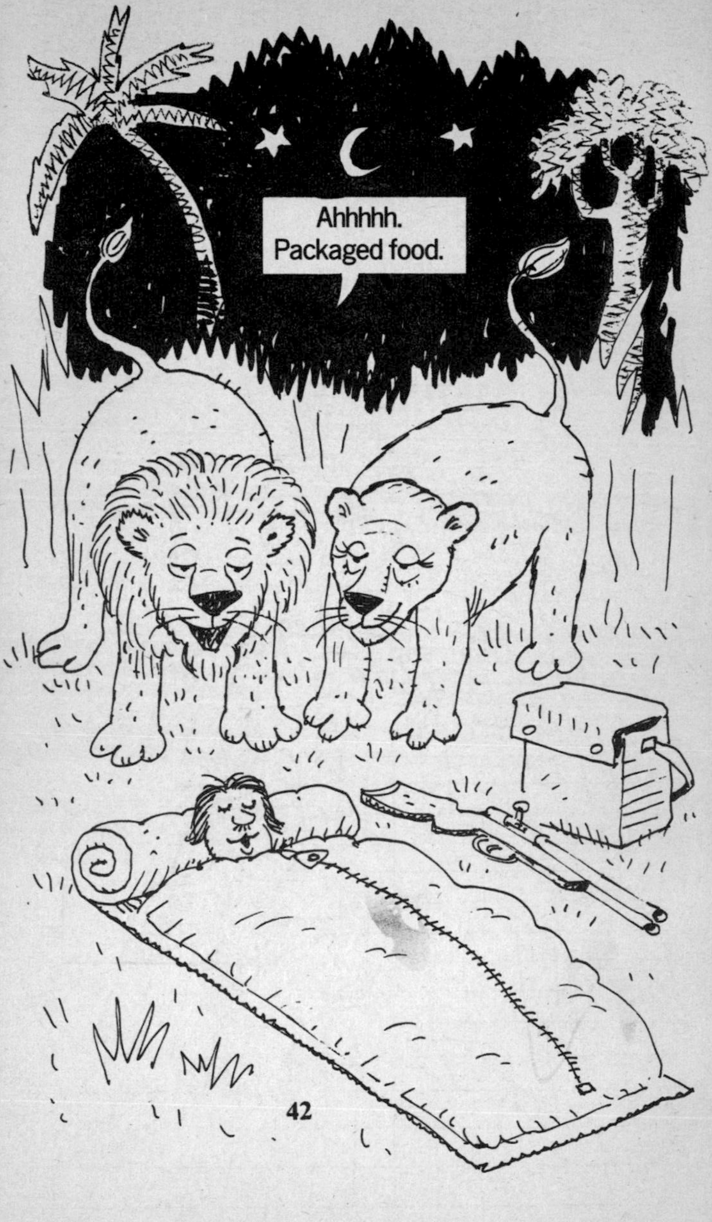
Ahhhhh.
Packaged food.

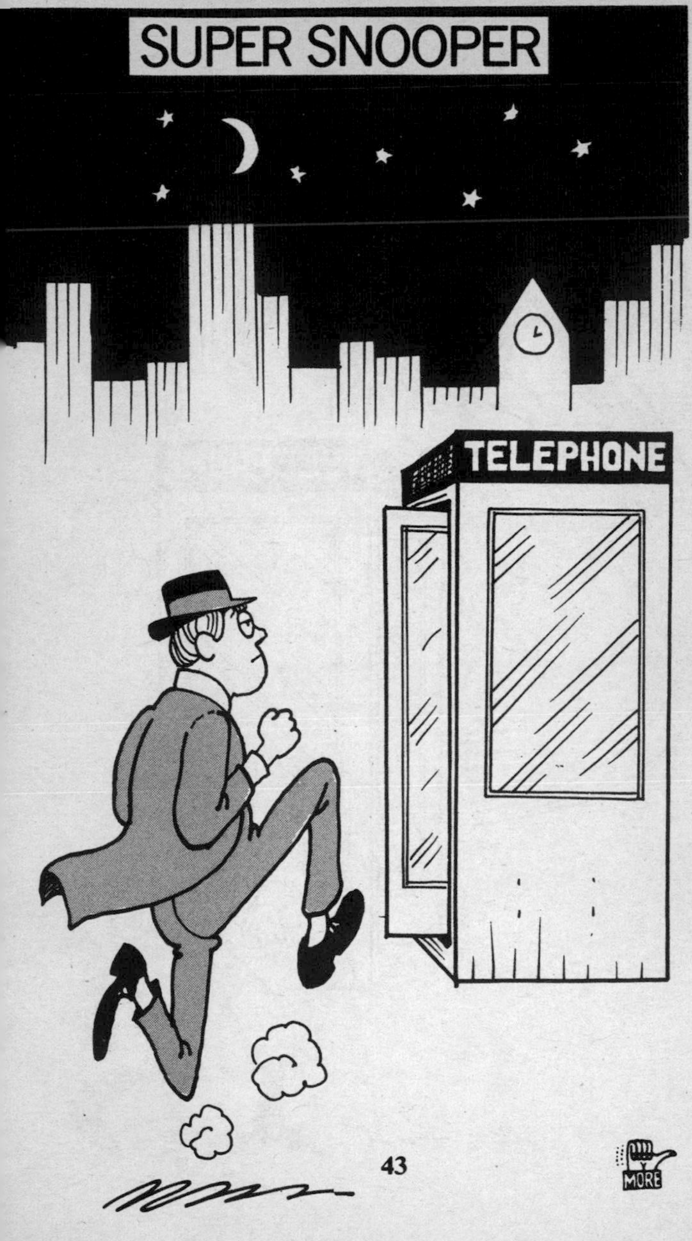
SUPER SNOOPER
TELEPHONE
MORE

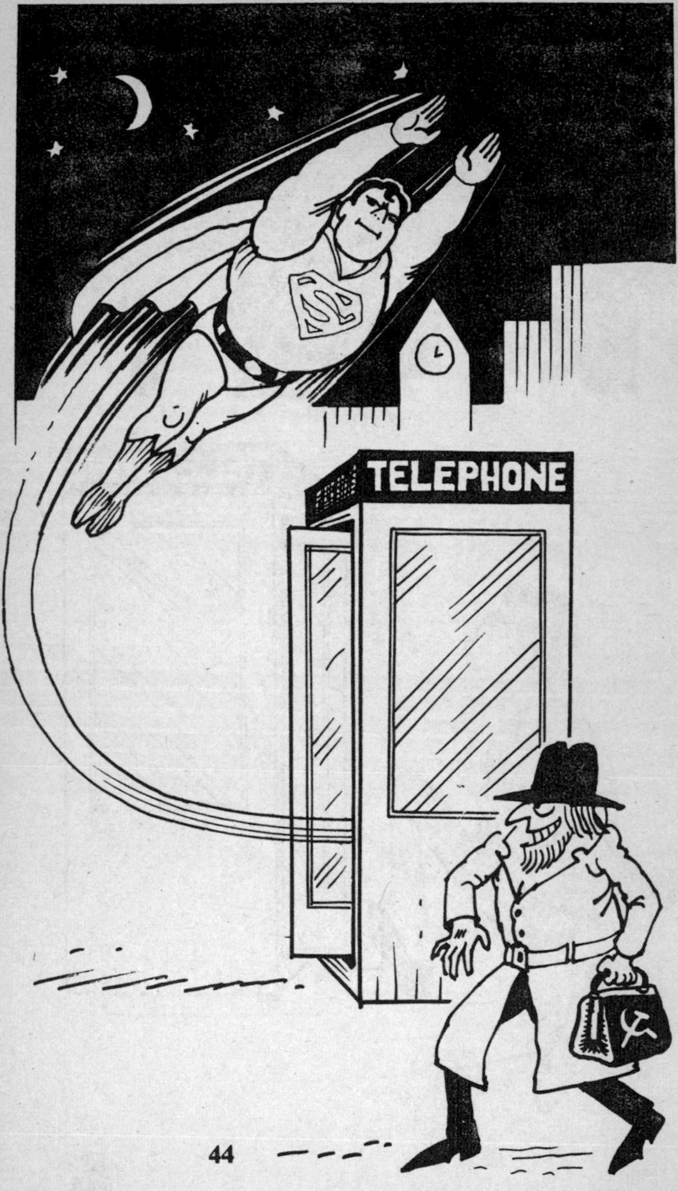
TELEPHONE

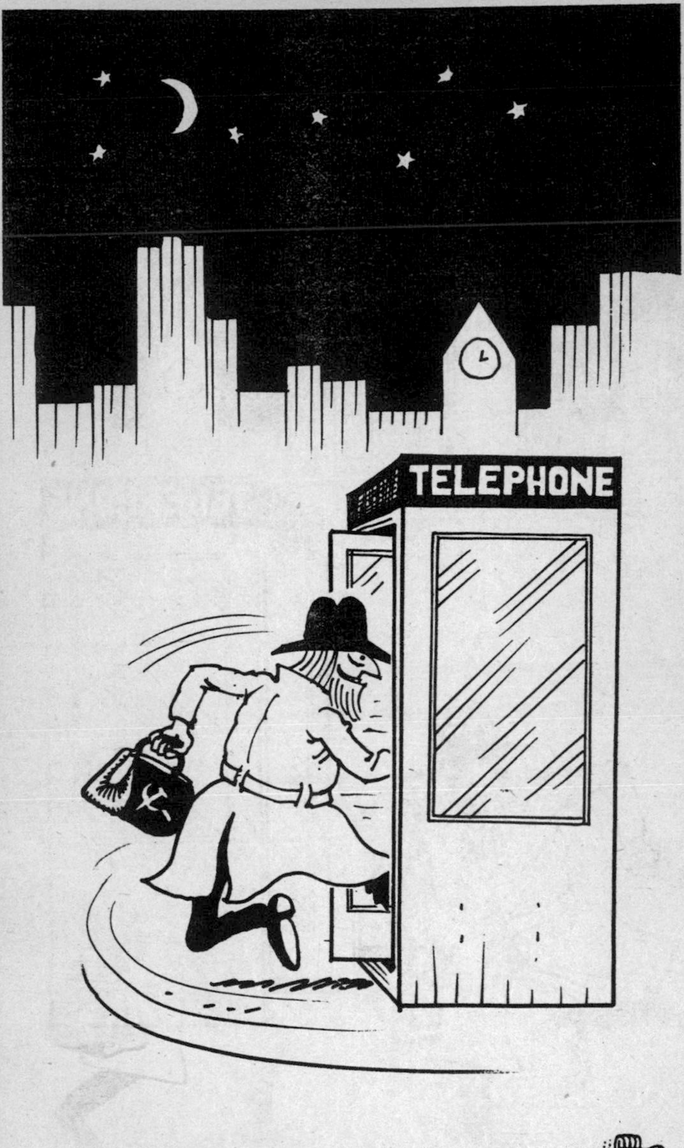
TELEPHONE
MORE

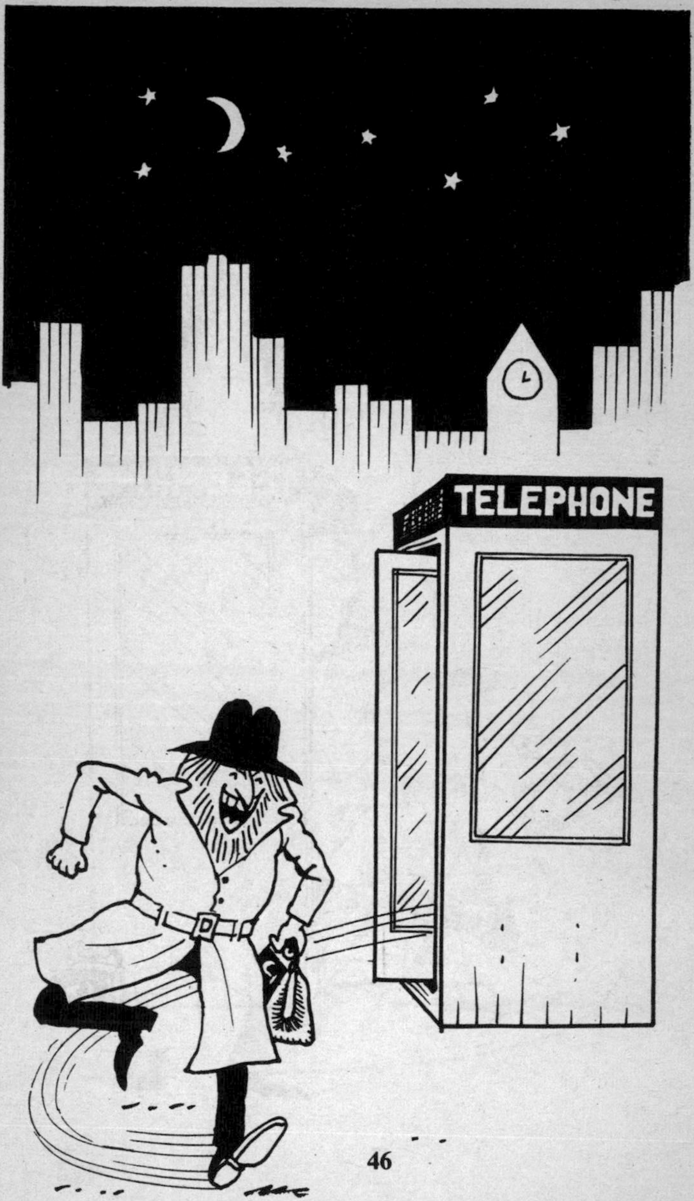
TELEPHONE

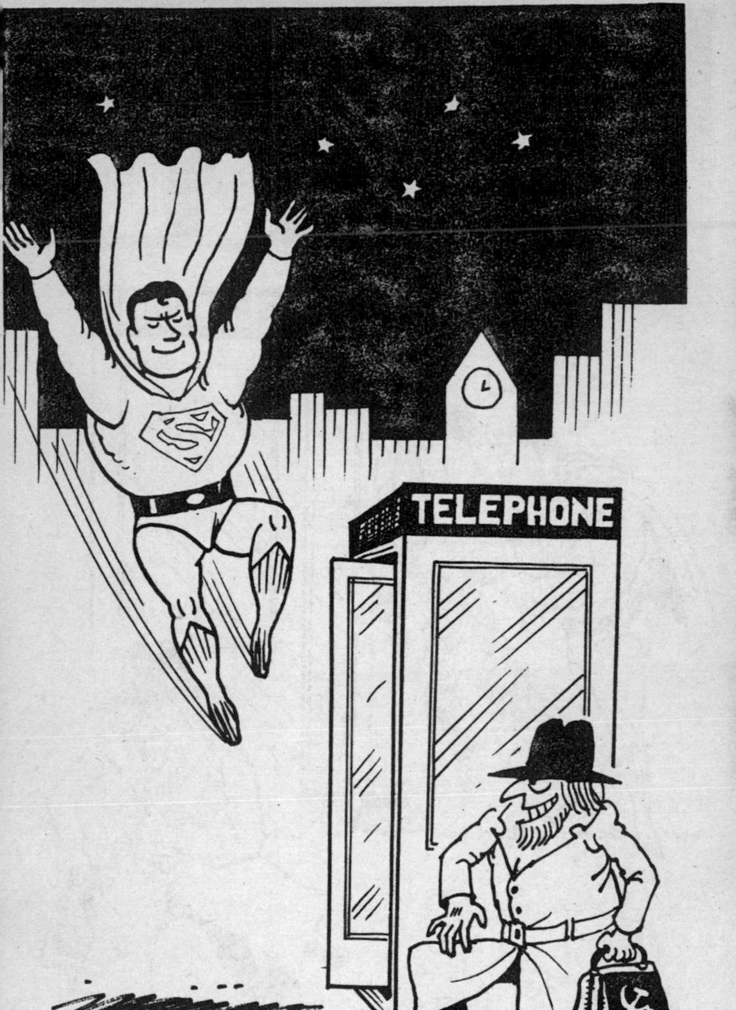
TELEPHONE

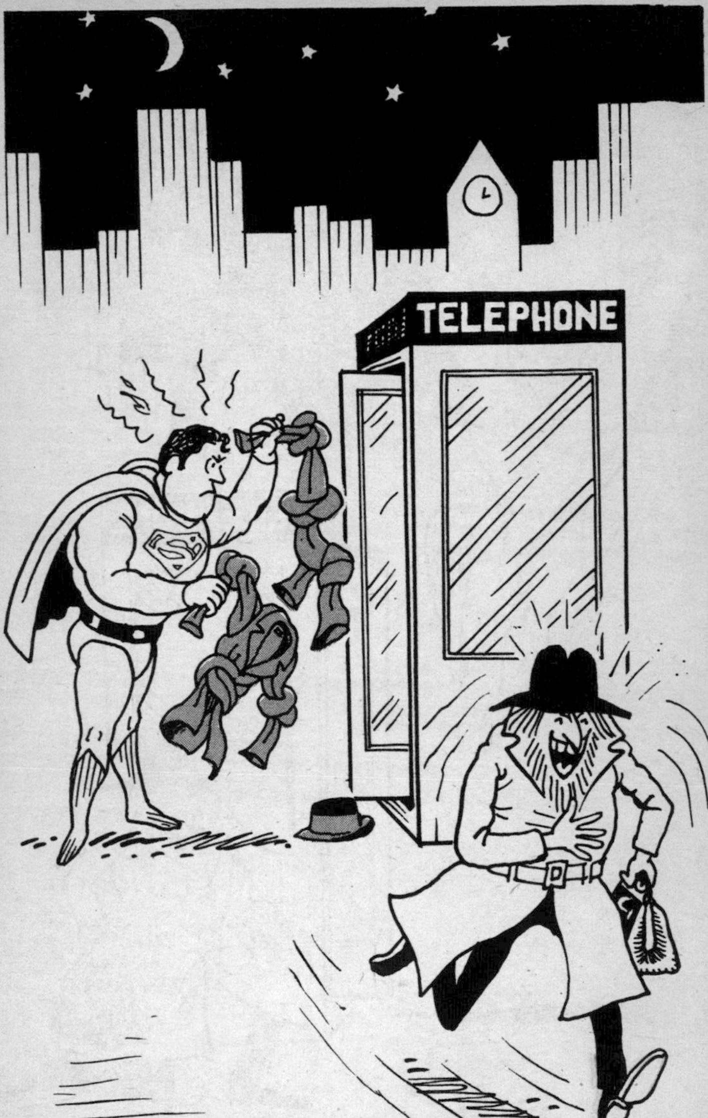
TELEPHONE

EYEFULL TRIFLE

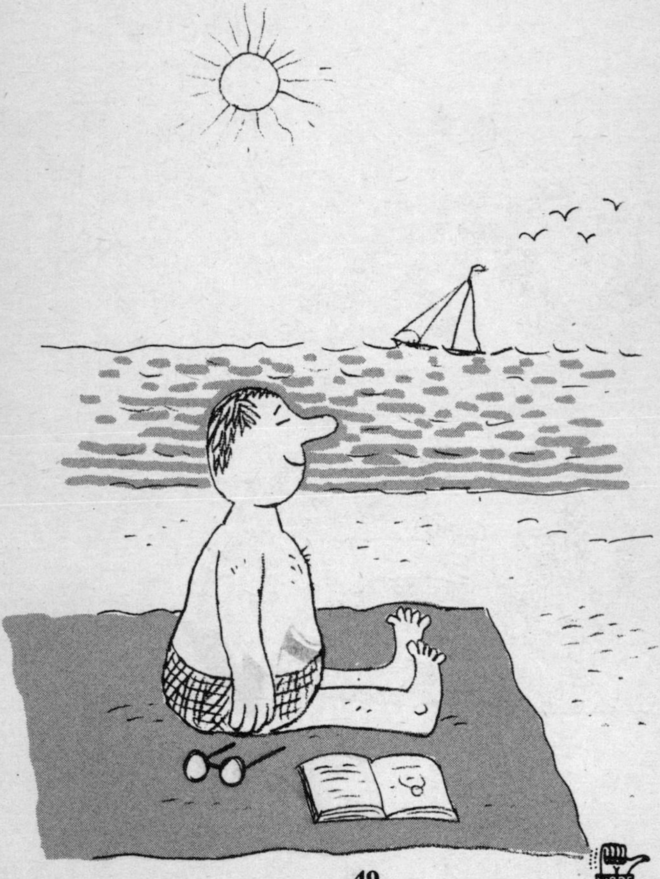

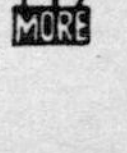
MORE

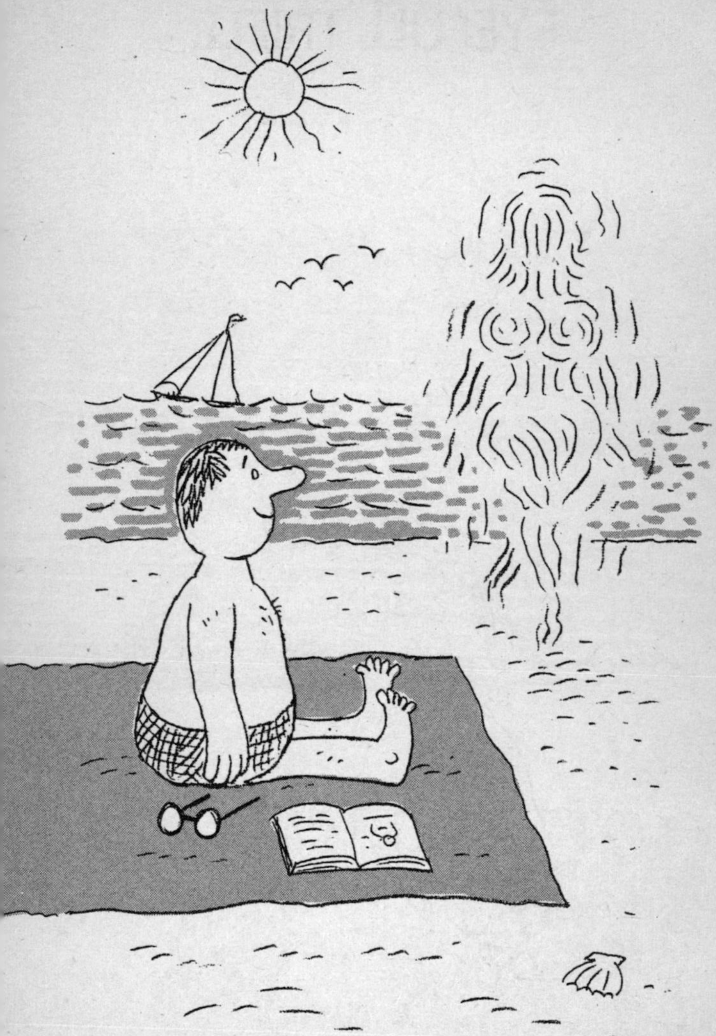

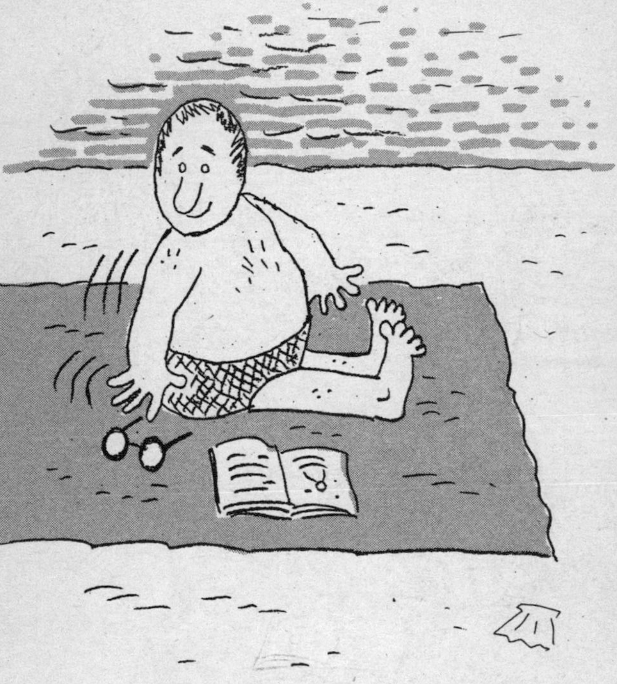

MORE

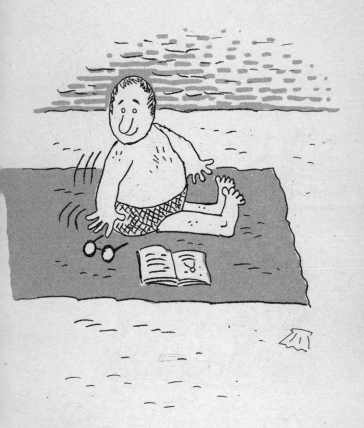

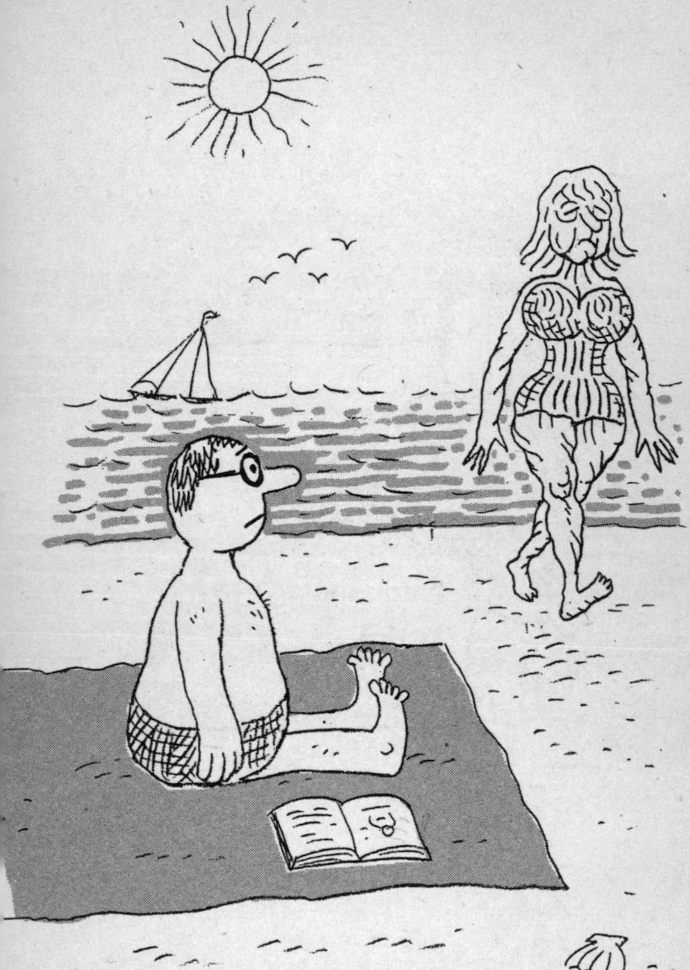

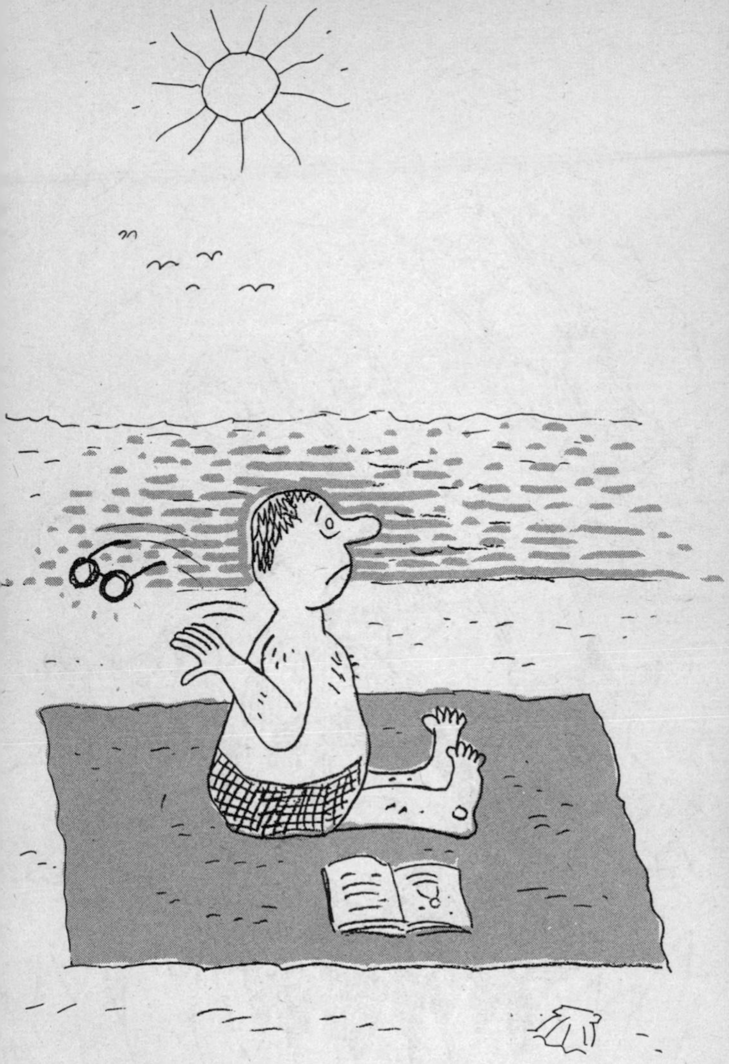

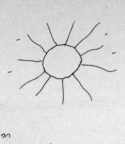

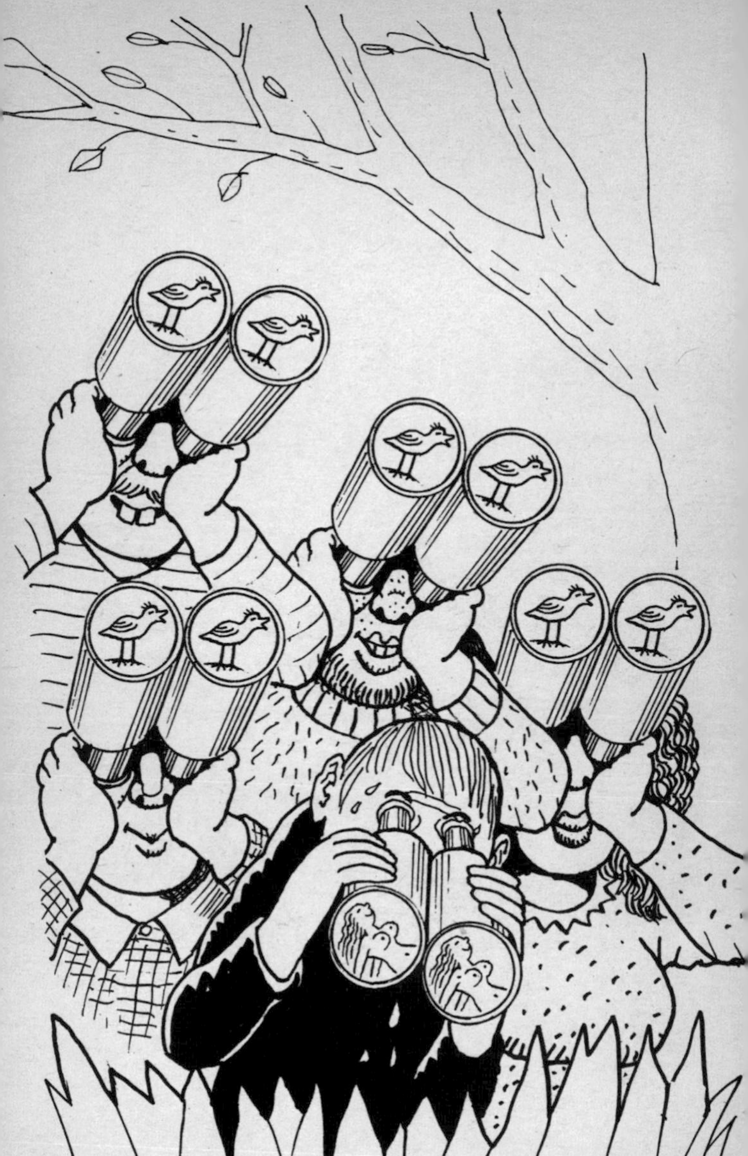

PHONEY PONY

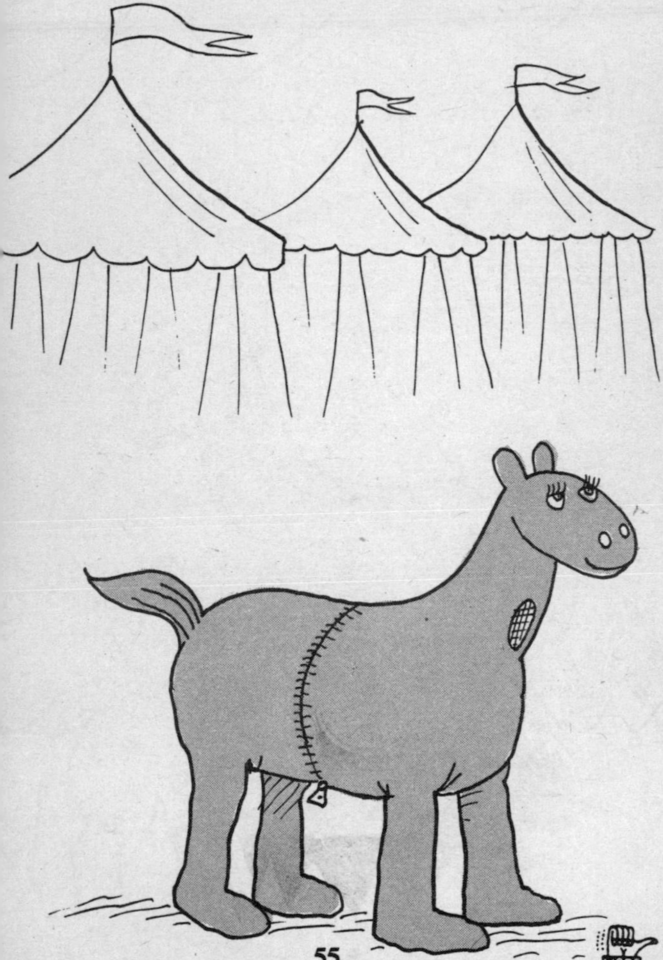

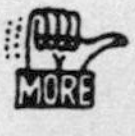
MORE

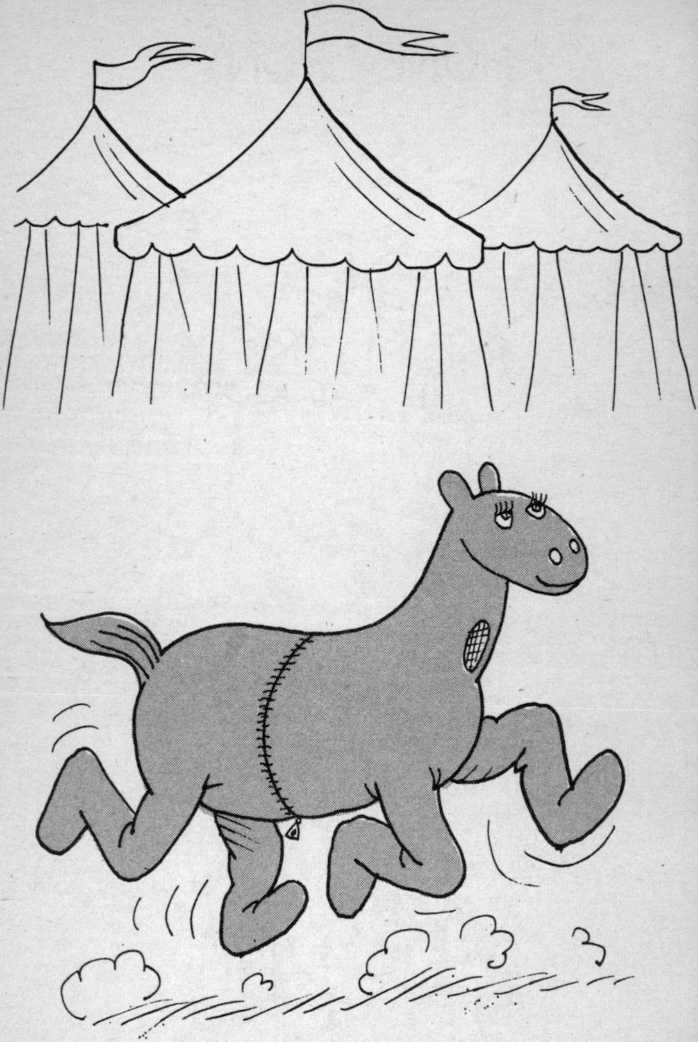

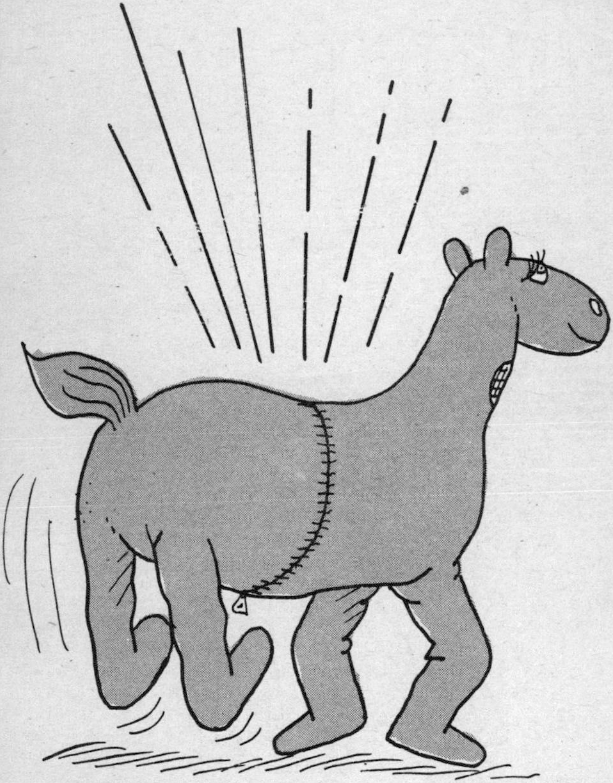

MORE

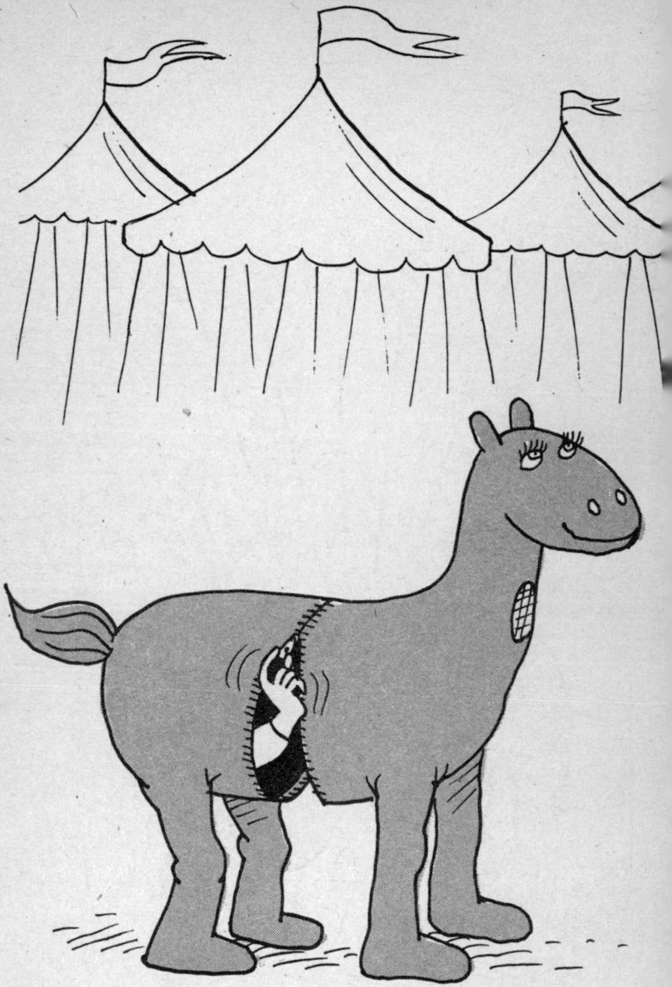

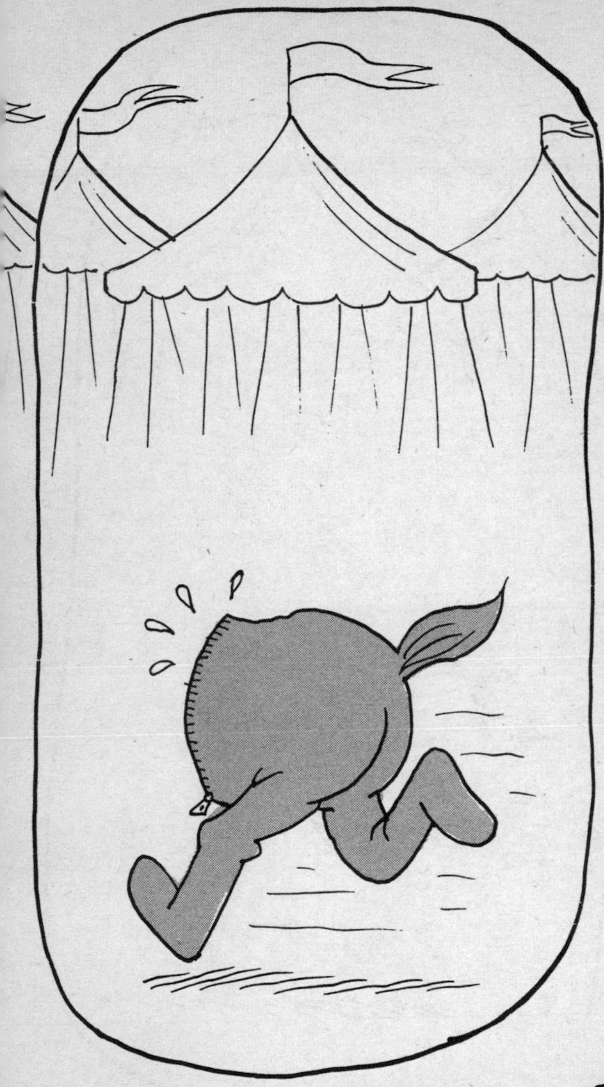

MORE

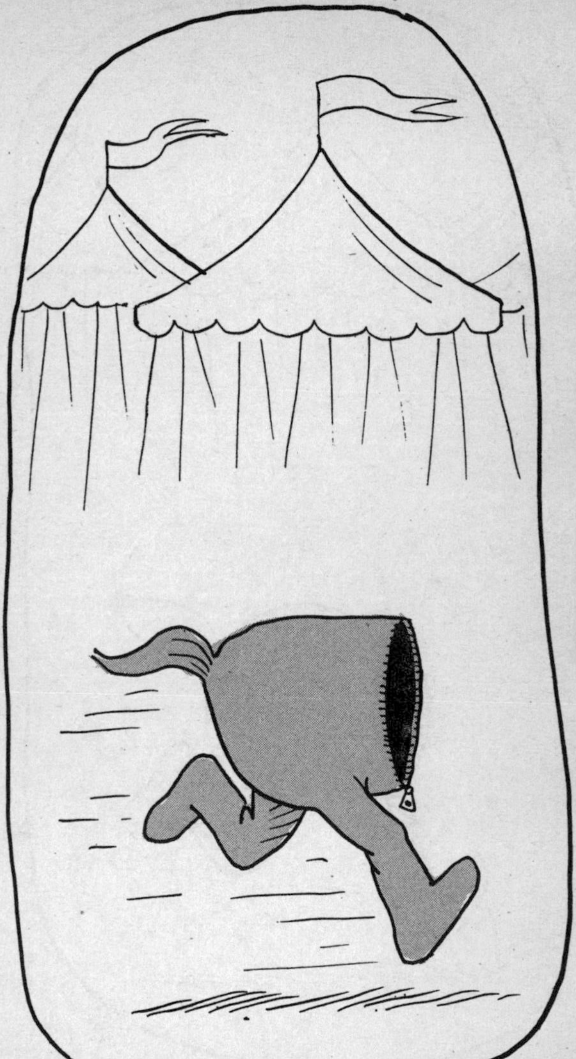

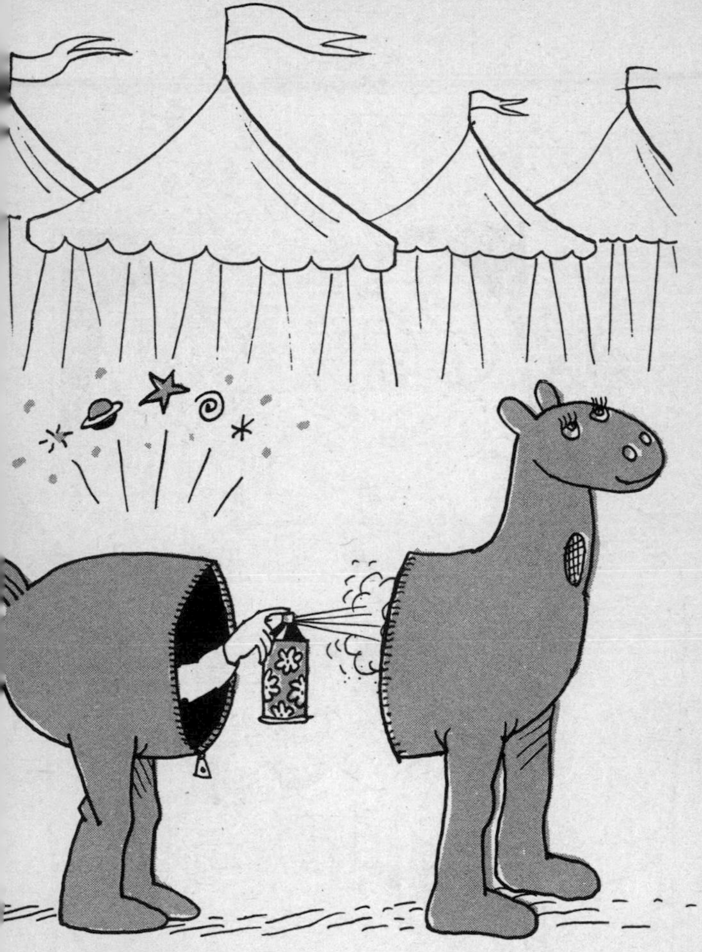

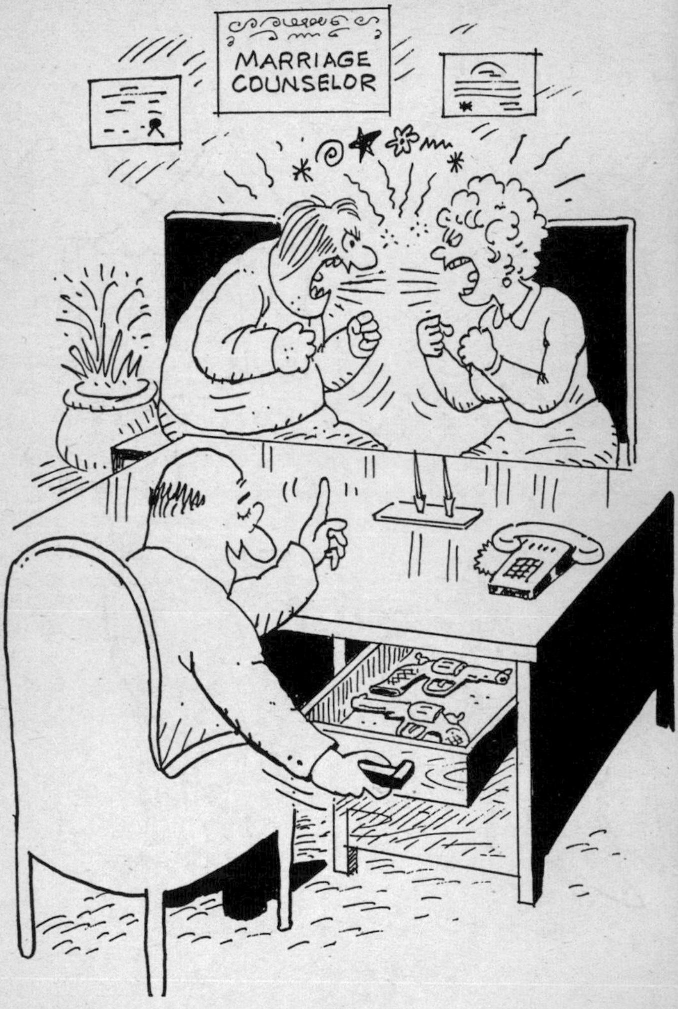
MARRIAGE
COUNSELOR

SUBDUED MOOD

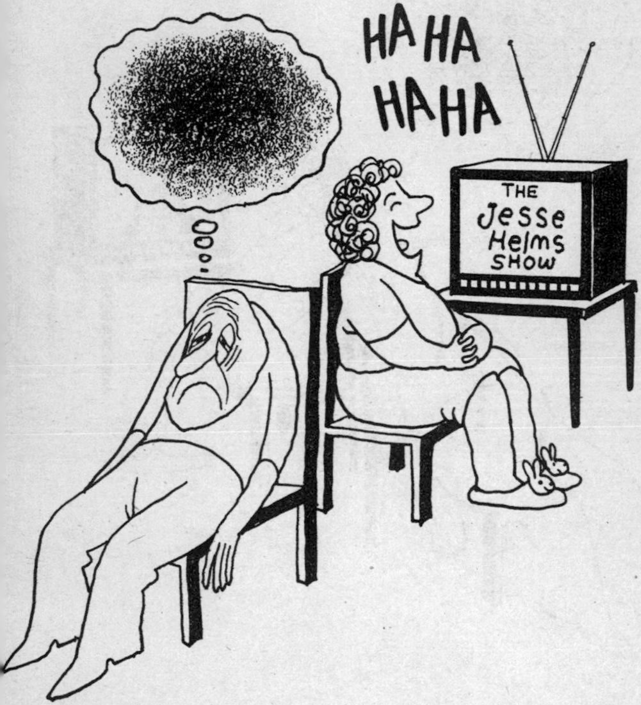
HA HA
HA HA
THE
Jesse
Helms
SHOW

MORE

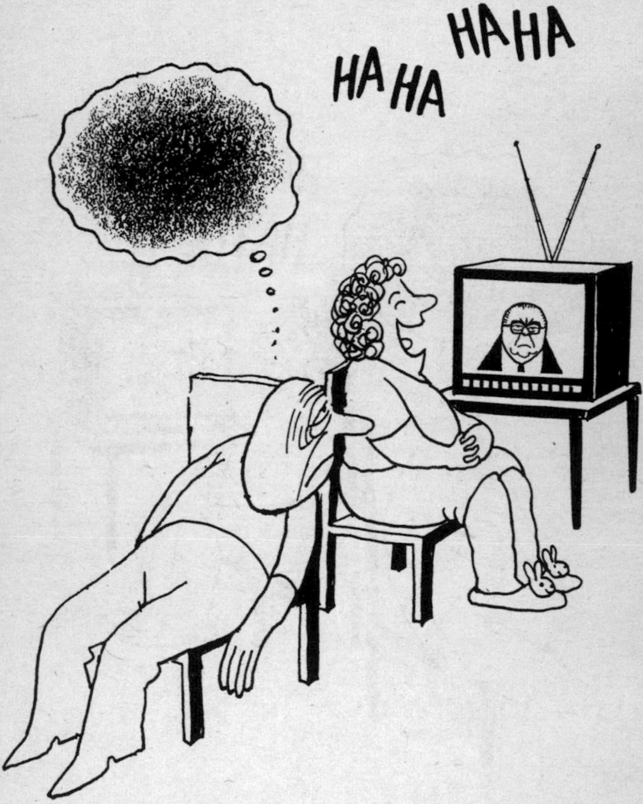
HAHA
HAHA

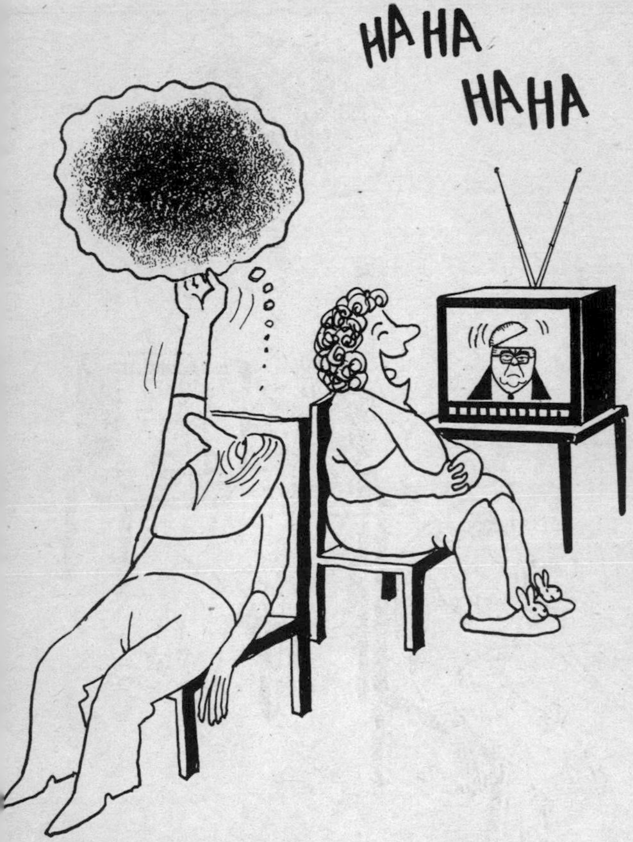
HA HA
HA HA

MORE

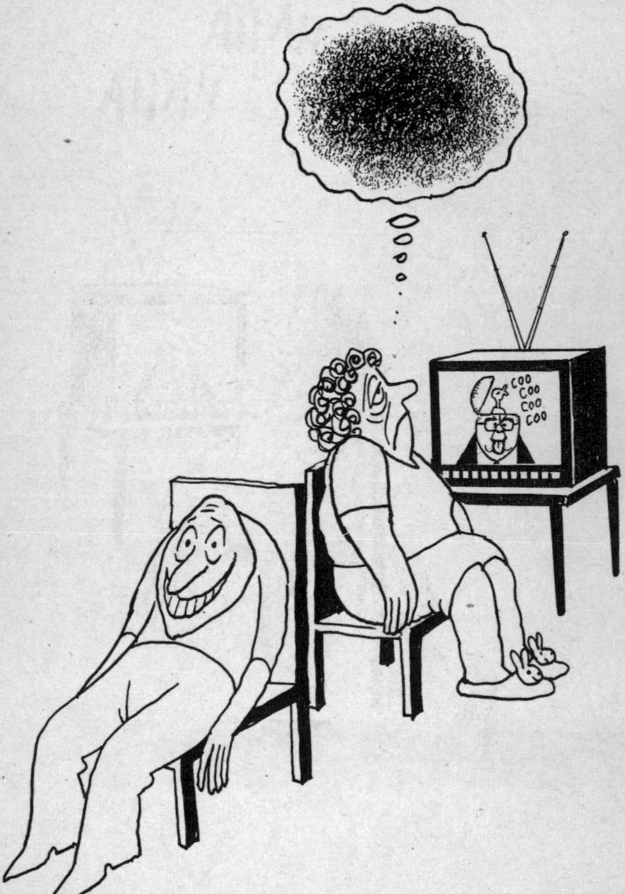
COO
COO
COO
COO

CRUISE BLUES

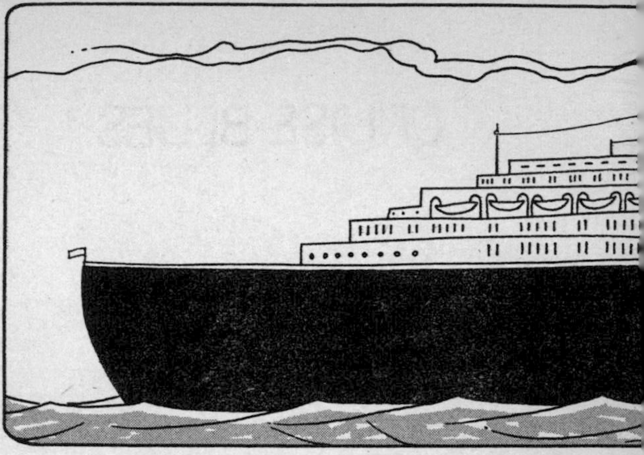

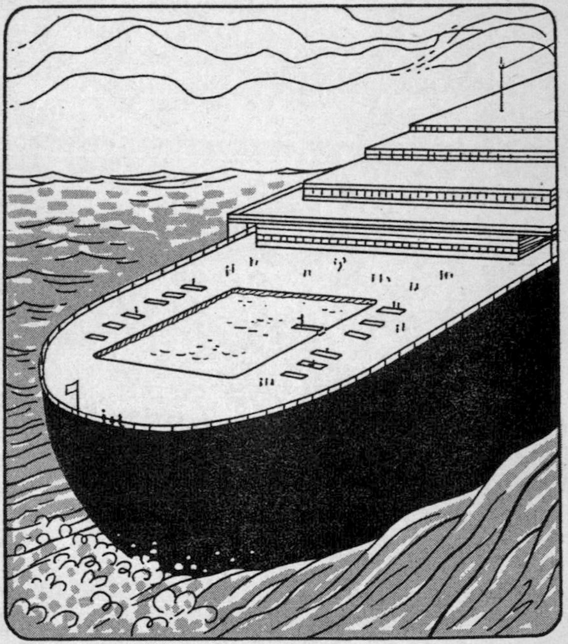

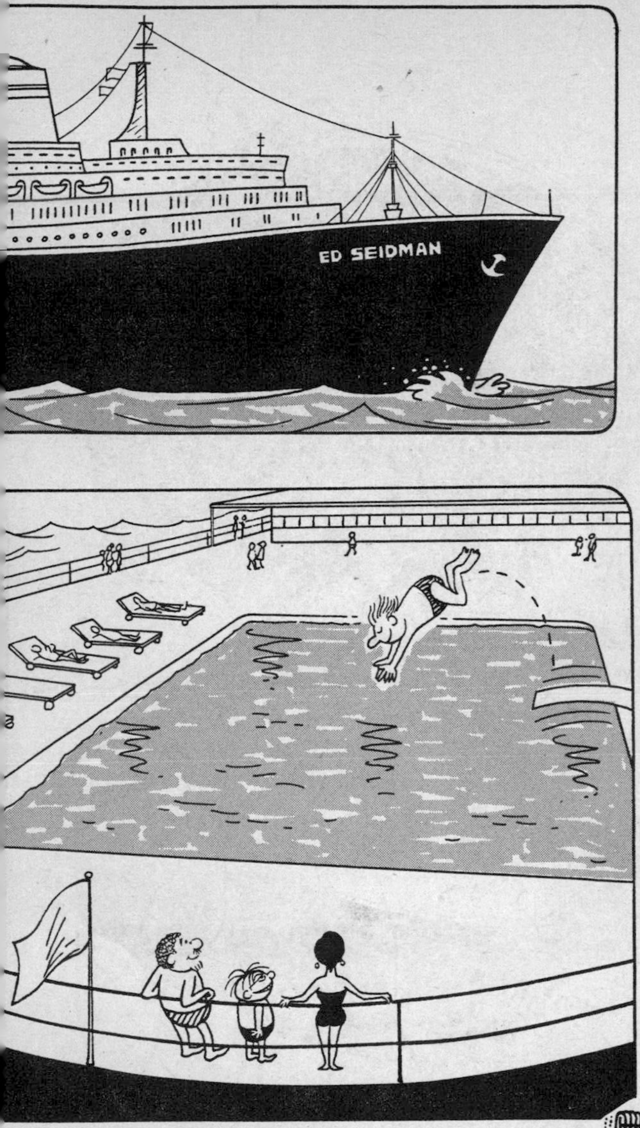
ED SEIDMAN

MORE

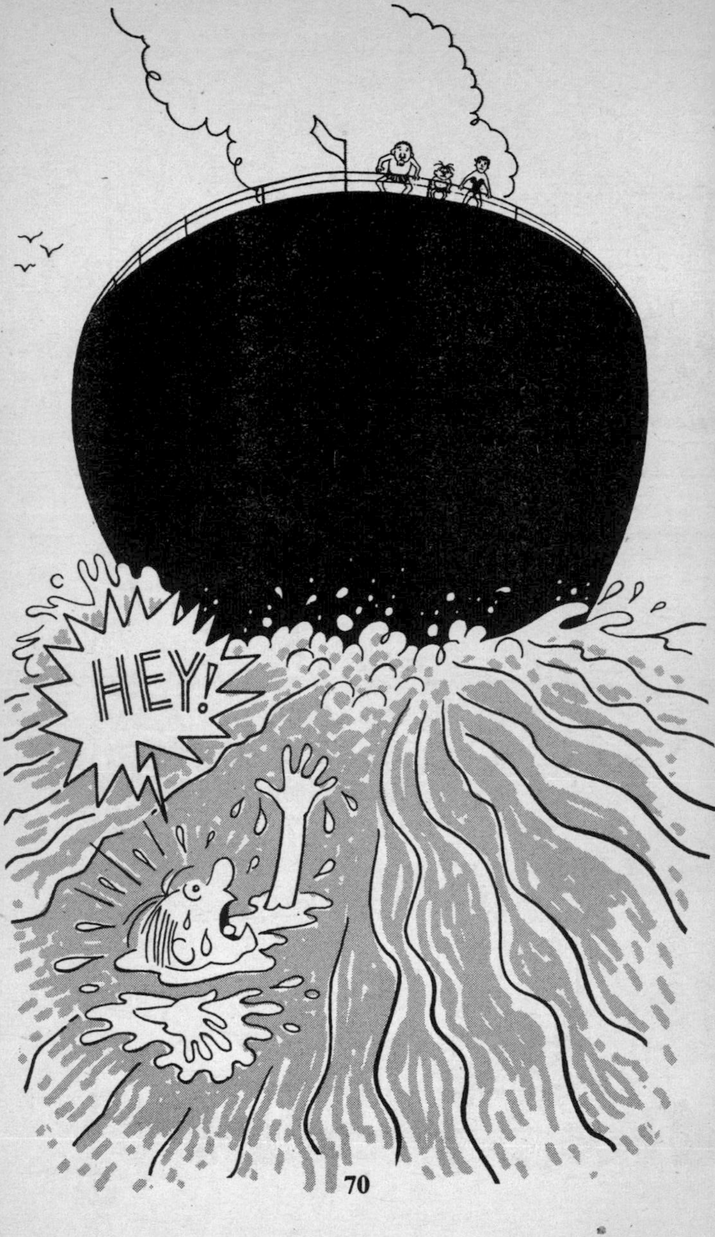
HEY!

WIFE STRIFE

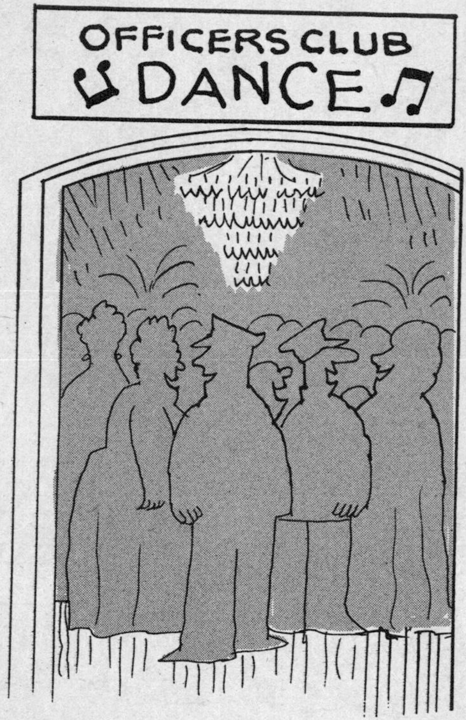
OFFICERS CLUB
DANCE

MORE

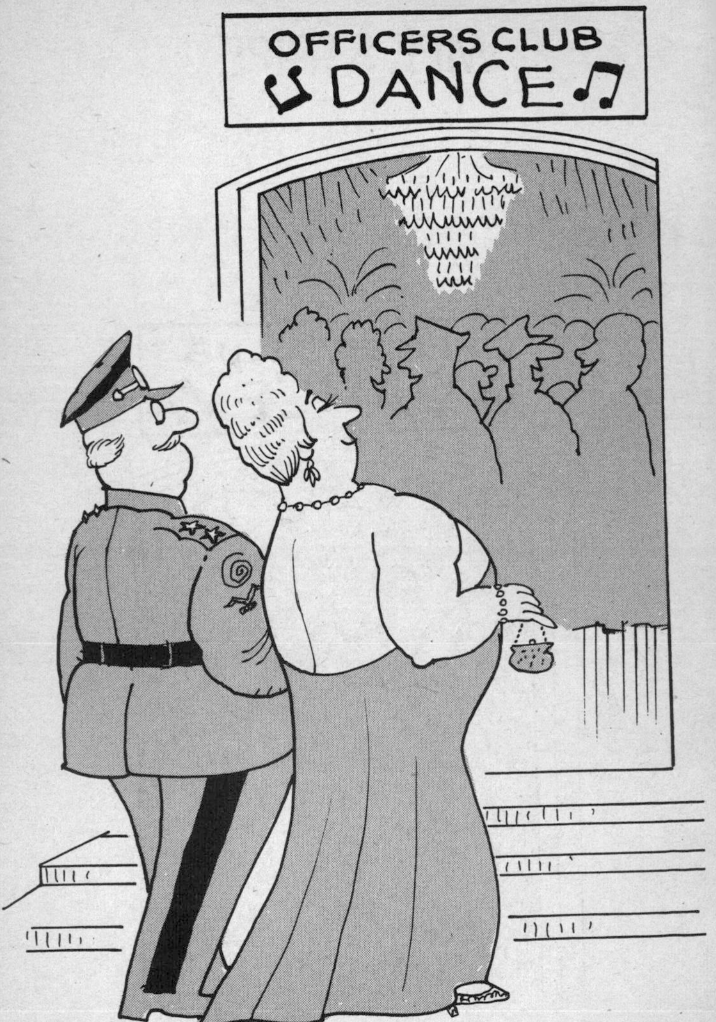
OFFICERS CLUB
DANCE

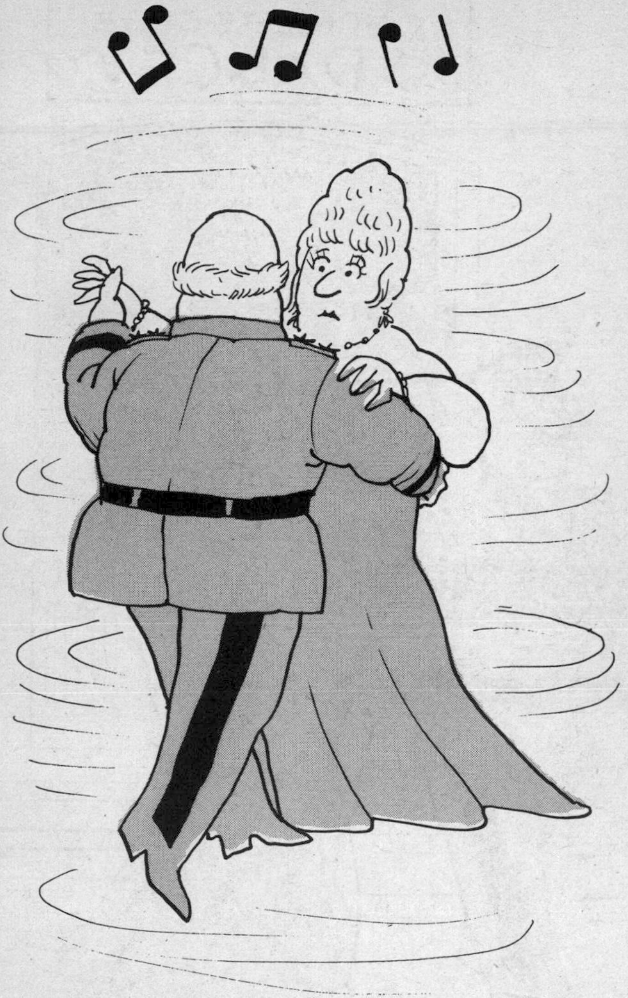

MORE

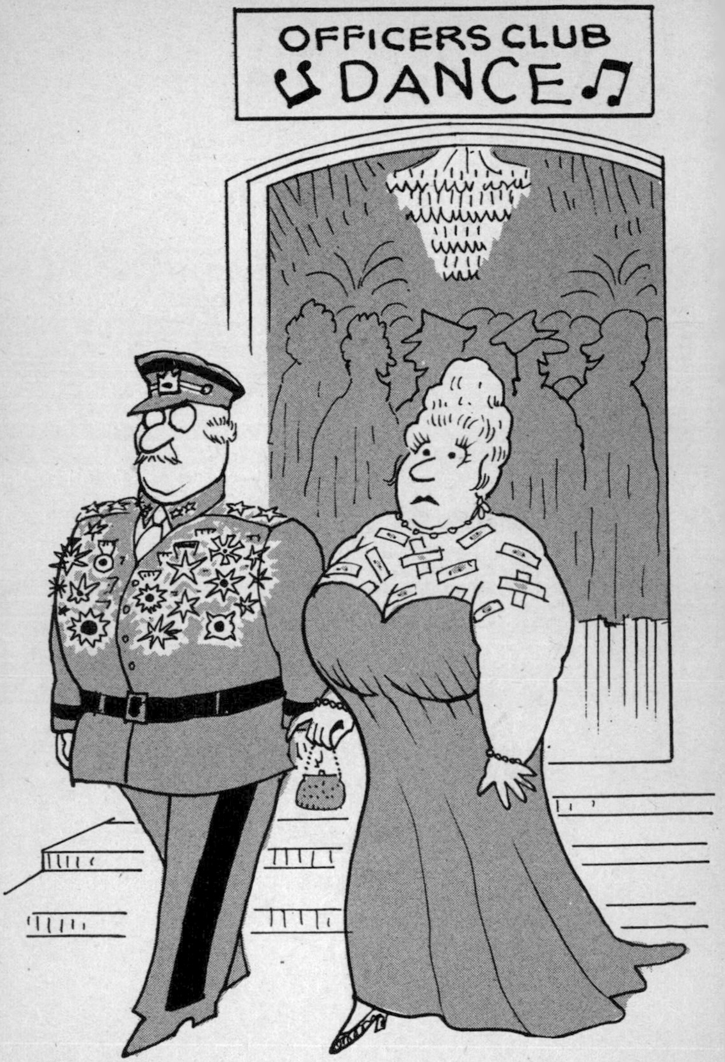
OFFICERS CLUB
DANCE

JAIL TALE

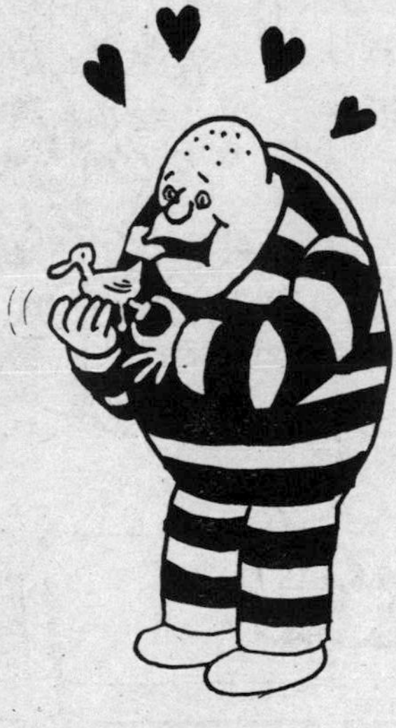

MORE

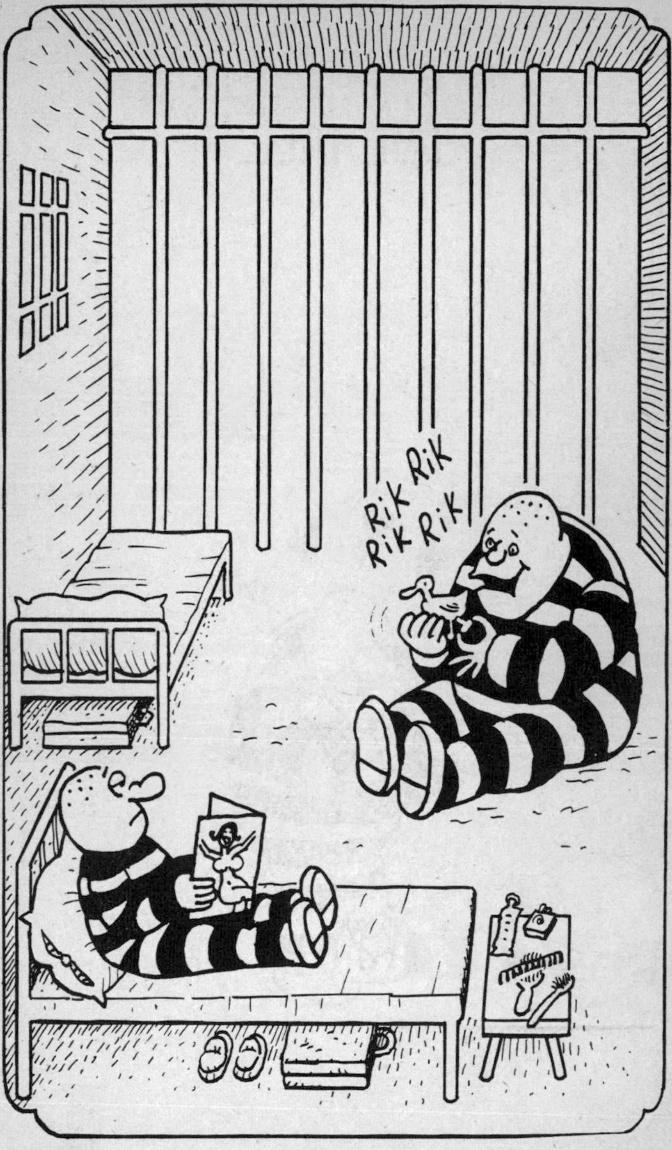
RiK RiK
RiK RiK

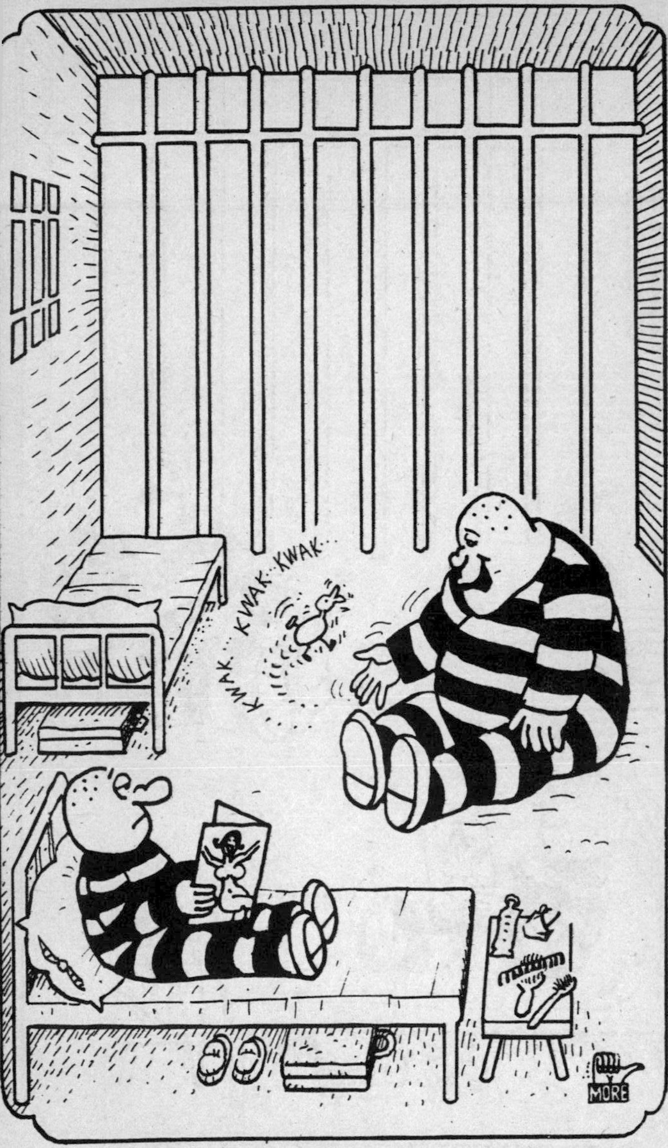
KWAK... KWAK... KWAK...

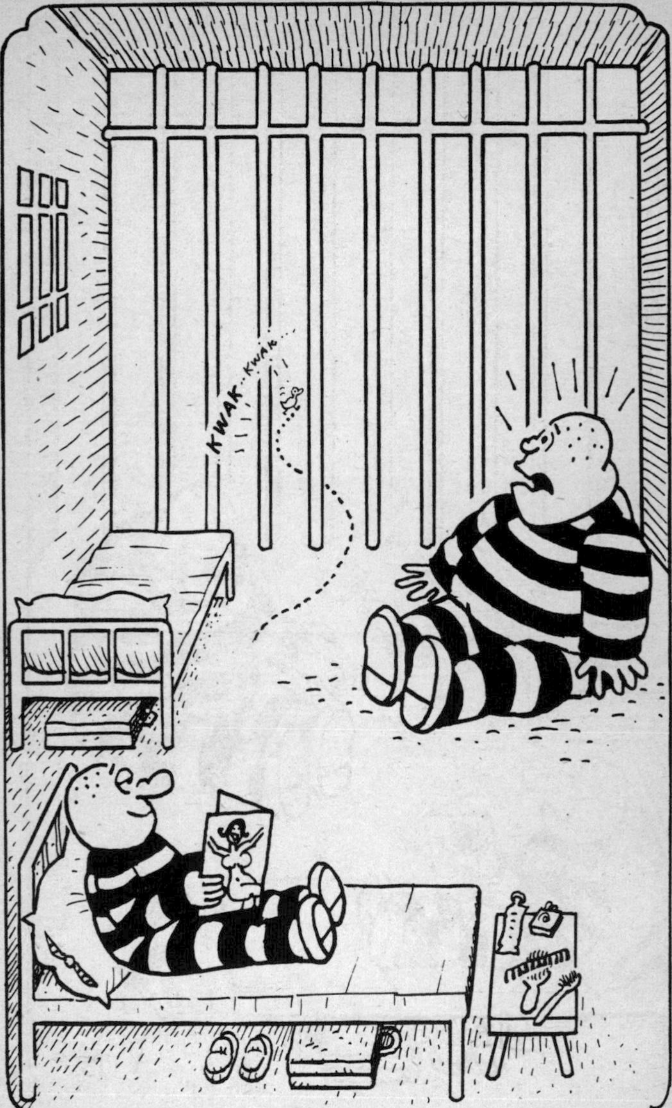
KWAK..KWAK...

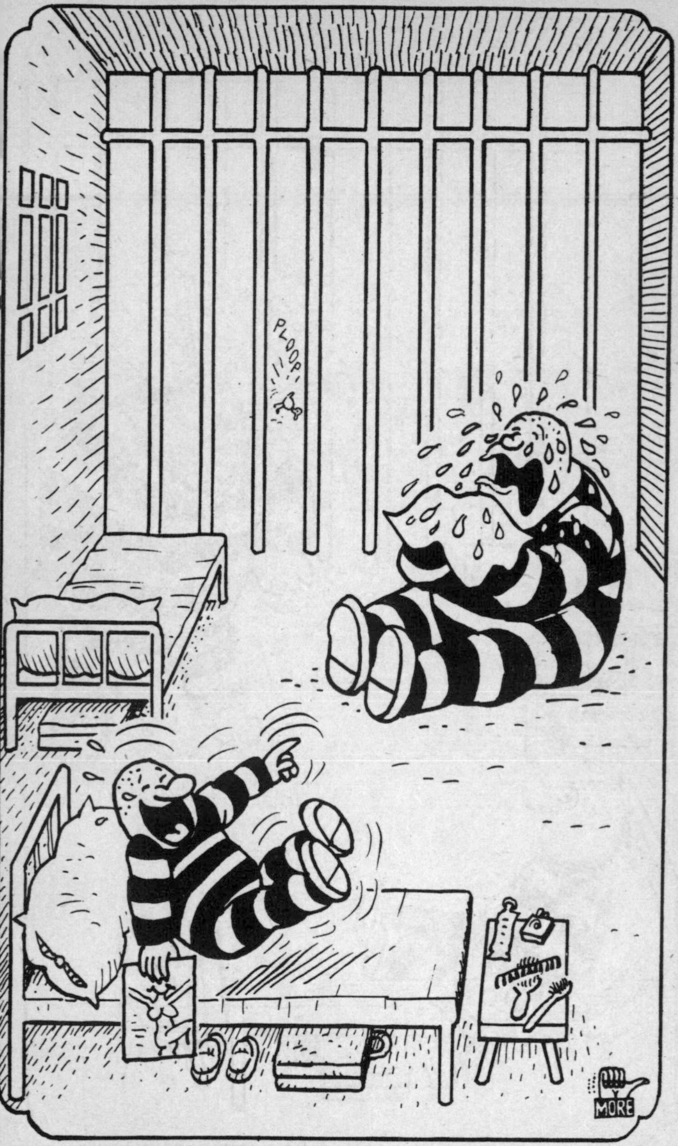
PLOOOP
MORE

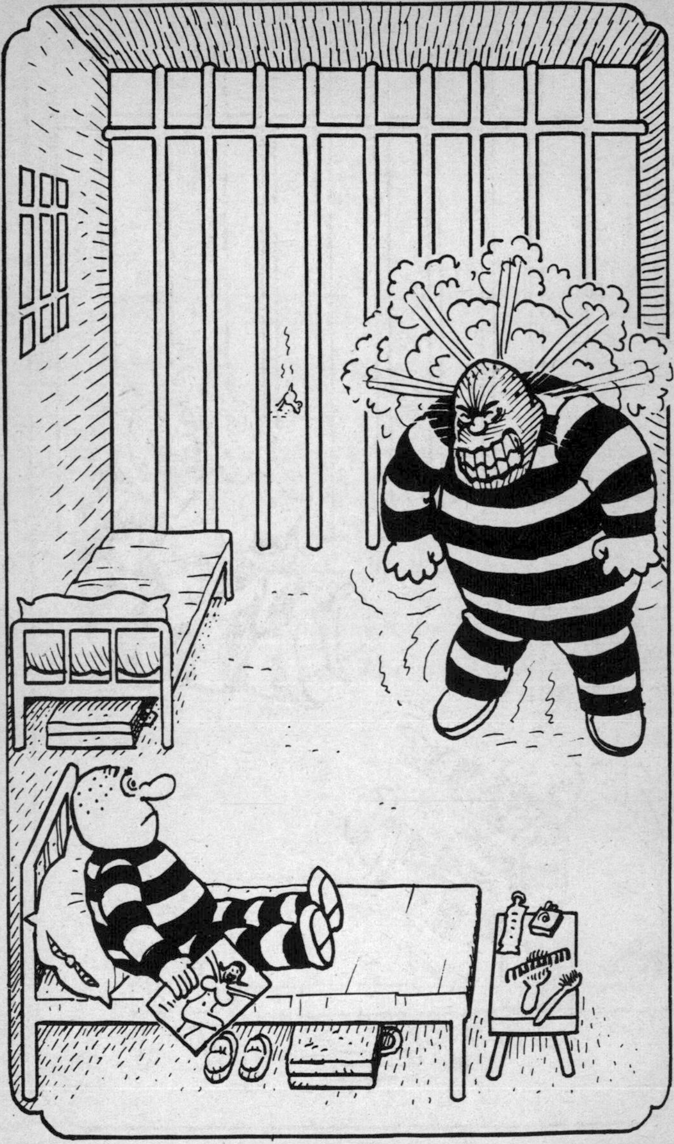

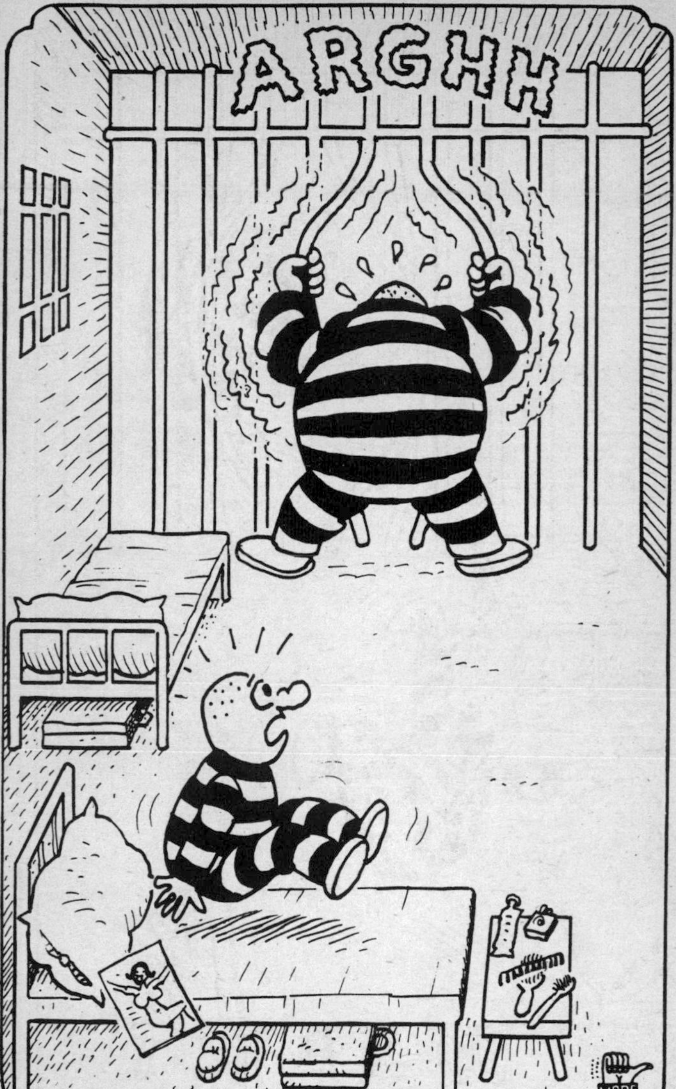
ARGHH
MORE

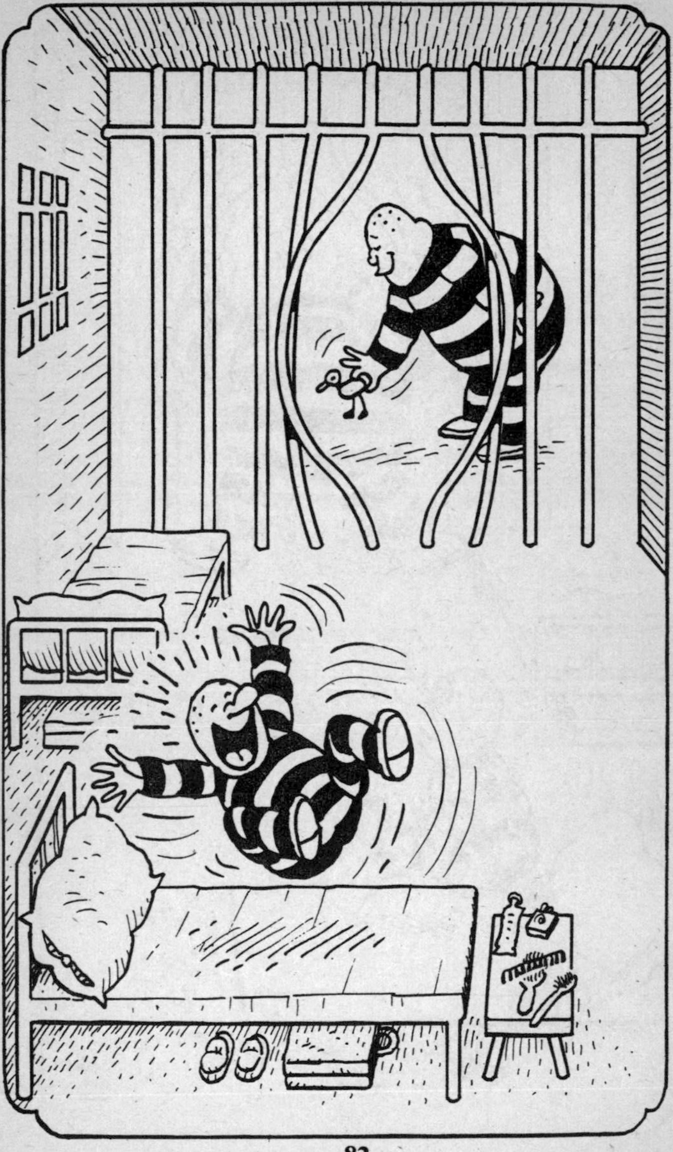

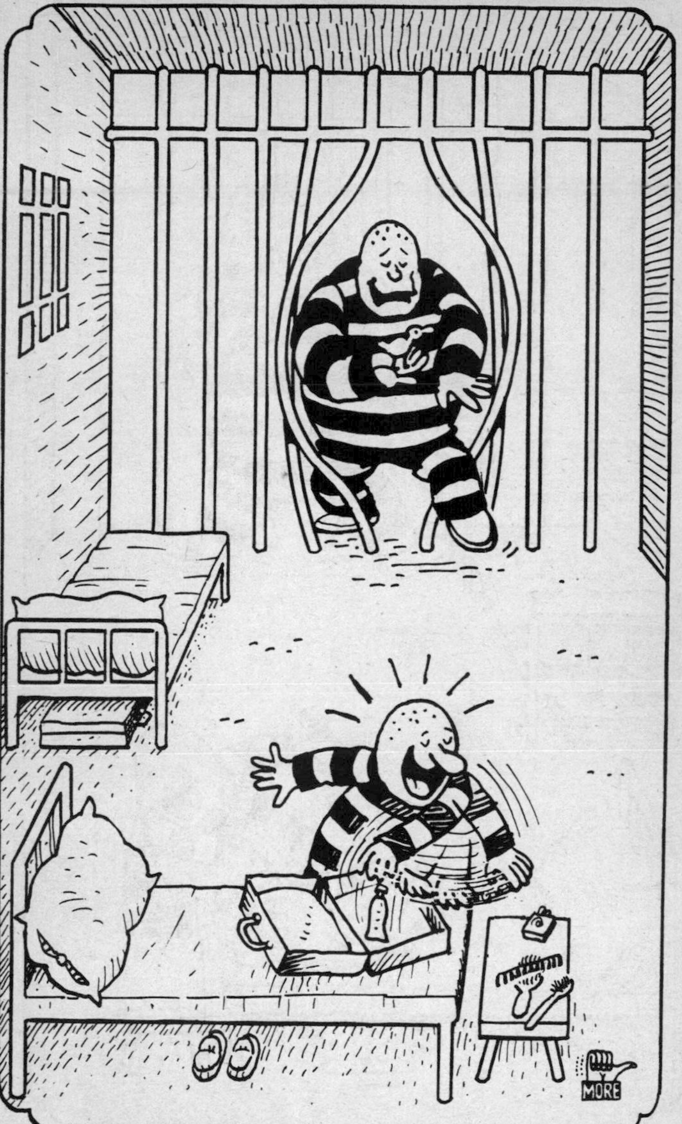
MORE

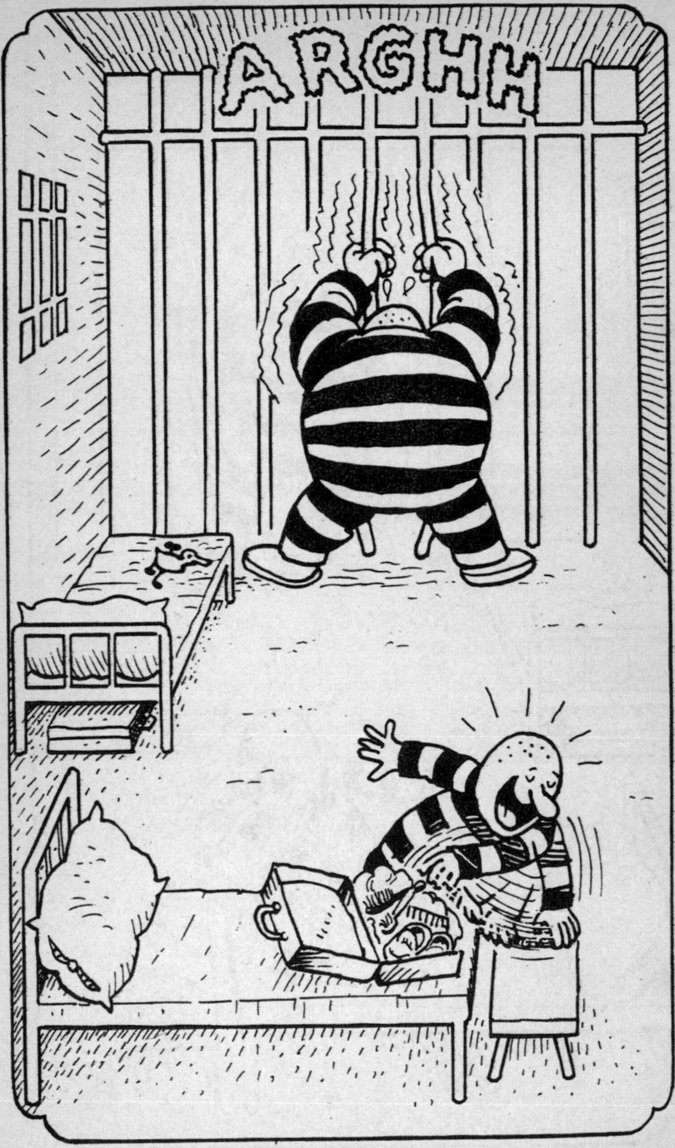
ARGHH

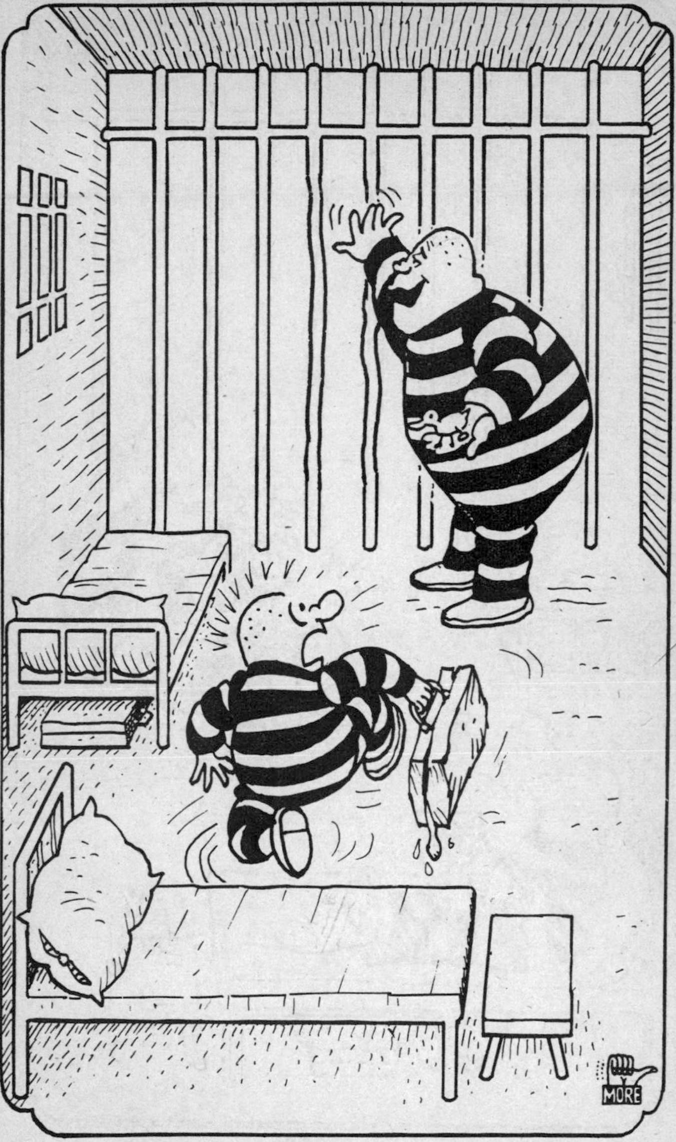
MORE

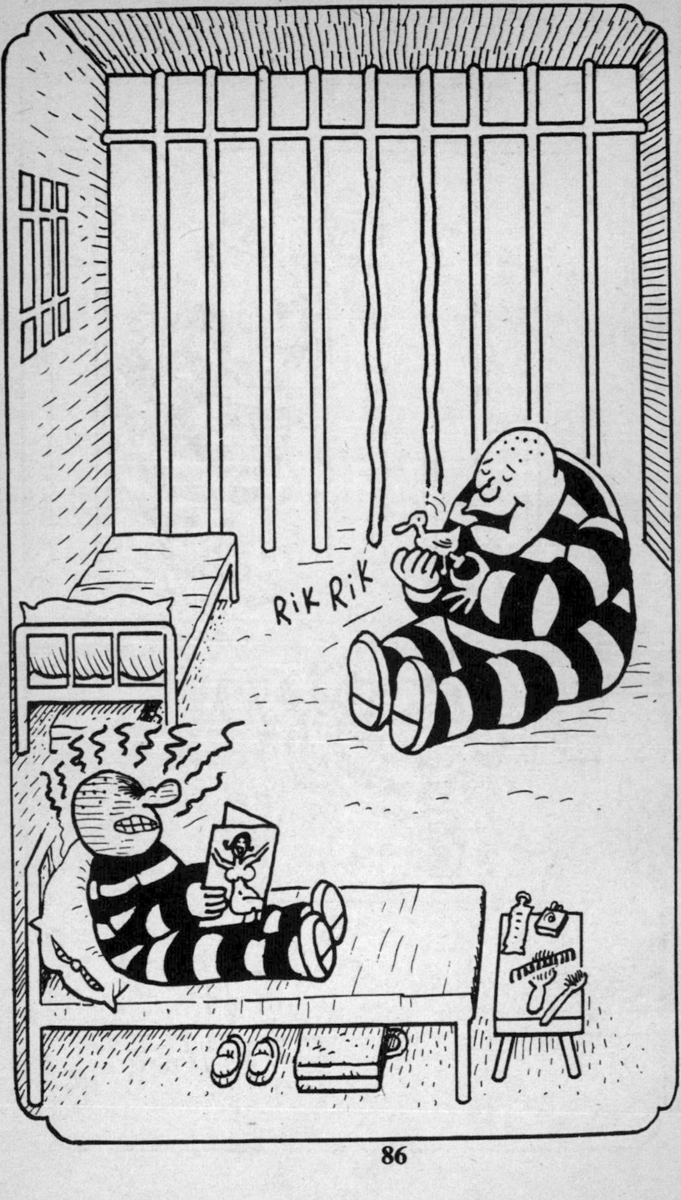
RIK RIK

JOKE STROKE

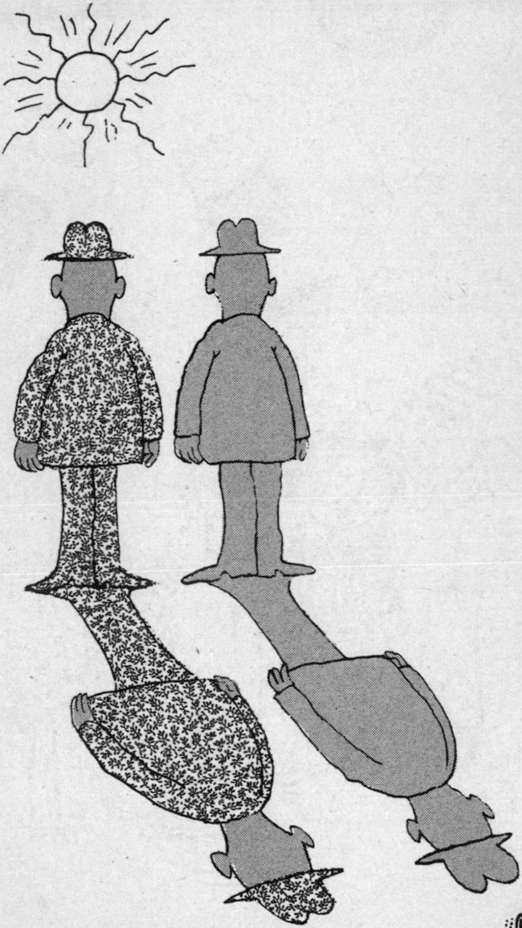

MORE

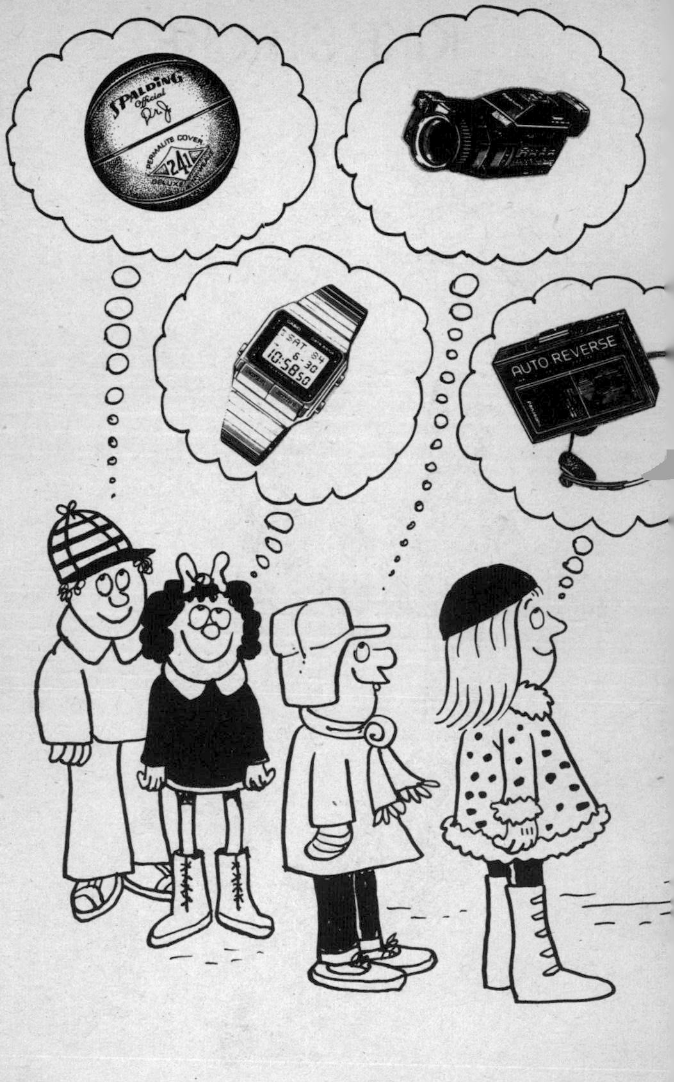
SPALDING
Official
PERMALITE COVER
241
DELUXE
SAT 84
6-30
10:58 50
AUTO REVERSE

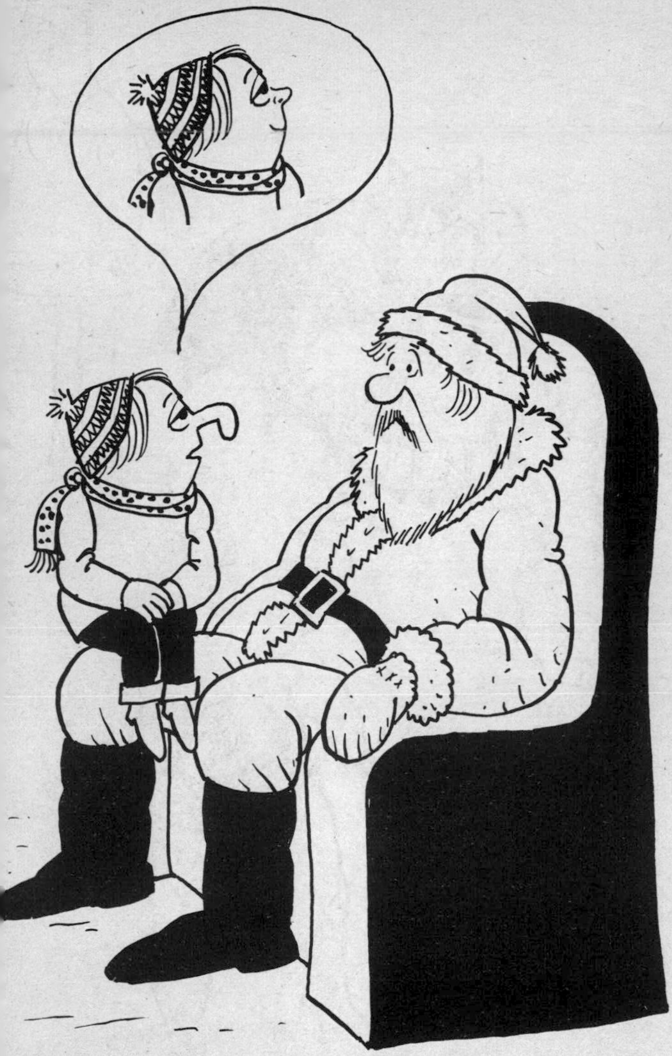

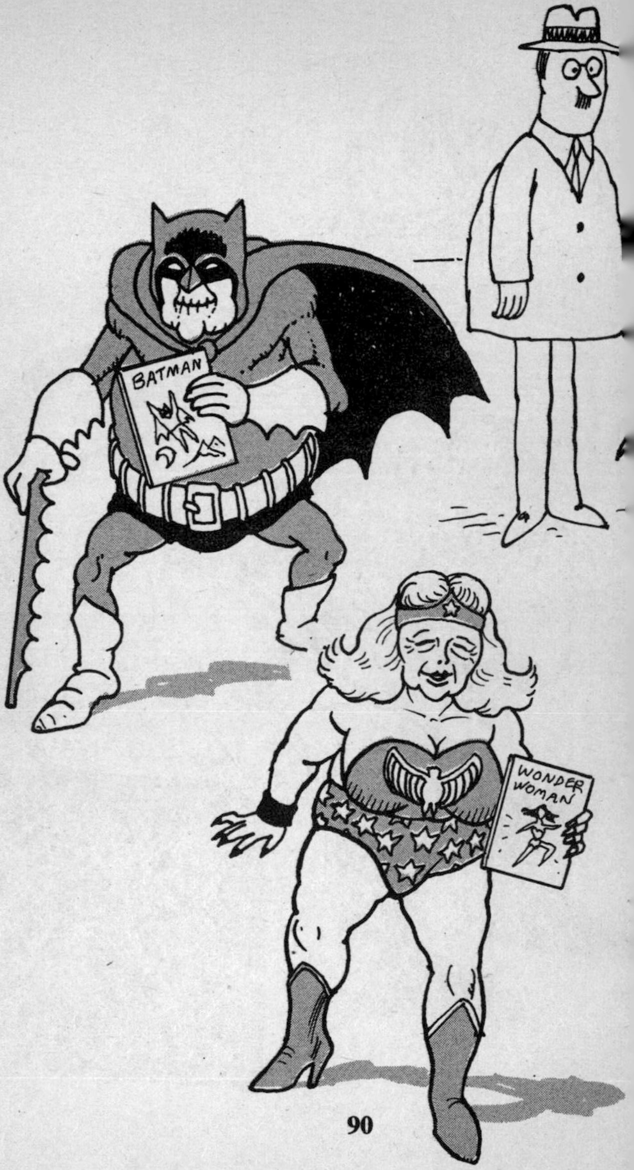
BATMAN
WONDER WOMAN

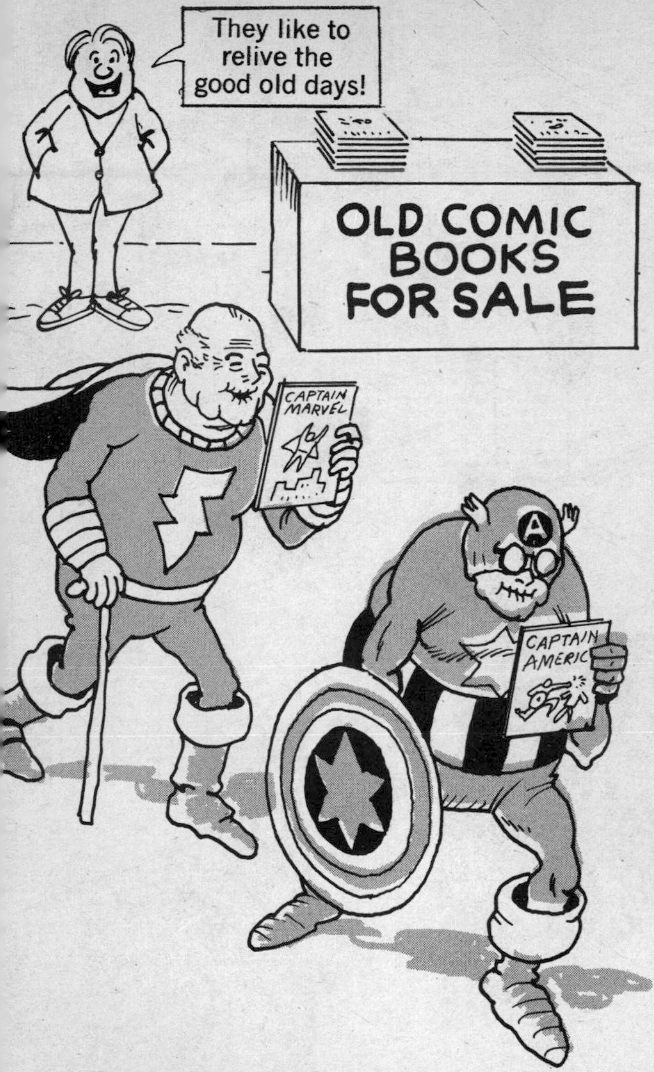
They like to relive the good old days!
OLD COMIC BOOKS FOR SALE
CAPTAIN MARVEL
CAPTAIN AMERIC

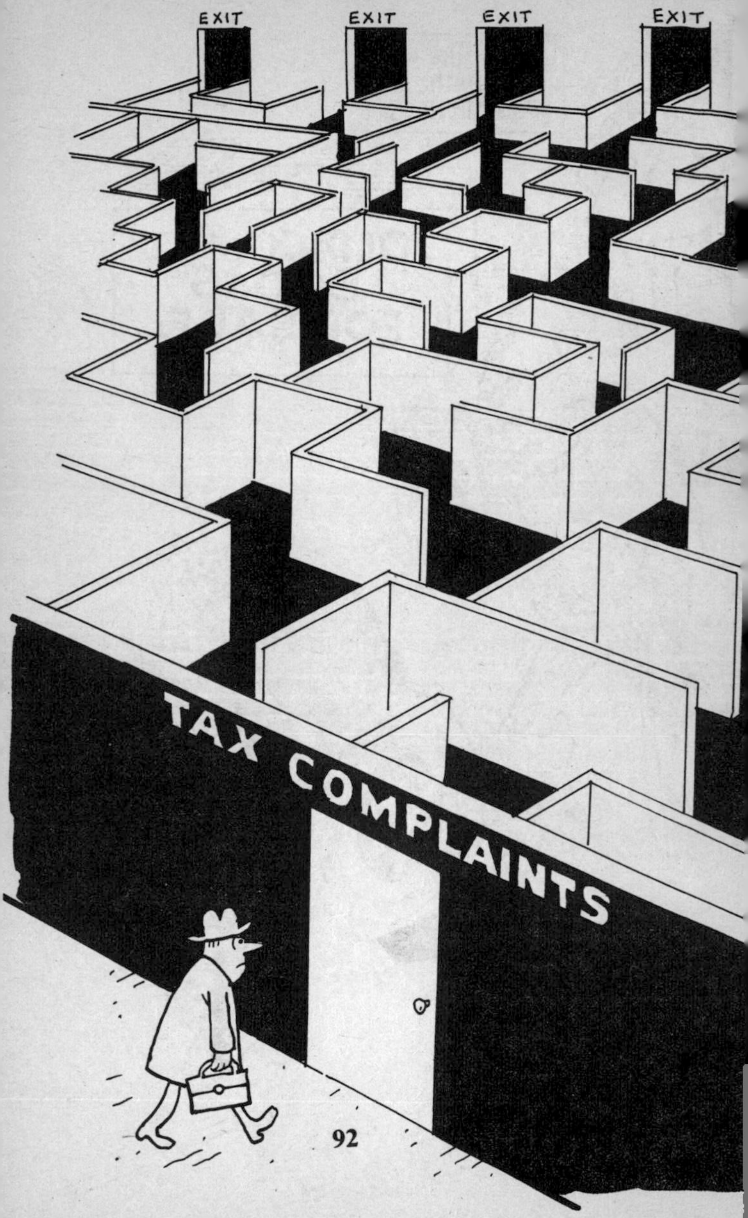
EXIT
EXIT
EXIT
EXIT
TAX COMPLAINTS

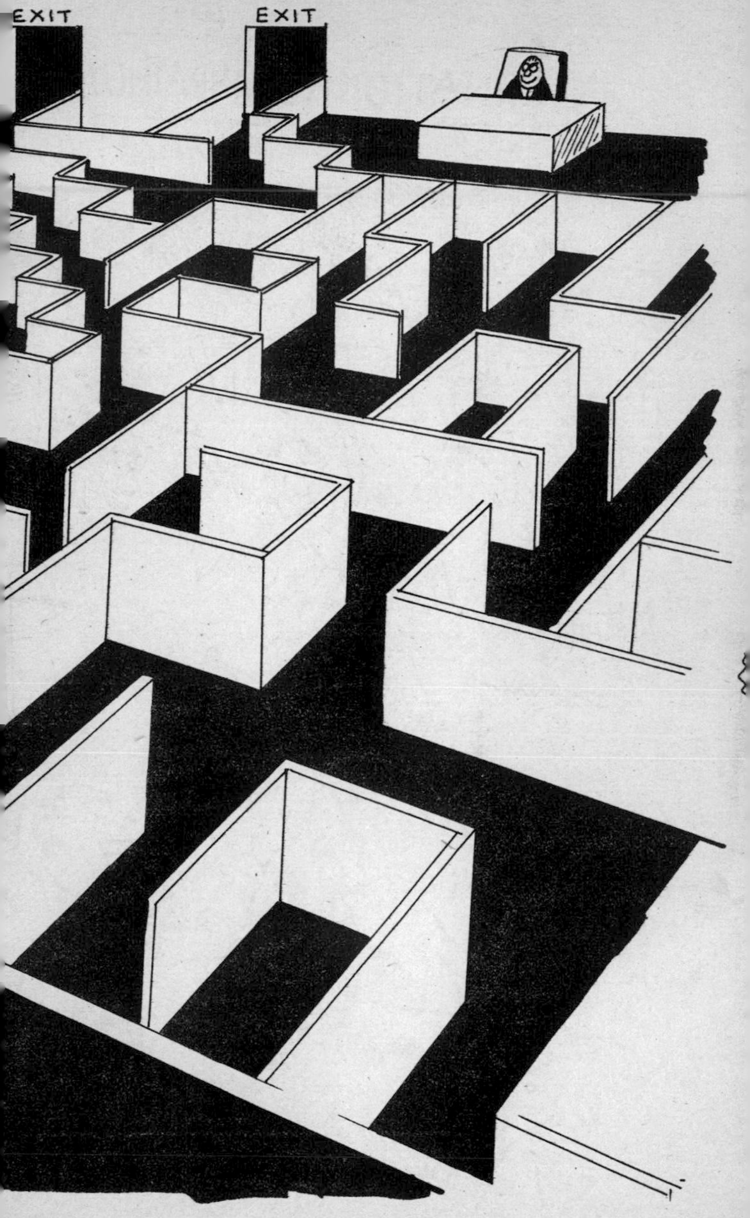
EXIT
EXIT

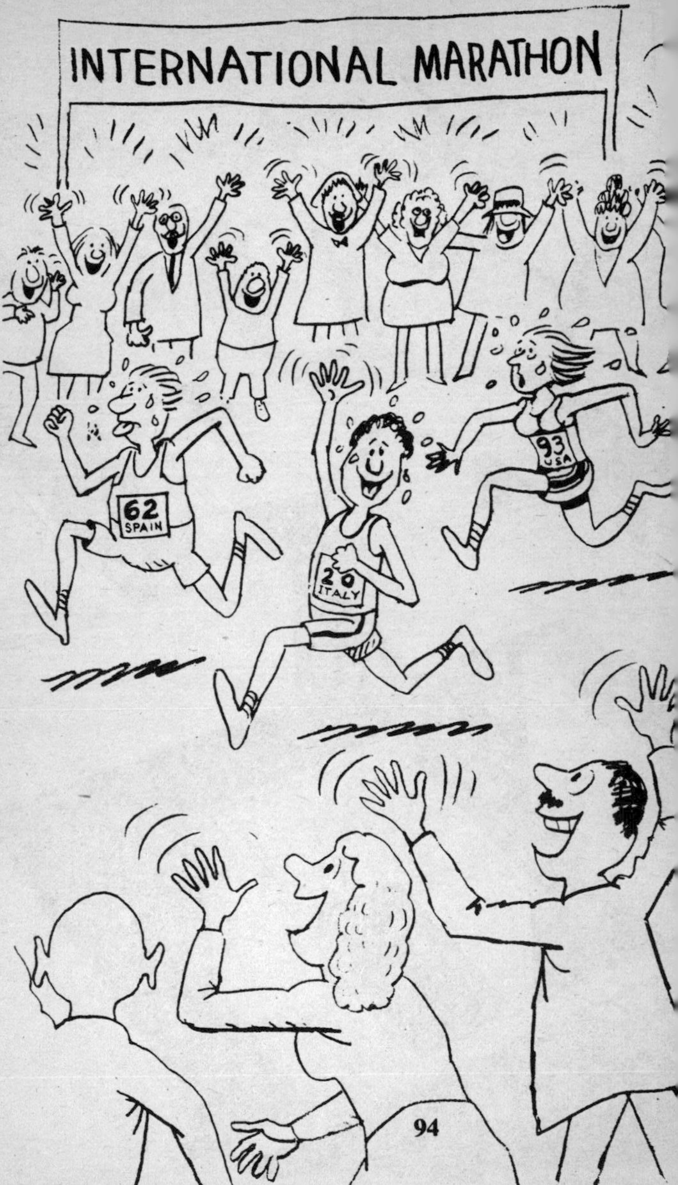
INTERNATIONAL MARATHON
62
SPAIN
20
ITALY
93
USA

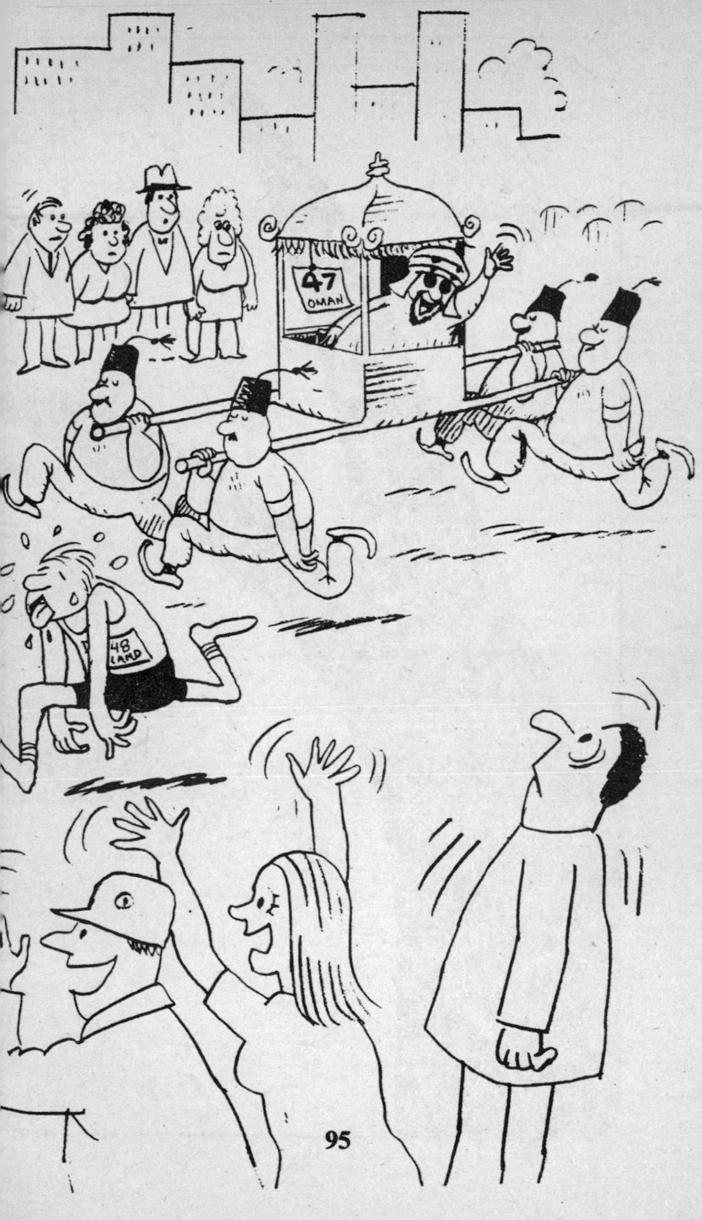
47
OMAN
48

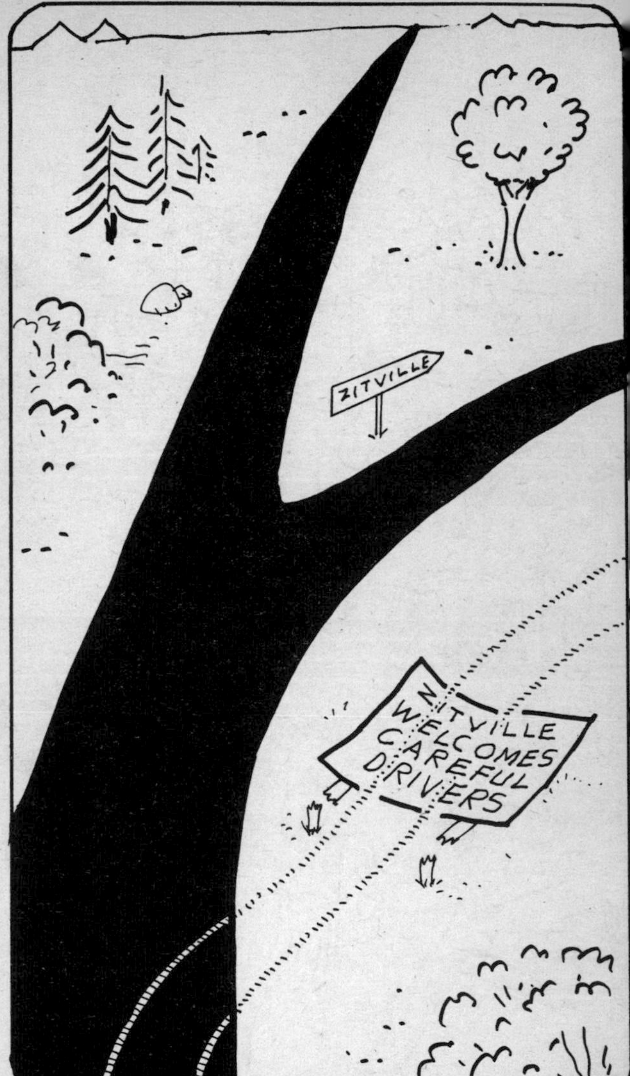
ZITVILLE
ZITVILLE WELCOMES CAREFUL DRIVERS

FILM FLIM FLAM

MORE

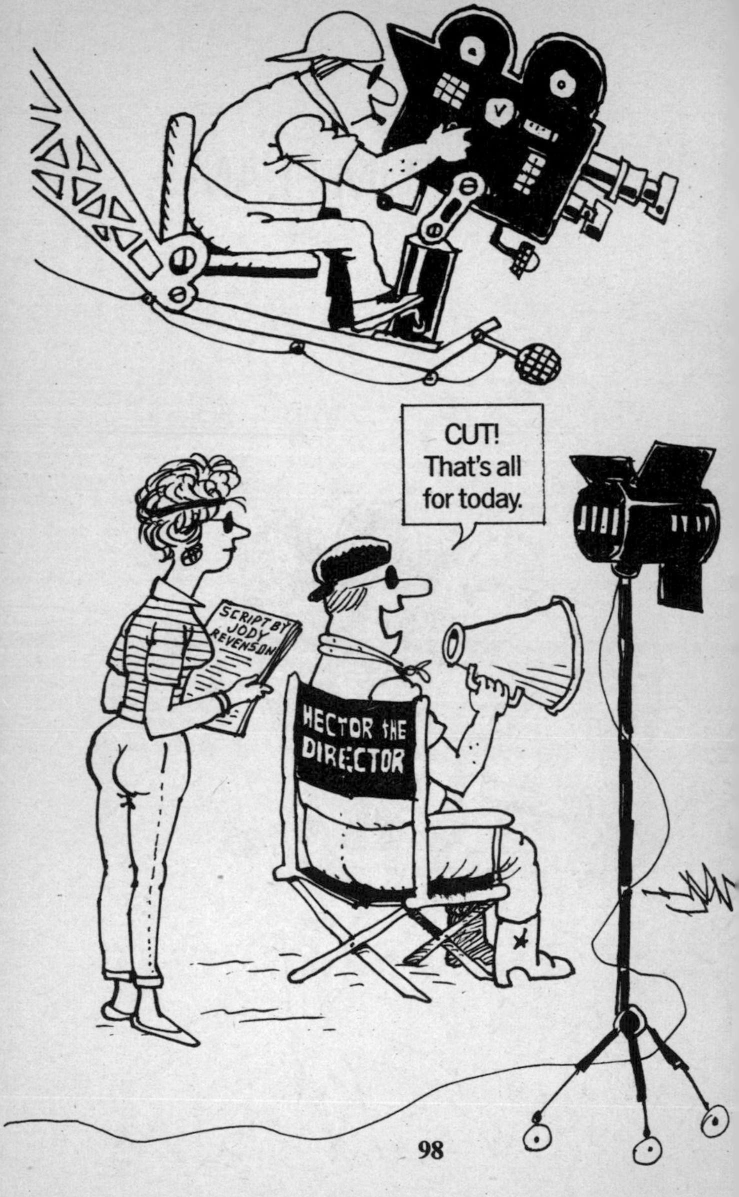
CUT!
That's all
for today.
SCRIPT BY
JODY
REVENSON
HECTOR THE
DIRECTOR

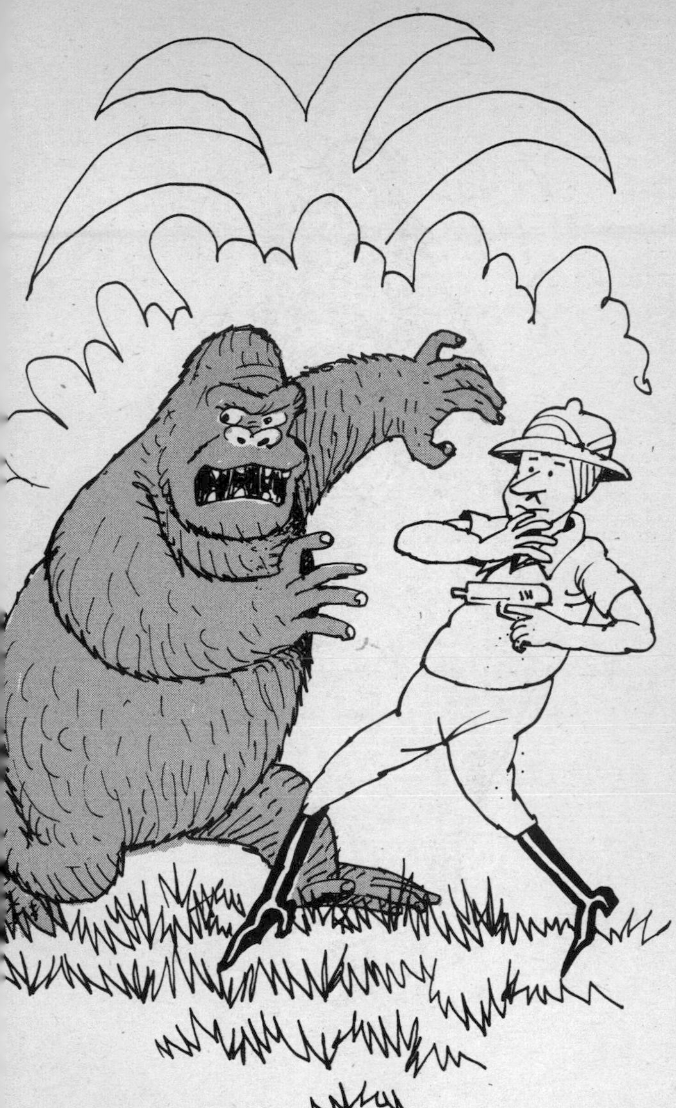

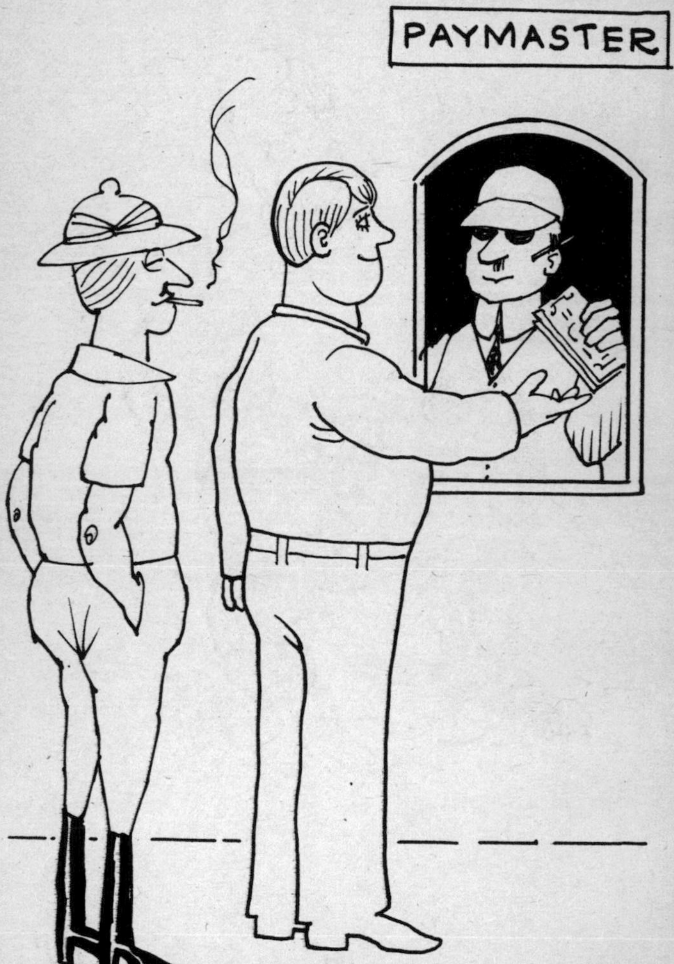
PAYMASTER

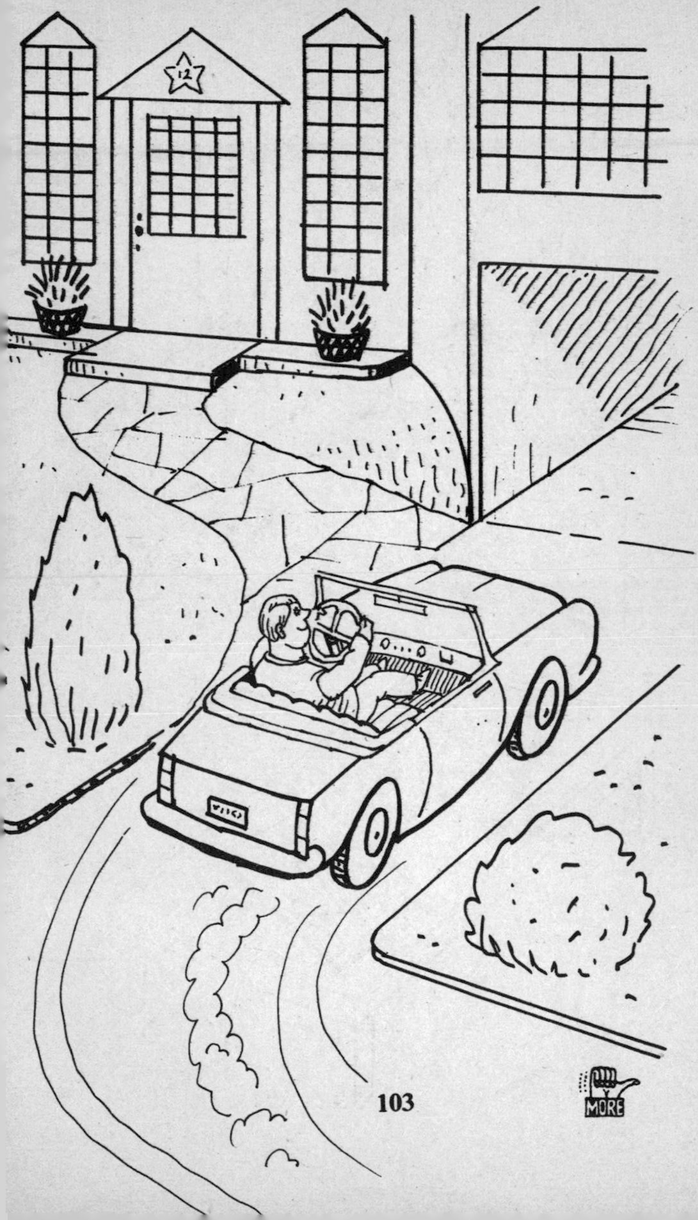
12

MORE

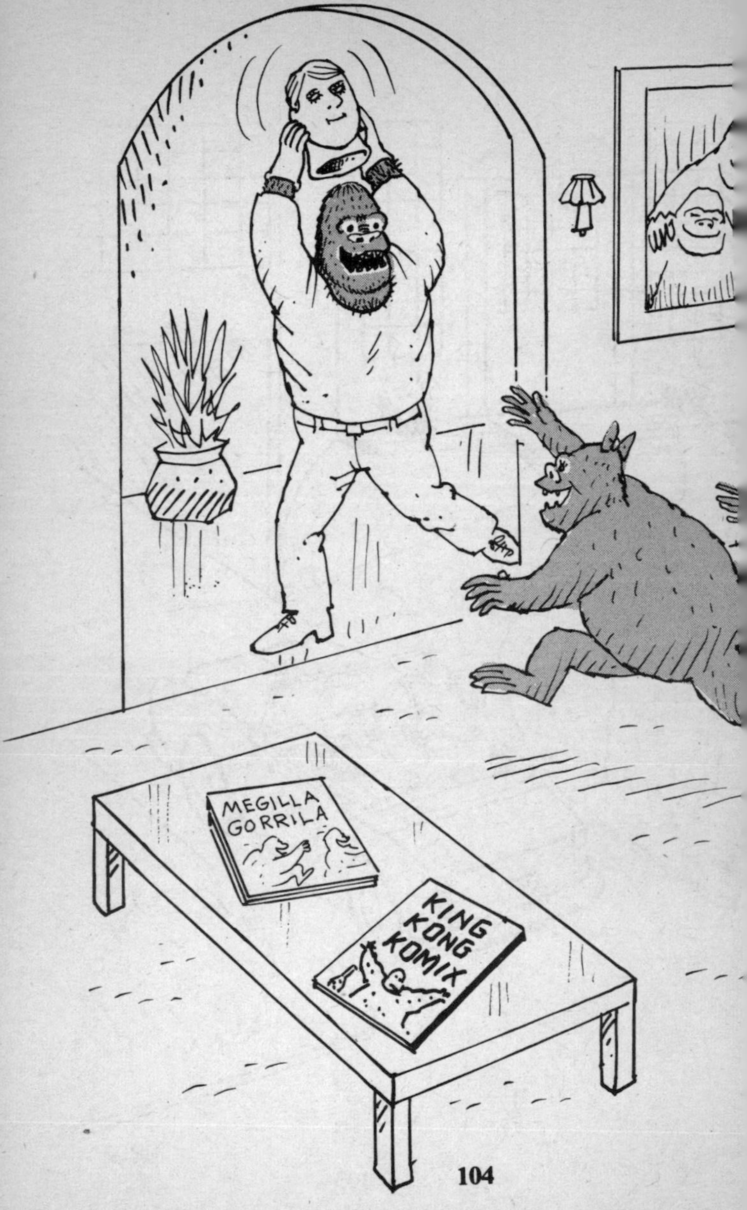
MEGILLA GORRILA
KING KONG KOMIX

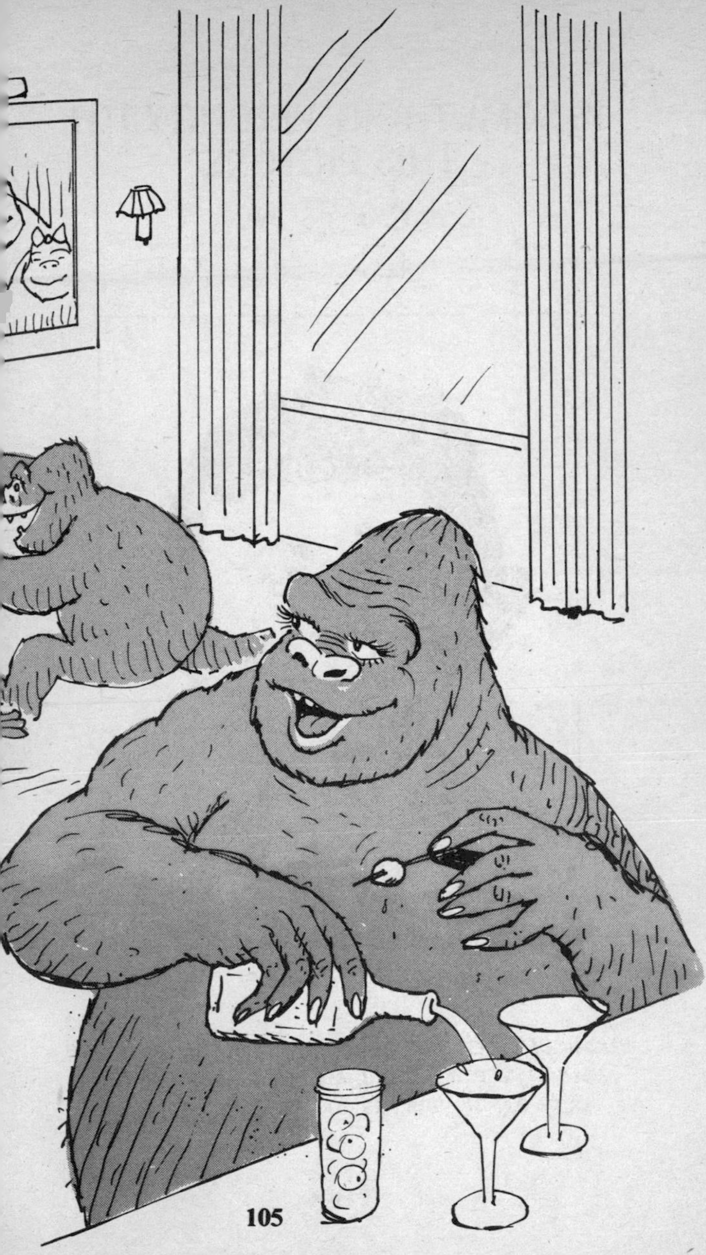

IS SOMETHING WRONG WITH THIS PICTURE?

YES   NO

☐   ☐

ANSWER: If your answer was "yes," you're wrong. There is nothing wrong with this picture. This is a picture of Marvin C. Neuman, Alfred E. Neuman's cousin.

BOOR TOUR

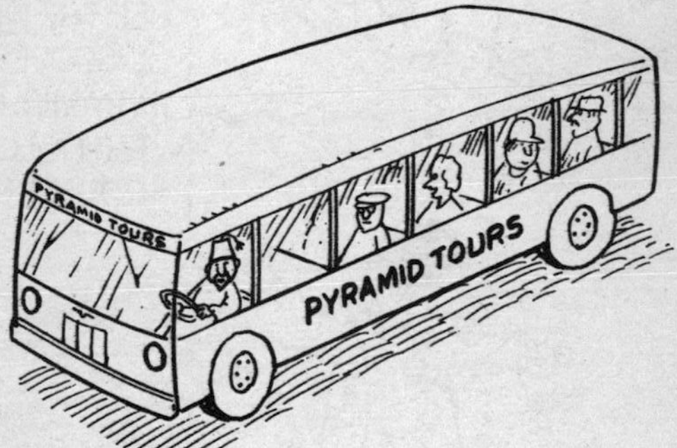
PYRAMID TOURS
PYRAMID TOURS

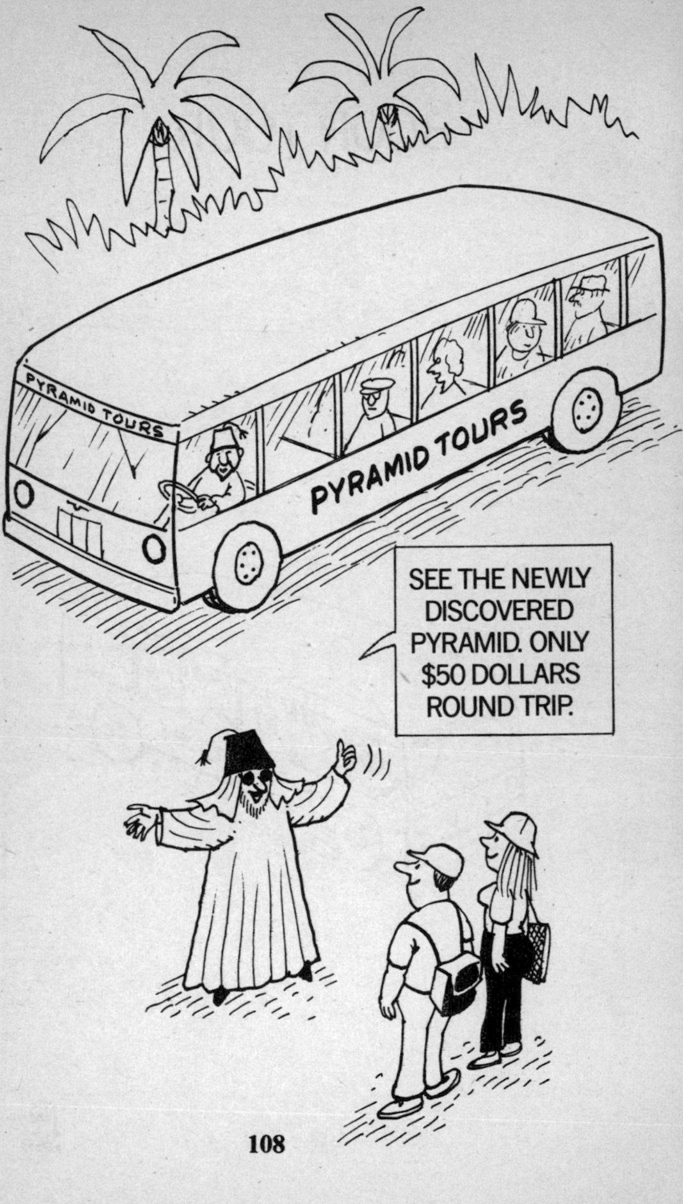
PYRAMID TOURS
PYRAMID TOURS
SEE THE NEWLY DISCOVERED PYRAMID. ONLY $50 DOLLARS ROUND TRIP.

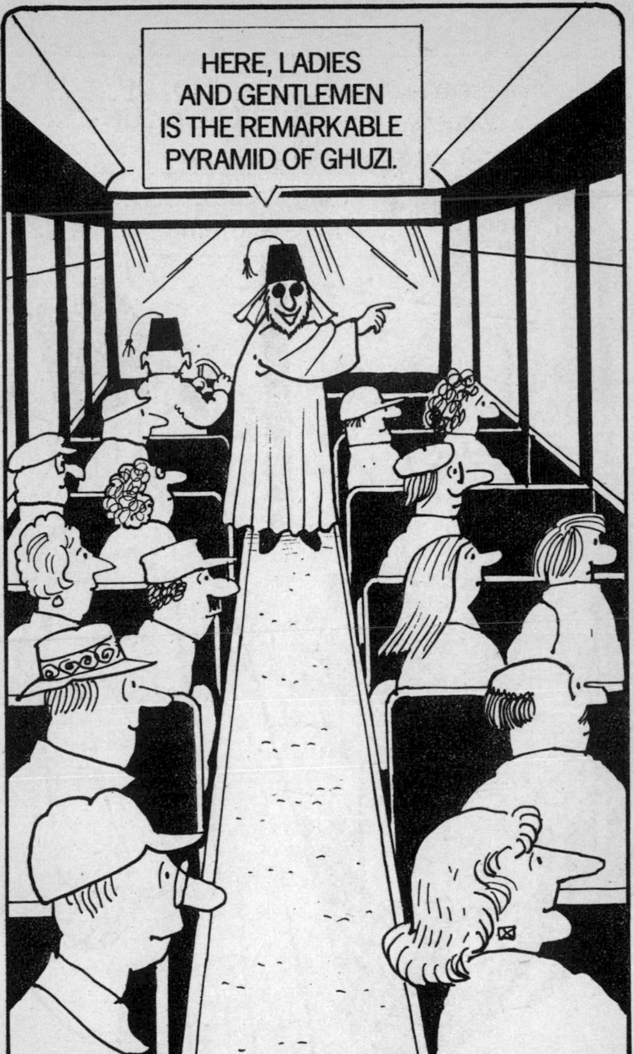
HERE, LADIES AND GENTLEMEN IS THE REMARKABLE PYRAMID OF GHUZI.

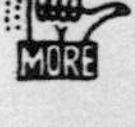
MORE

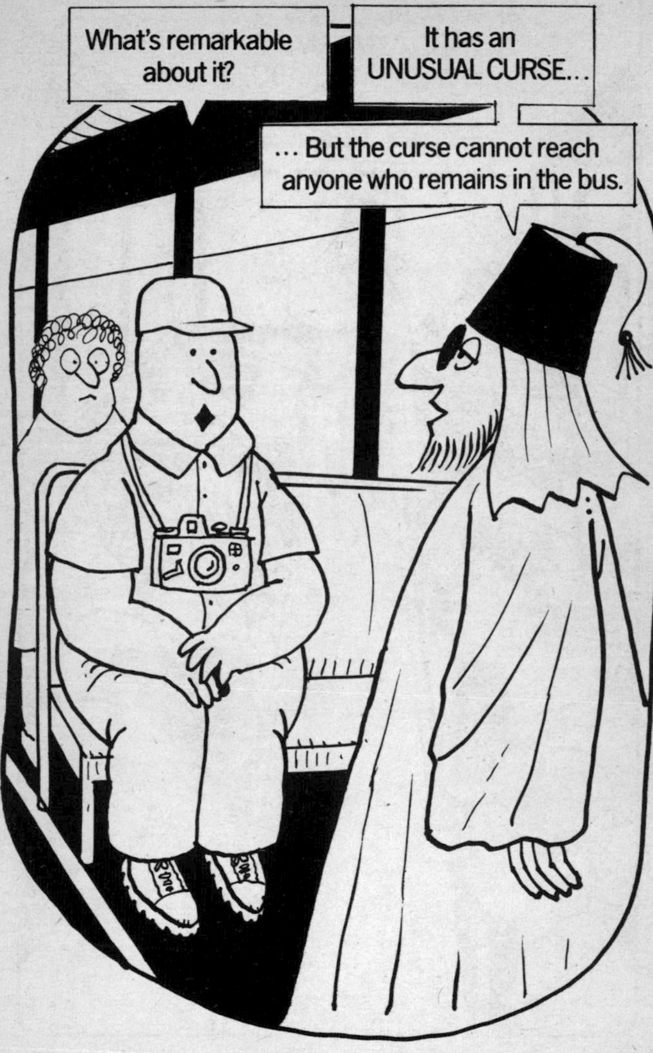
What's remarkable about it?
It has an UNUSUAL CURSE...
... But the curse cannot reach anyone who remains in the bus.

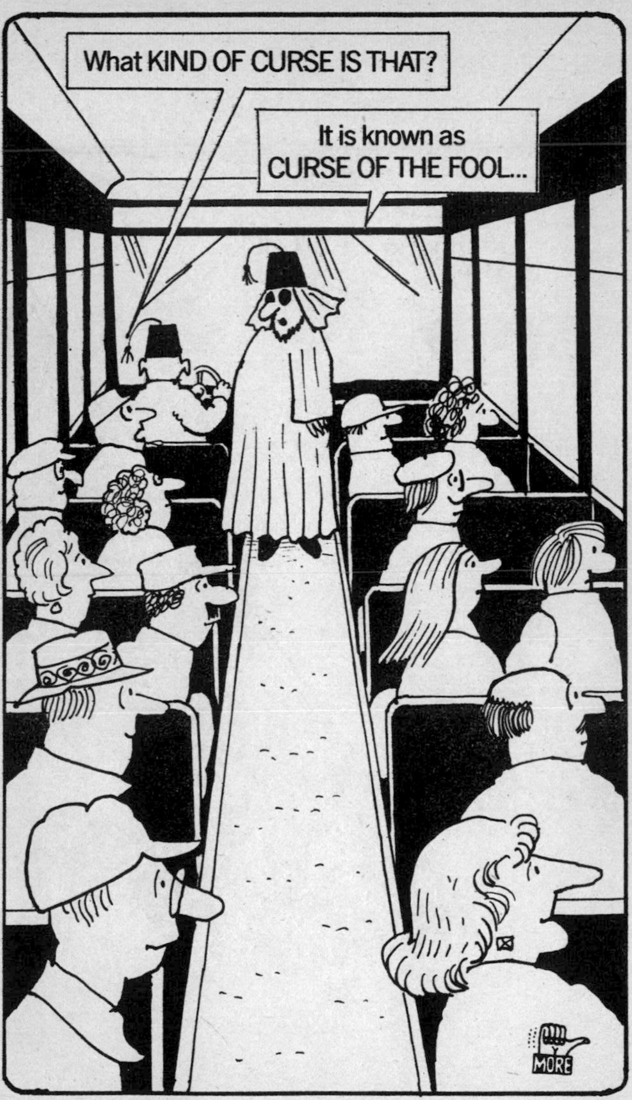
What KIND OF CURSE IS THAT?
It is known as CURSE OF THE FOOL...
MORE

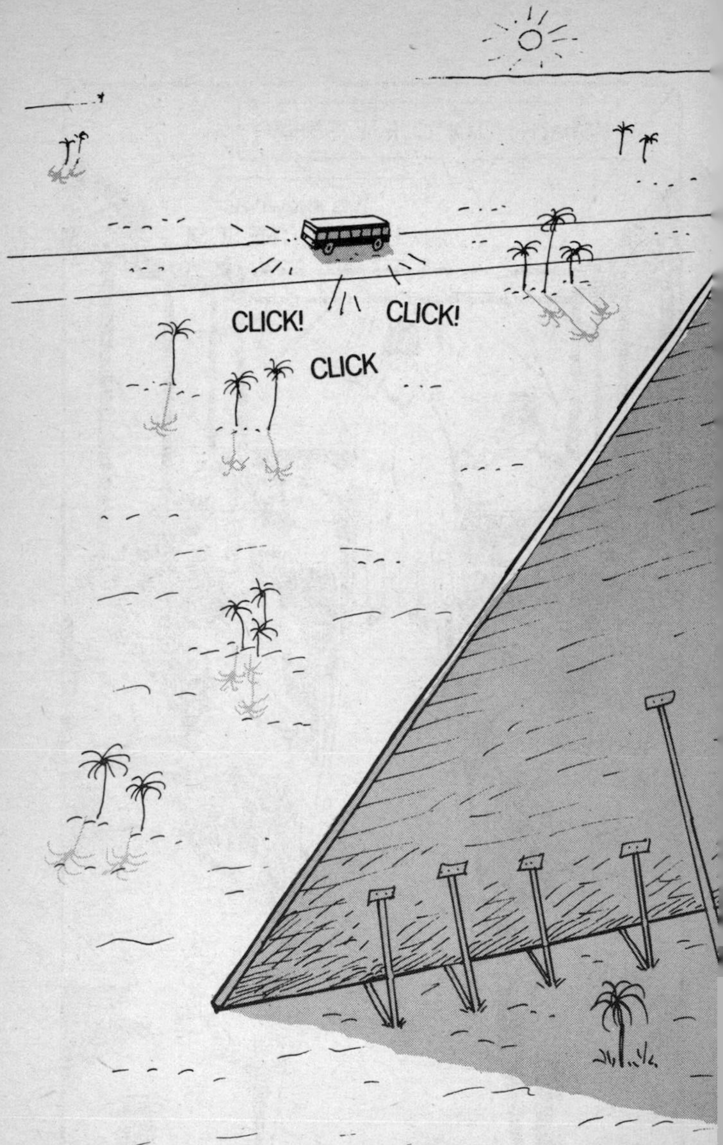
CLICK!
CLICK!
CLICK

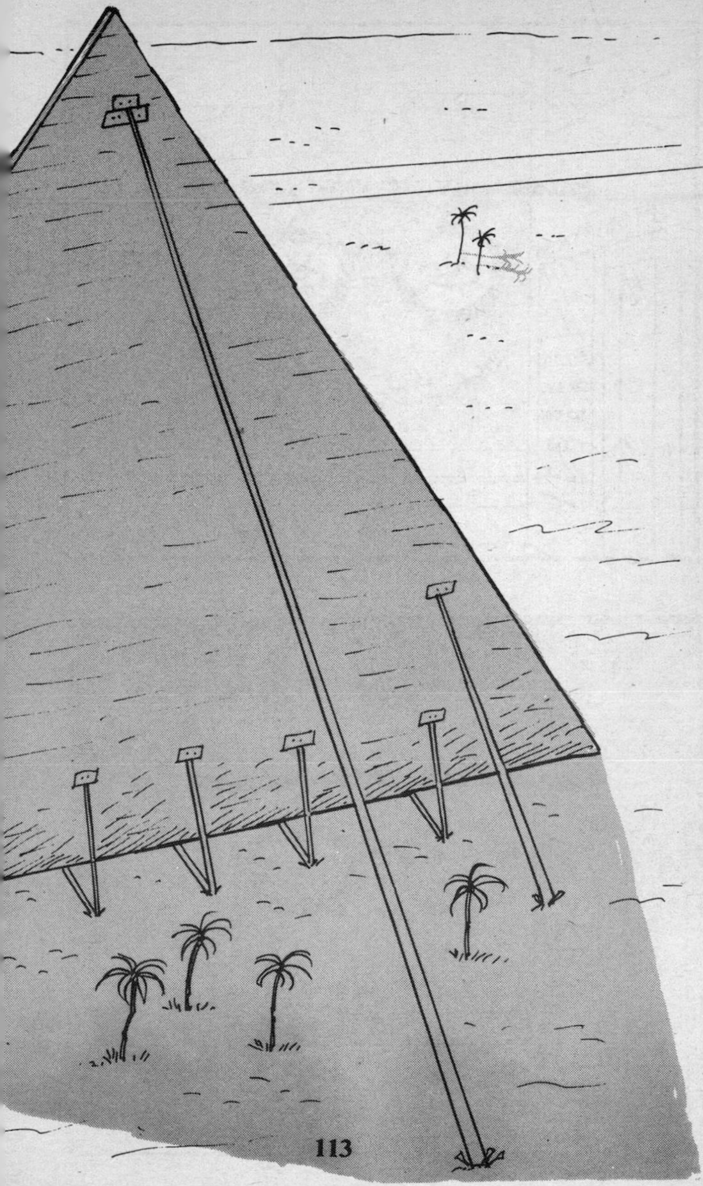

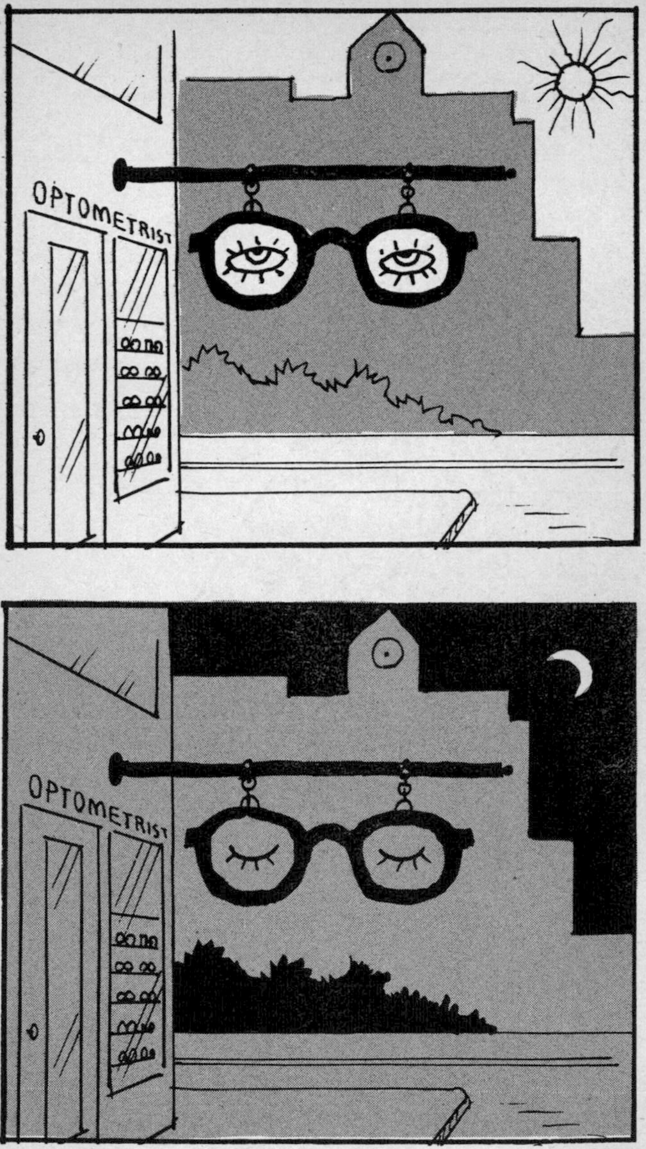
OPTOMETRIST
OPTOMETRIST

FRIGHT FLIGHT

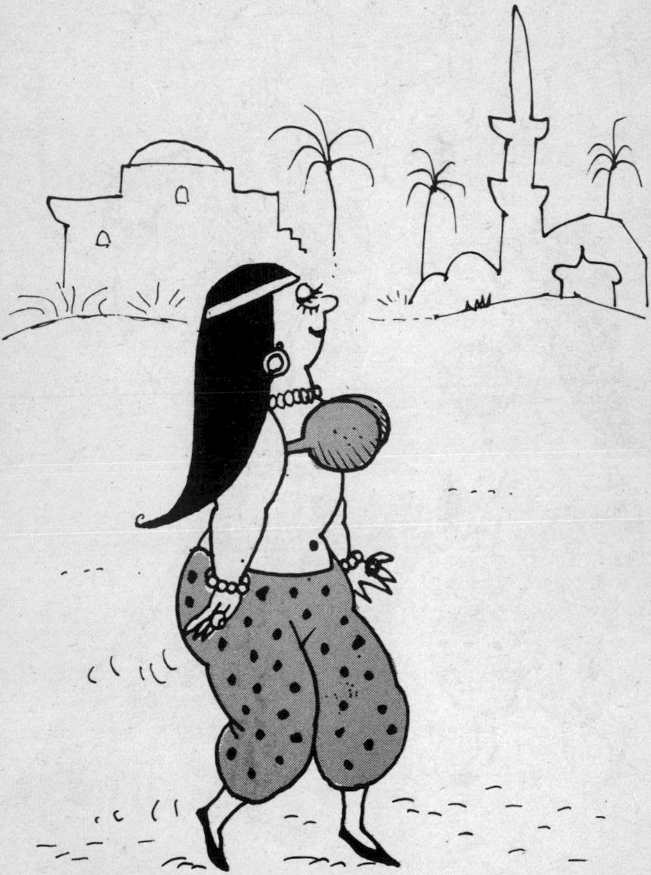

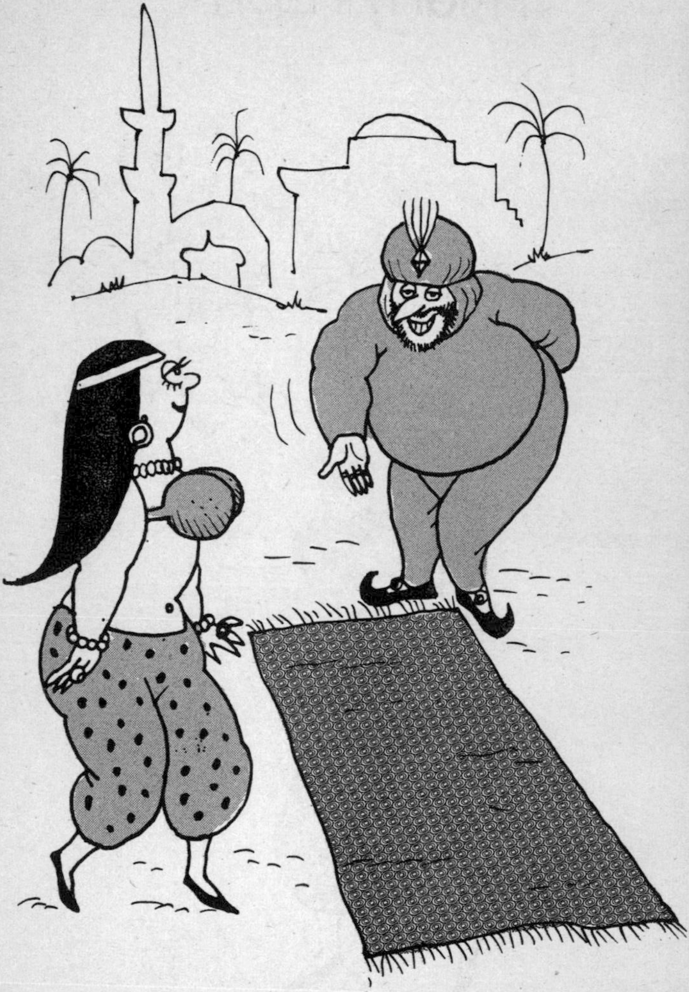

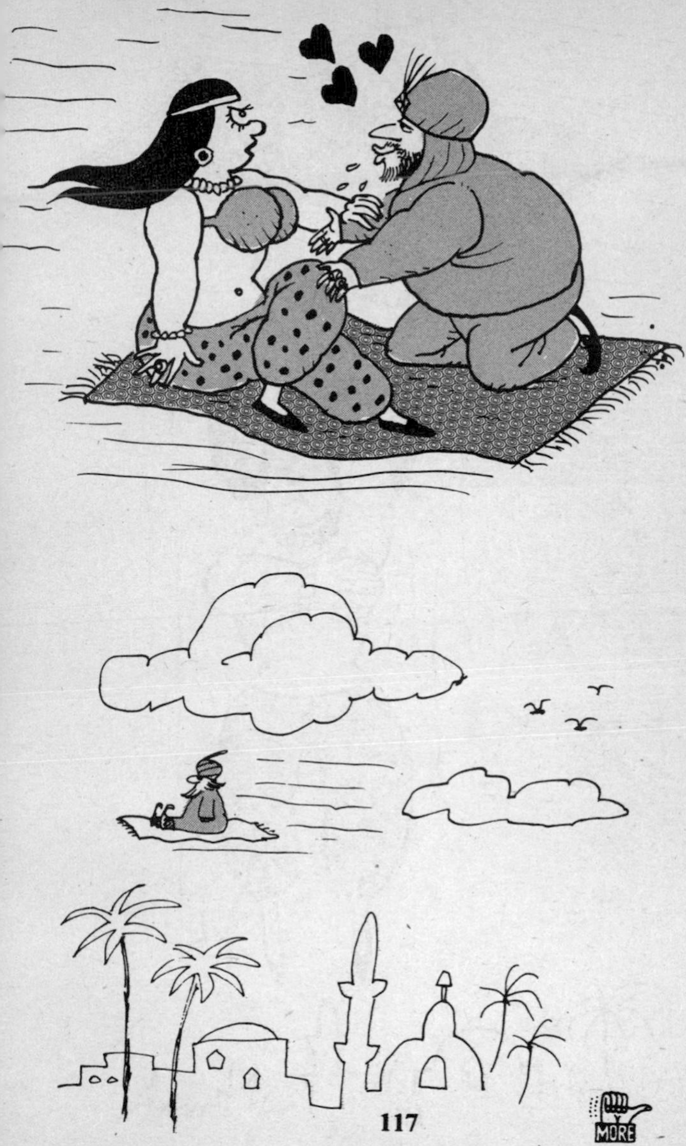
MORE

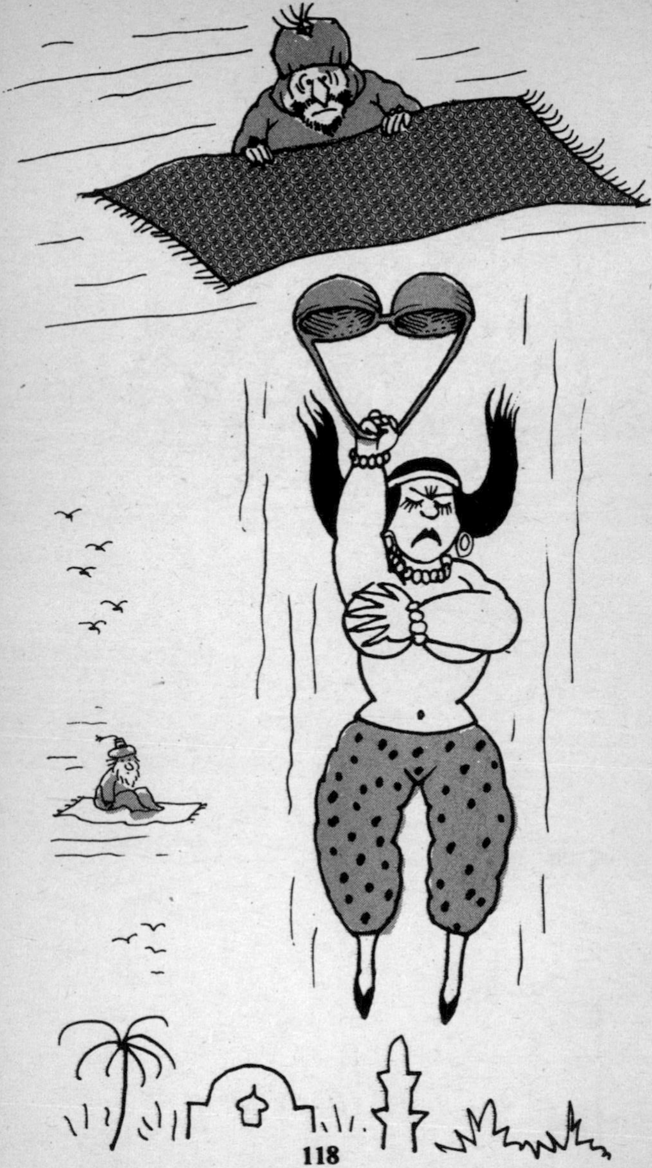

WALK TALK

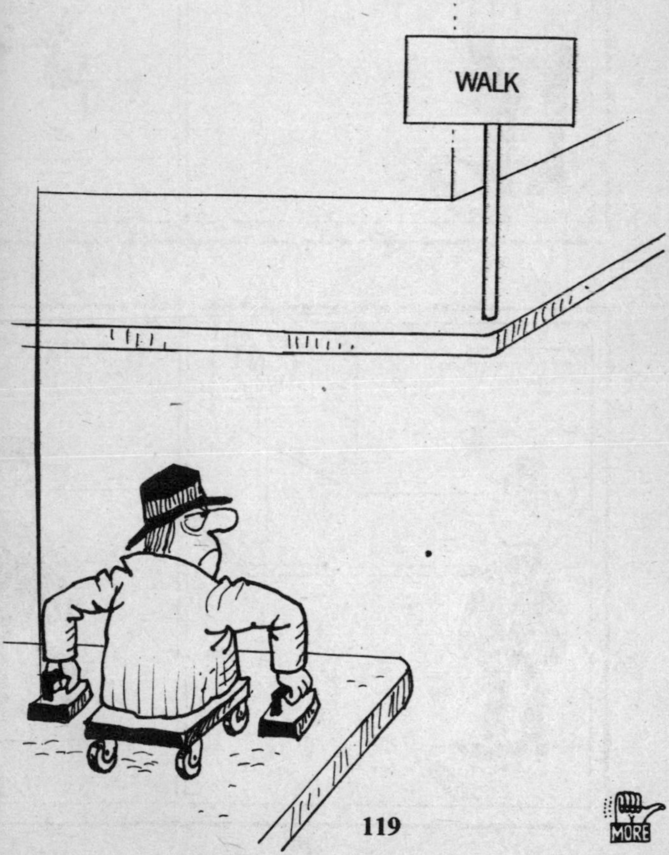
WALK

MORE

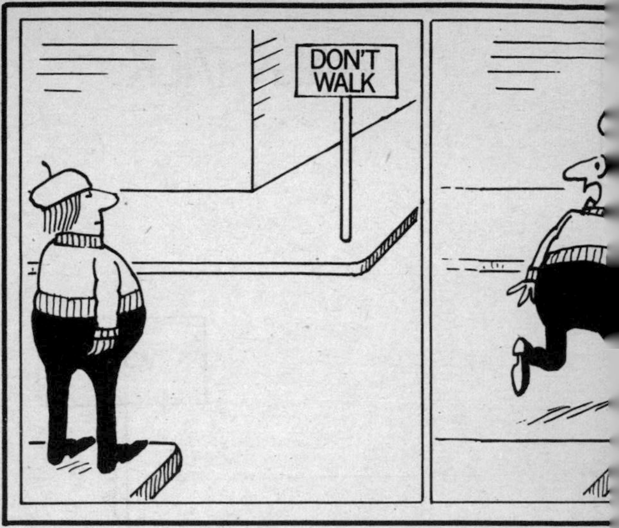
DON'T WALK

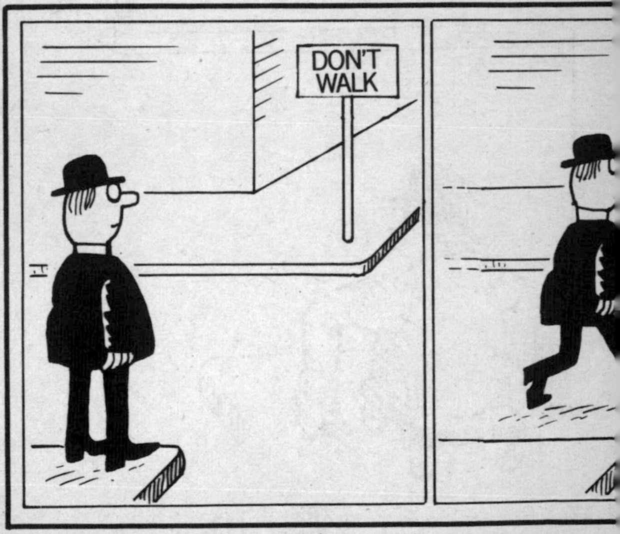
DON'T WALK

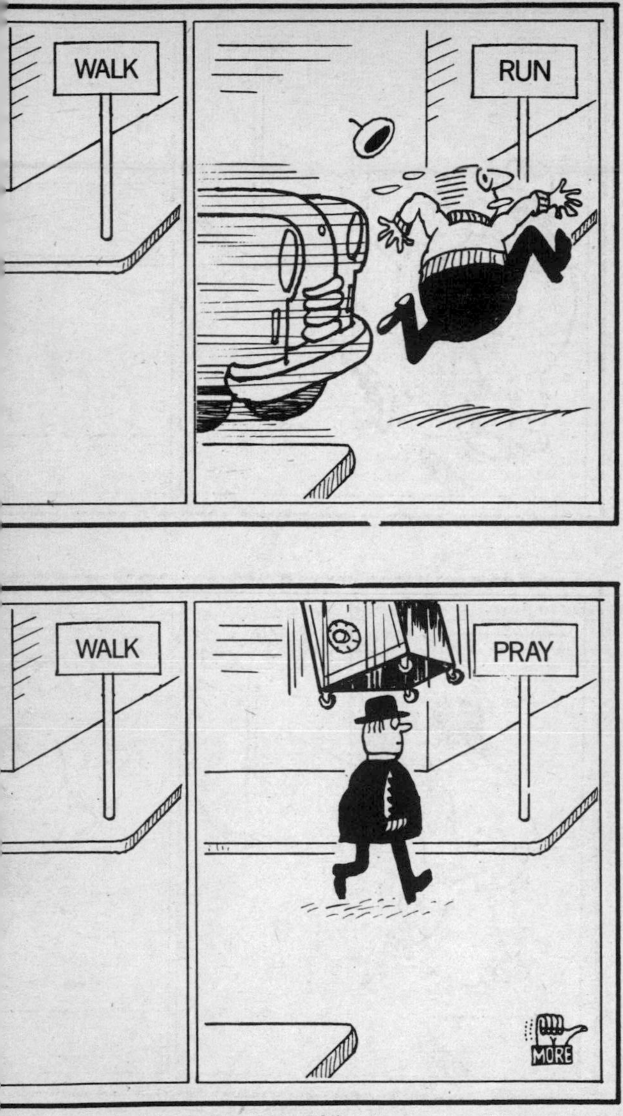
WALK
RUN
WALK
PRAY
MORE

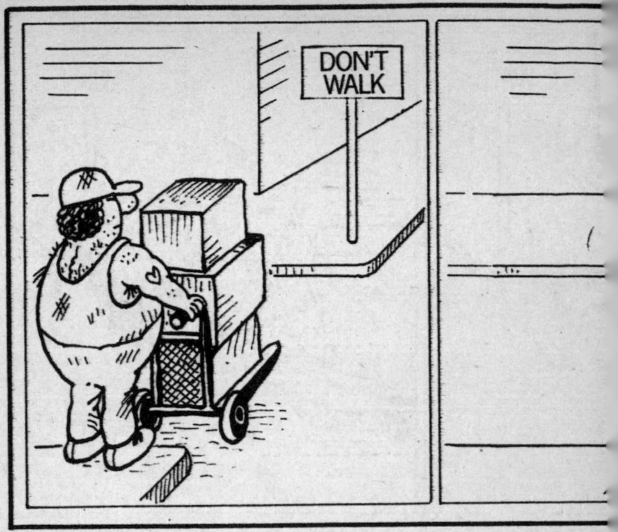
DON'T
WALK

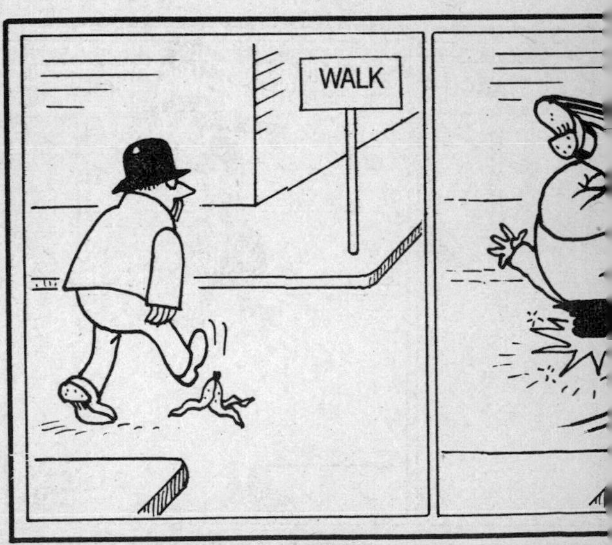
WALK

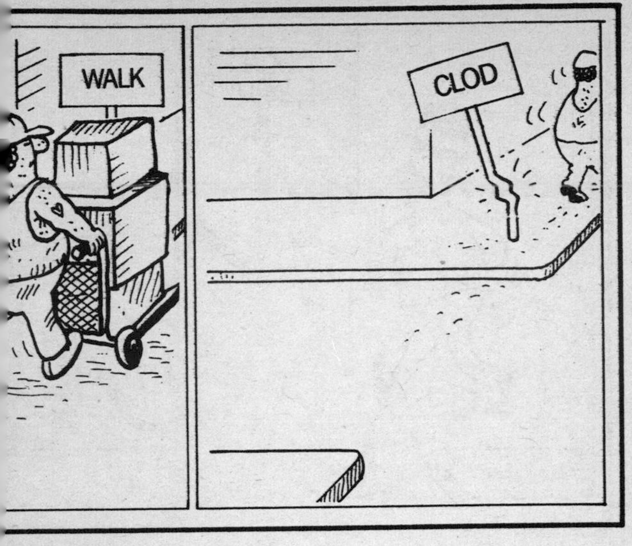
WALK
CLOD

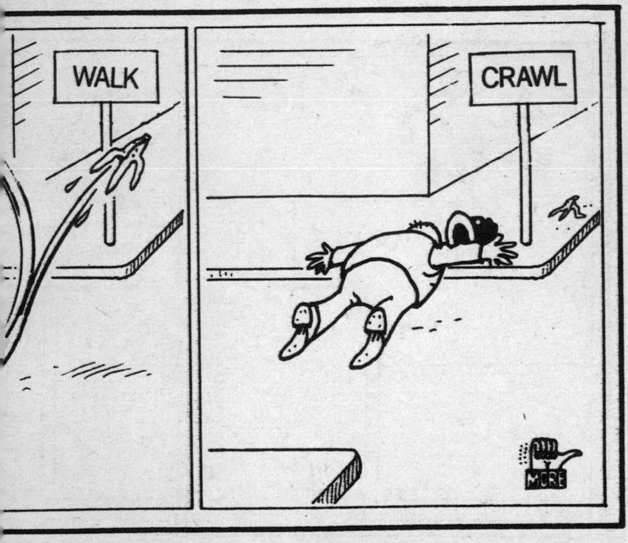
WALK
CRAWL
MORE

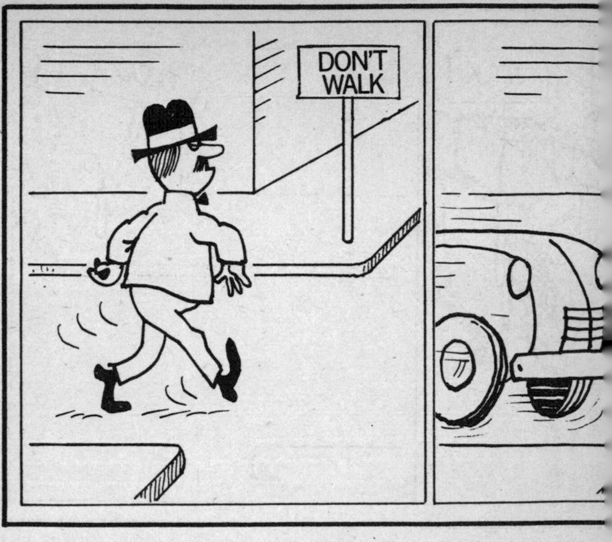
DON'T
WALK

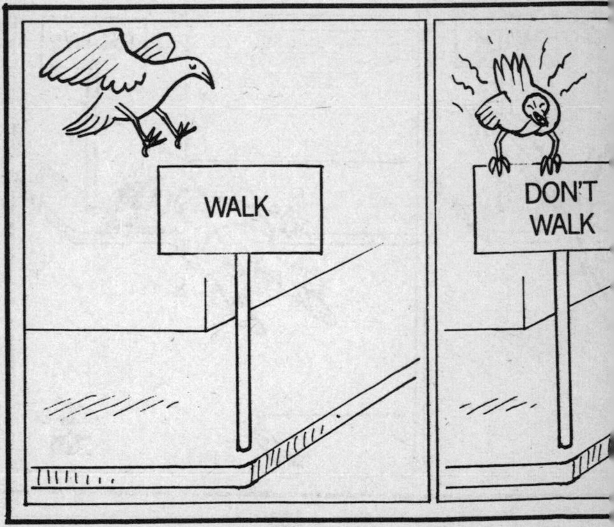
WALK
DON'T
WALK

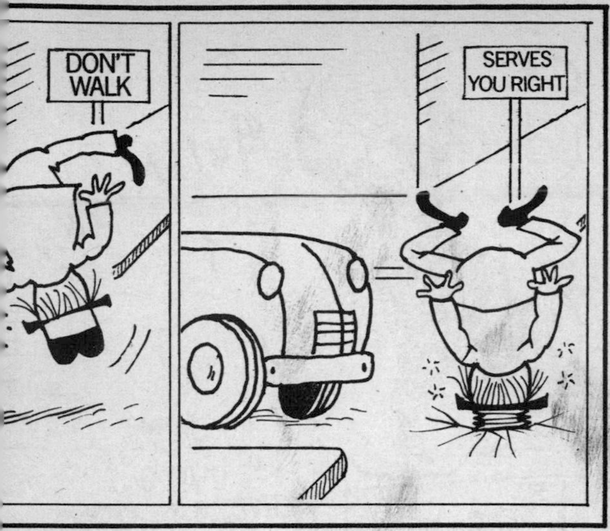
DON'T WALK
SERVES YOU RIGHT

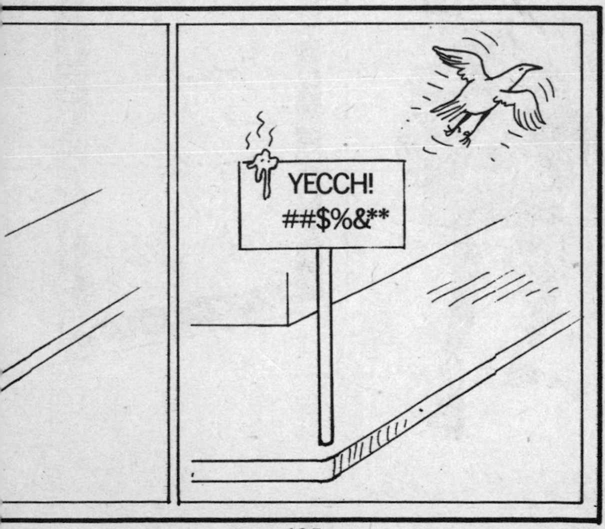
YECCH!
##$%&**

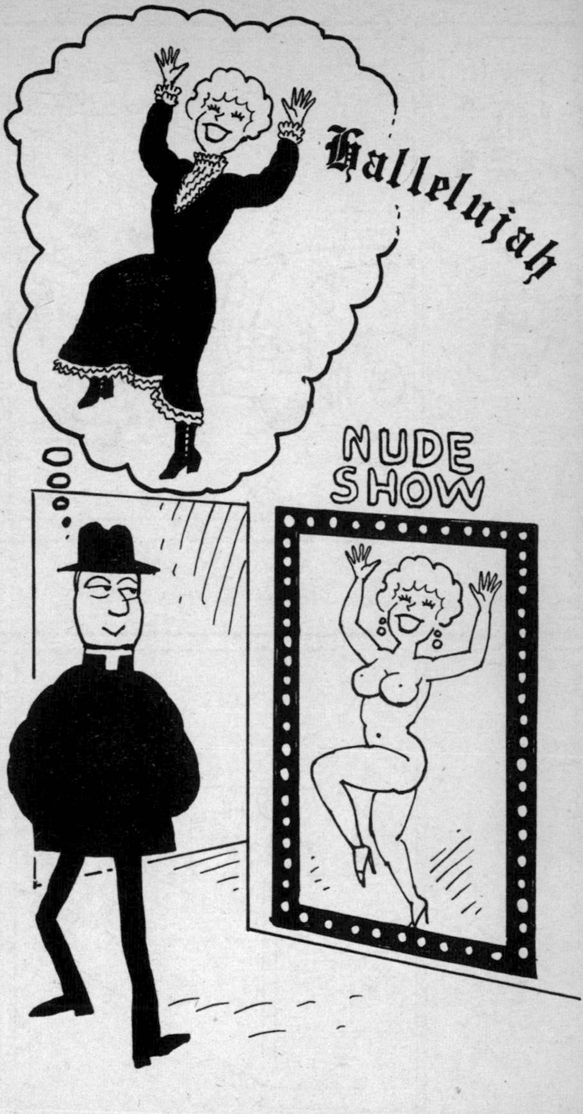
Hallelujah
NUDE SHOW

REFLECTION PERFECTION

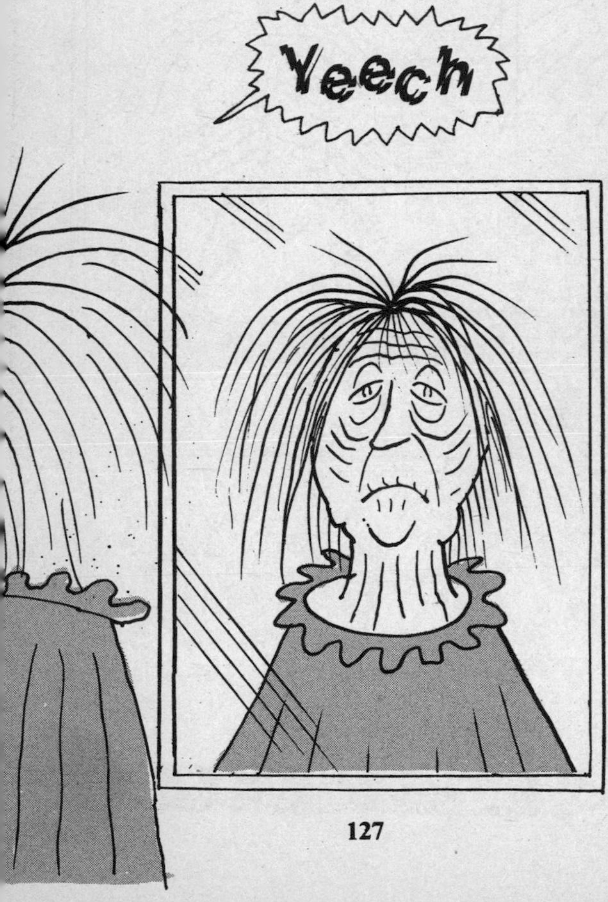
Yeech

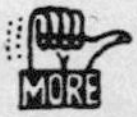
MORE

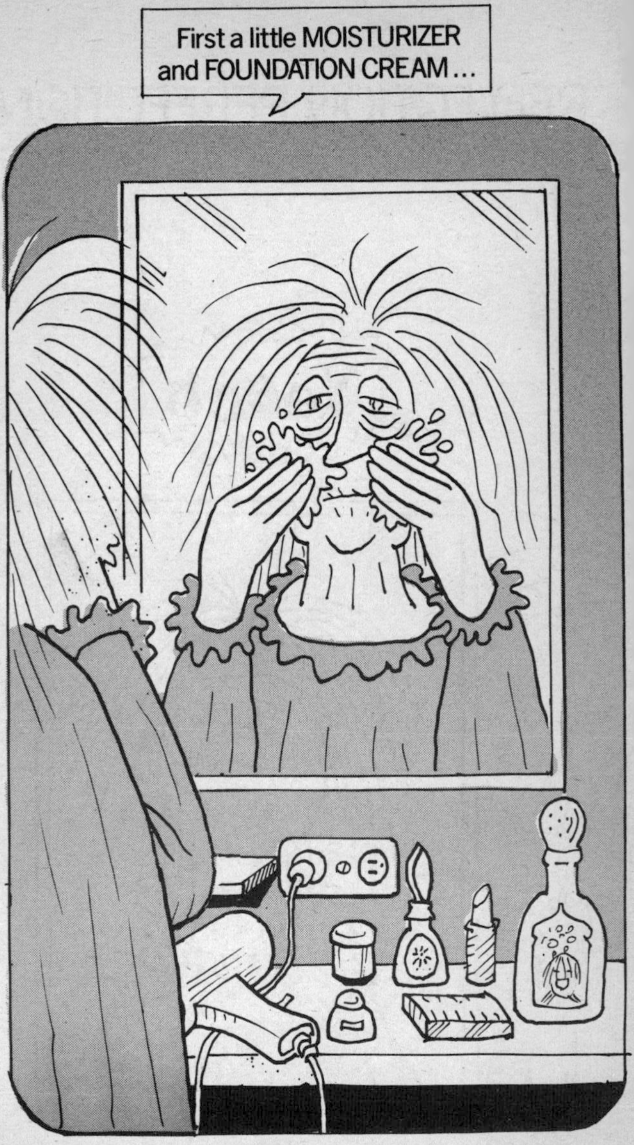
First a little MOISTURIZER
and FOUNDATION CREAM . . .

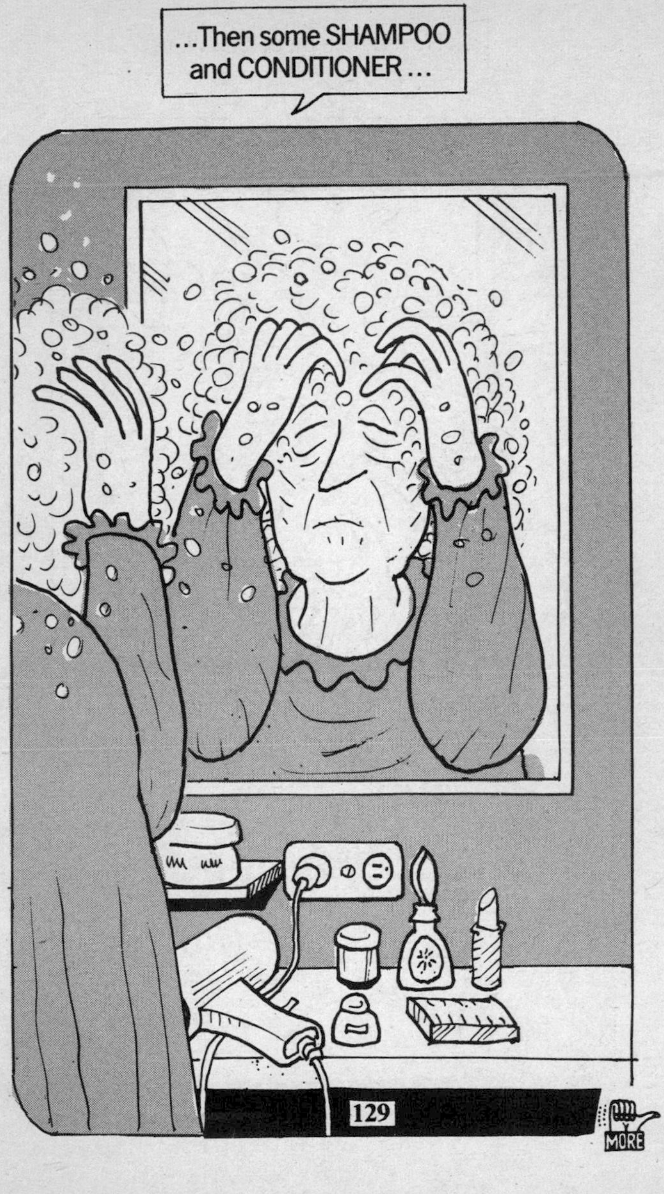
...Then some SHAMPOO and CONDITIONER...
MORE

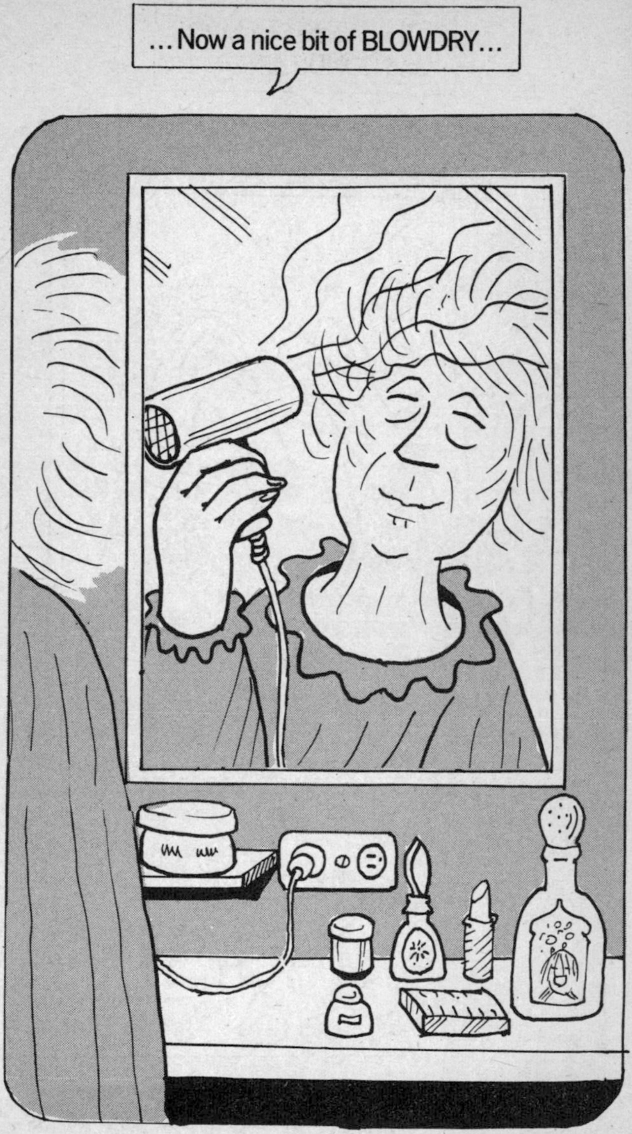
...Now a nice bit of BLOWDRY...

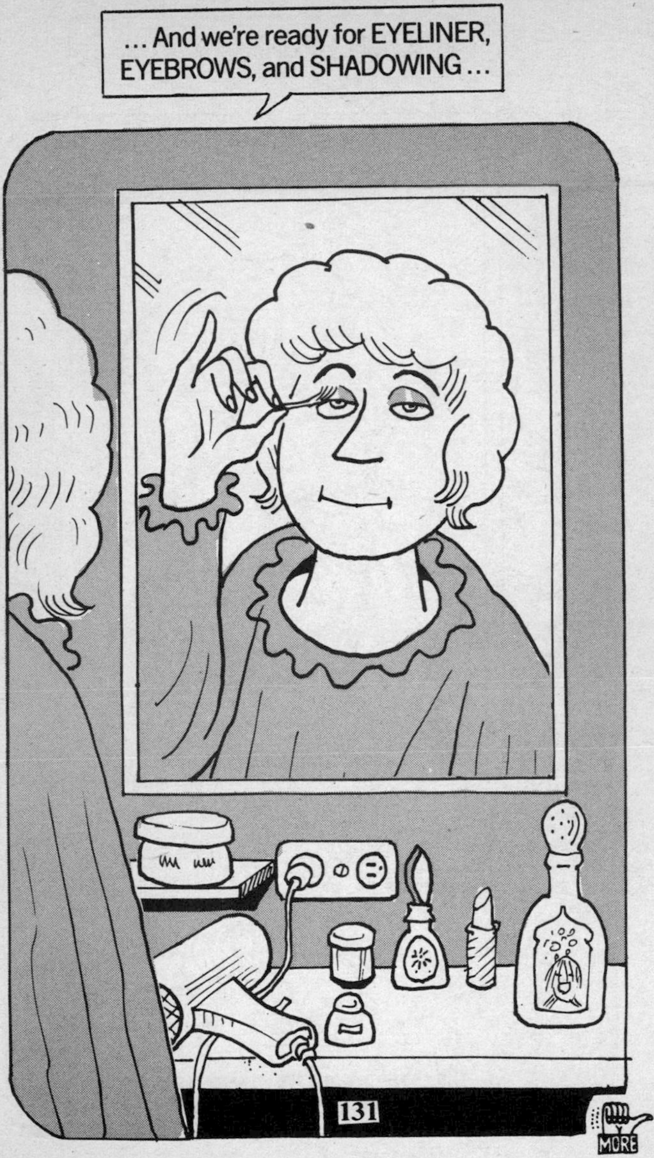
... And we're ready for EYELINER, EYEBROWS, and SHADOWING ...
MORE

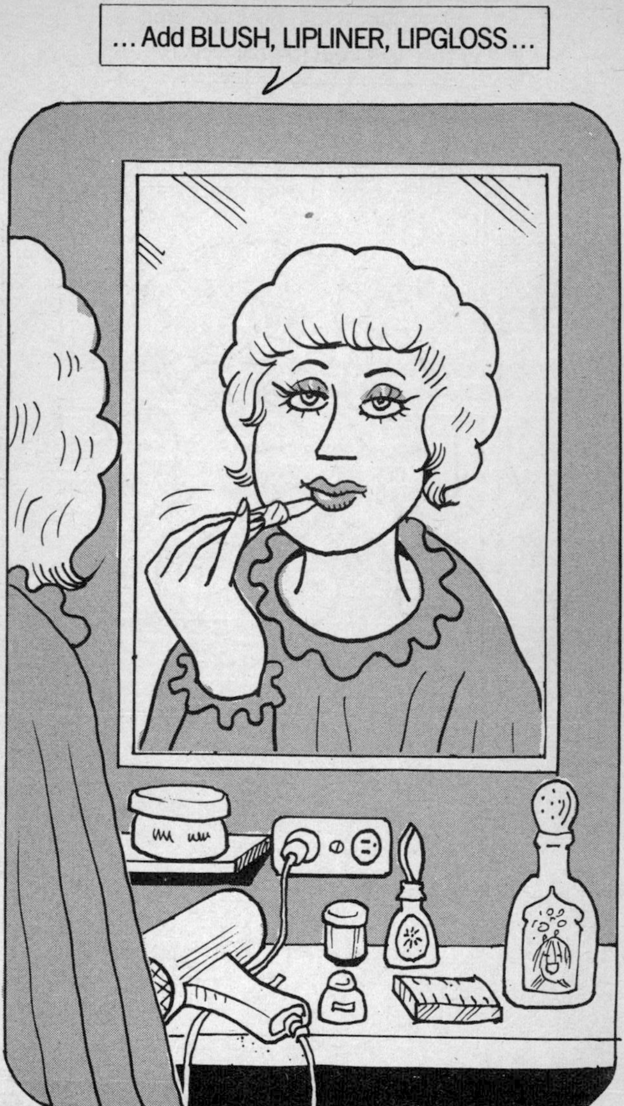
... Add BLUSH, LIPLINER, LIPGLOSS ...

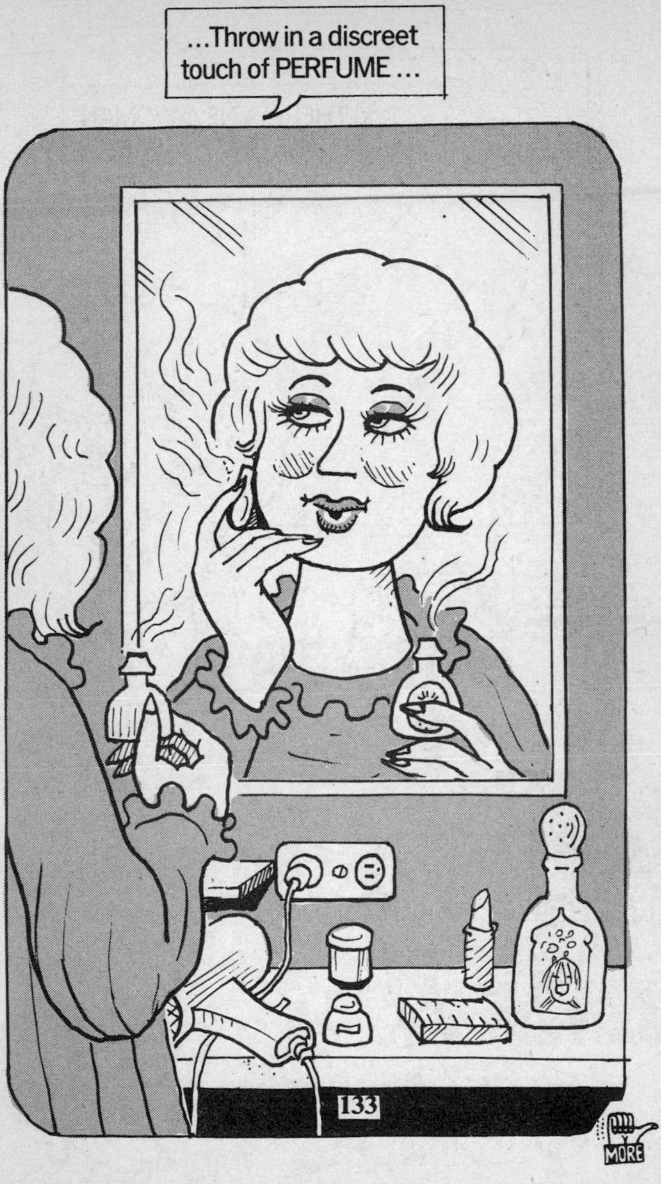
...Throw in a discreet touch of PERFUME ...
MORE

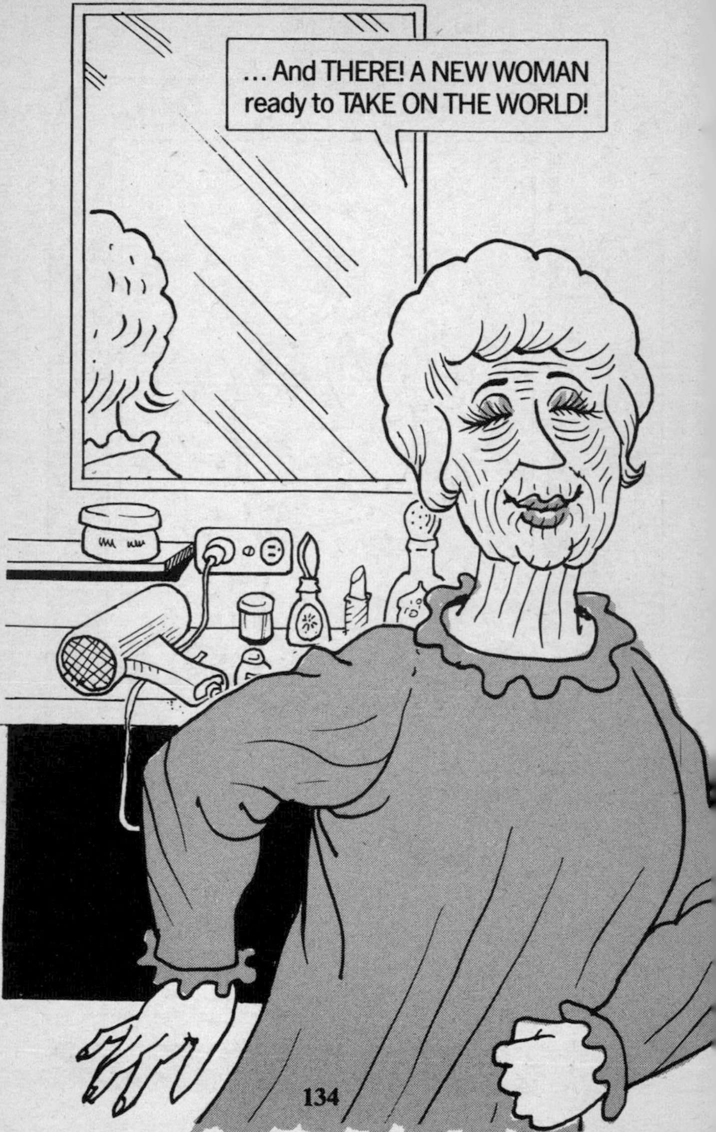
... And THERE! A NEW WOMAN ready to TAKE ON THE WORLD!

PRISON VISIONS

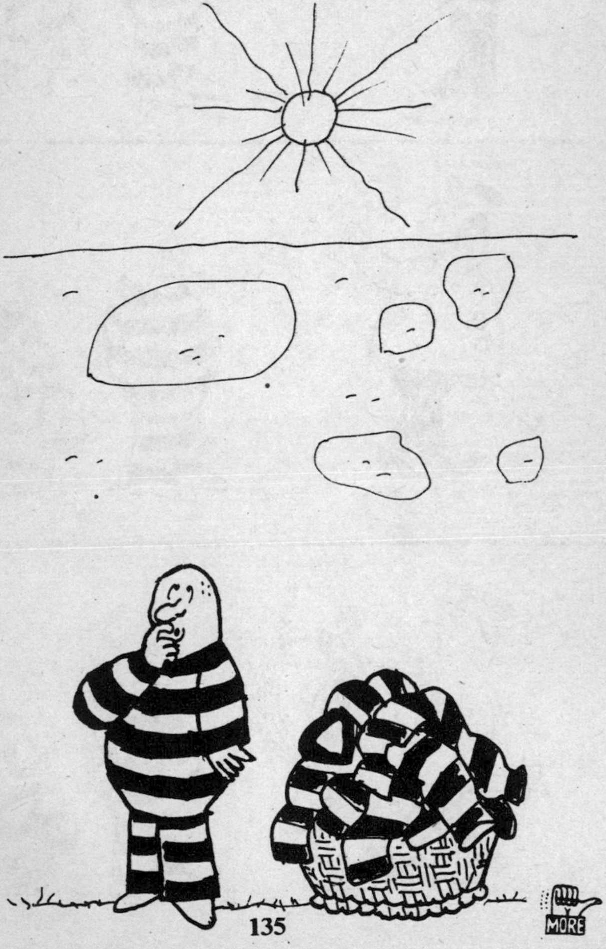
MORE

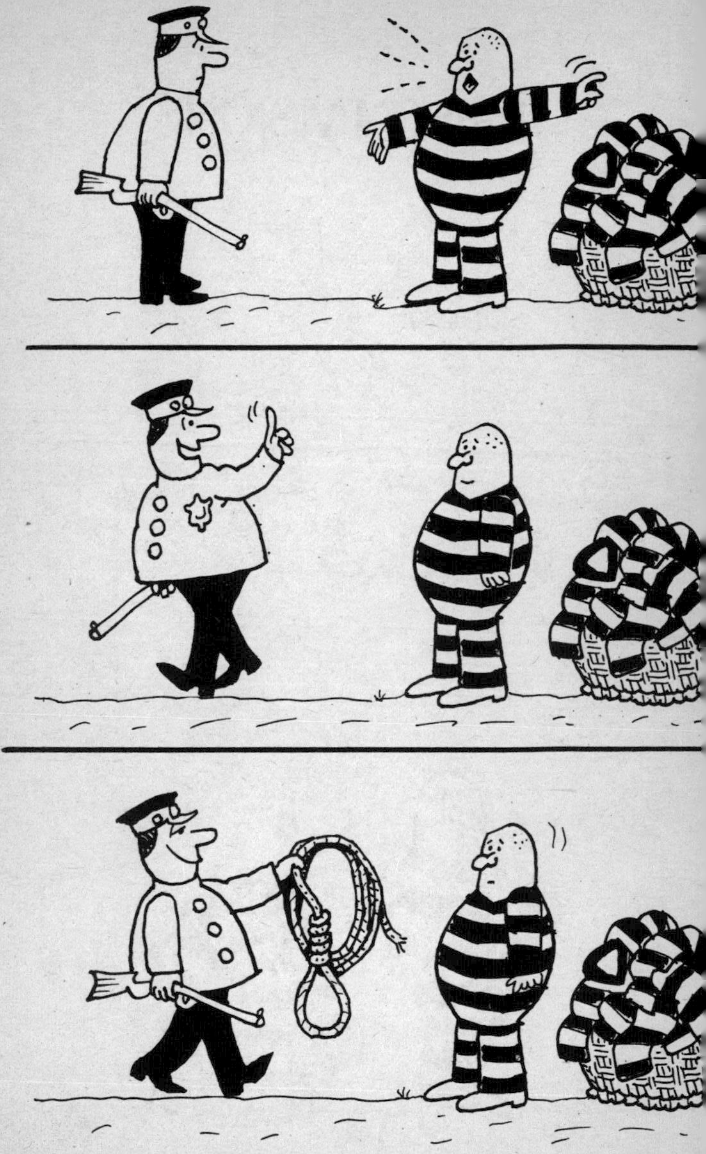

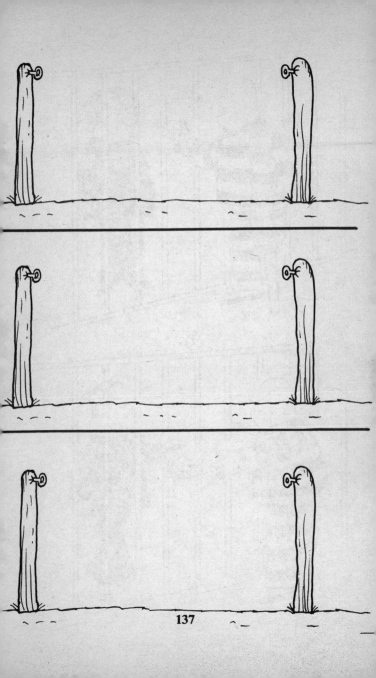

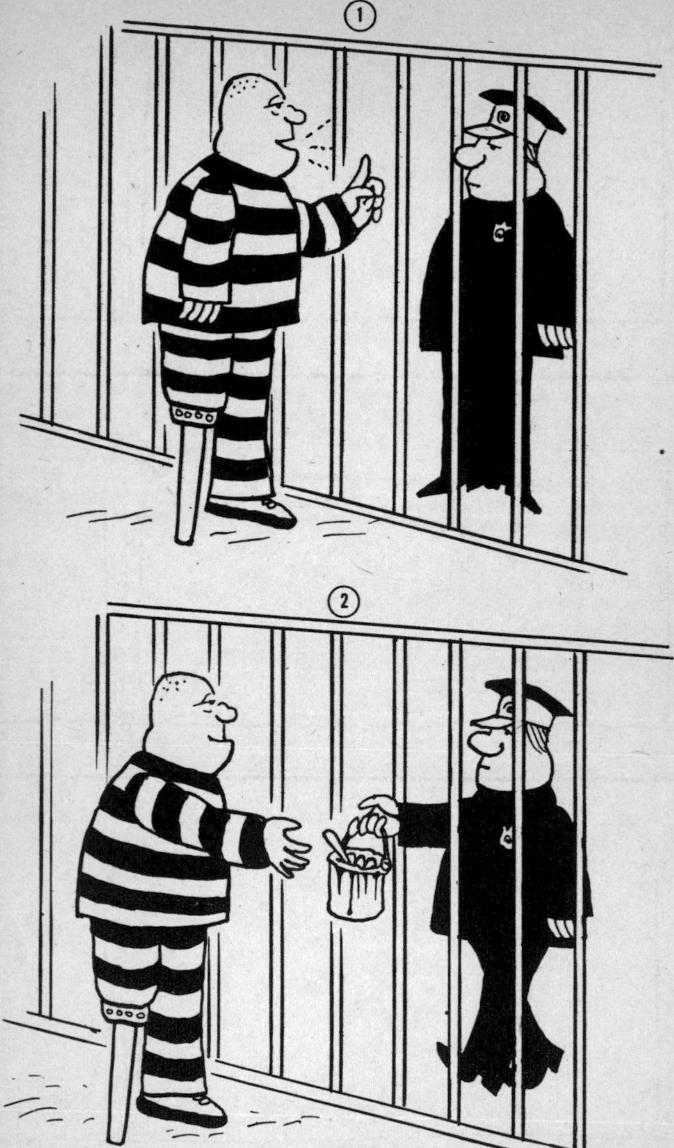
1
2

③

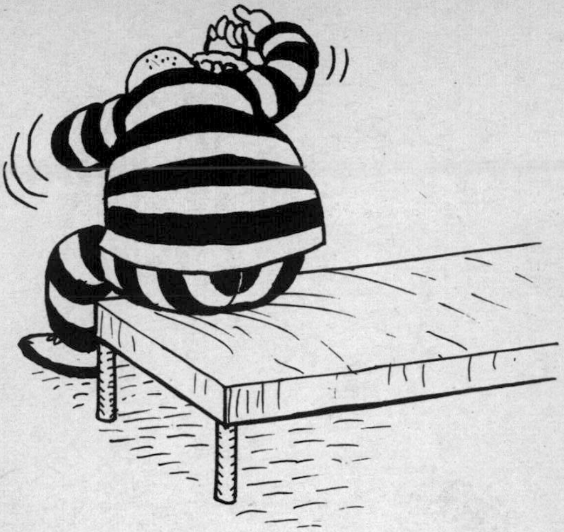

④

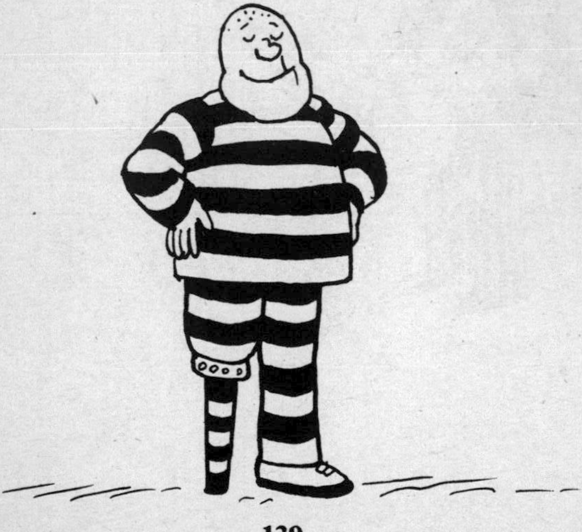

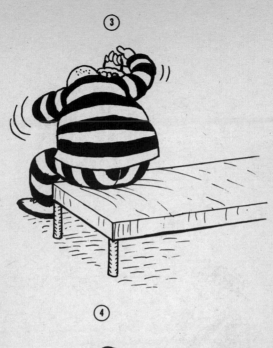

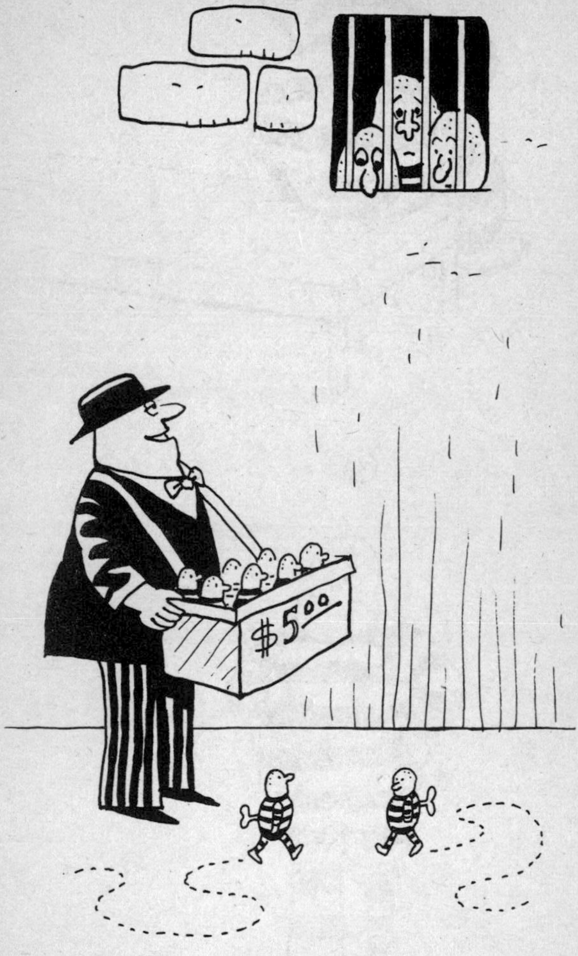
$5.00

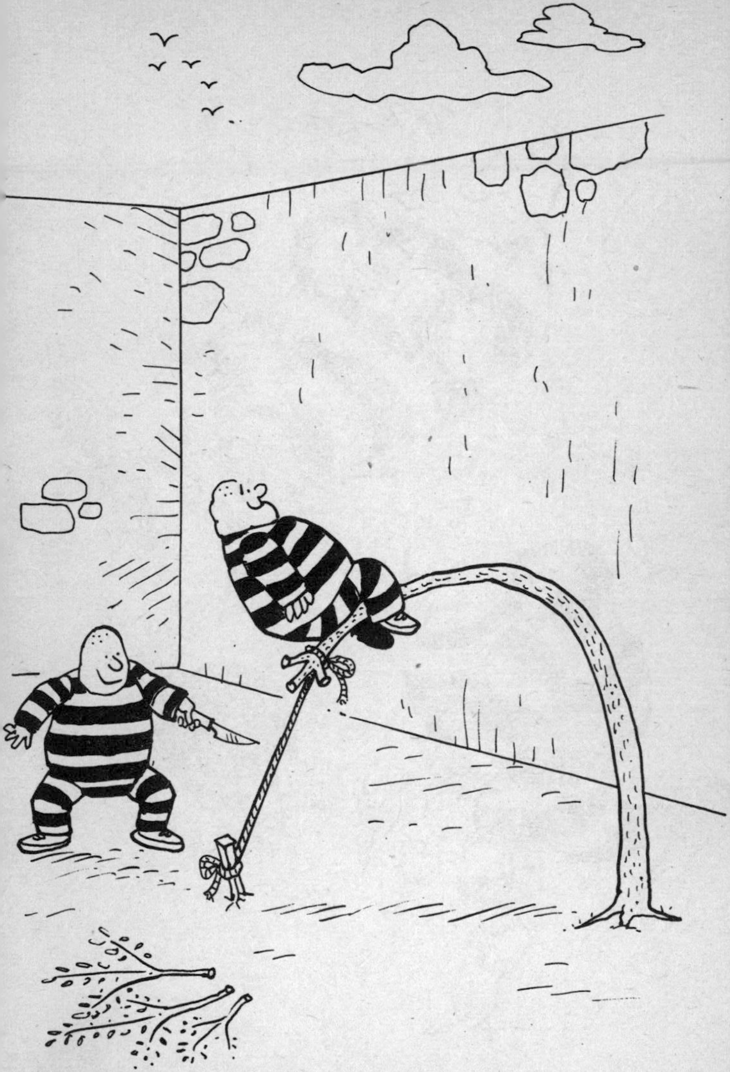

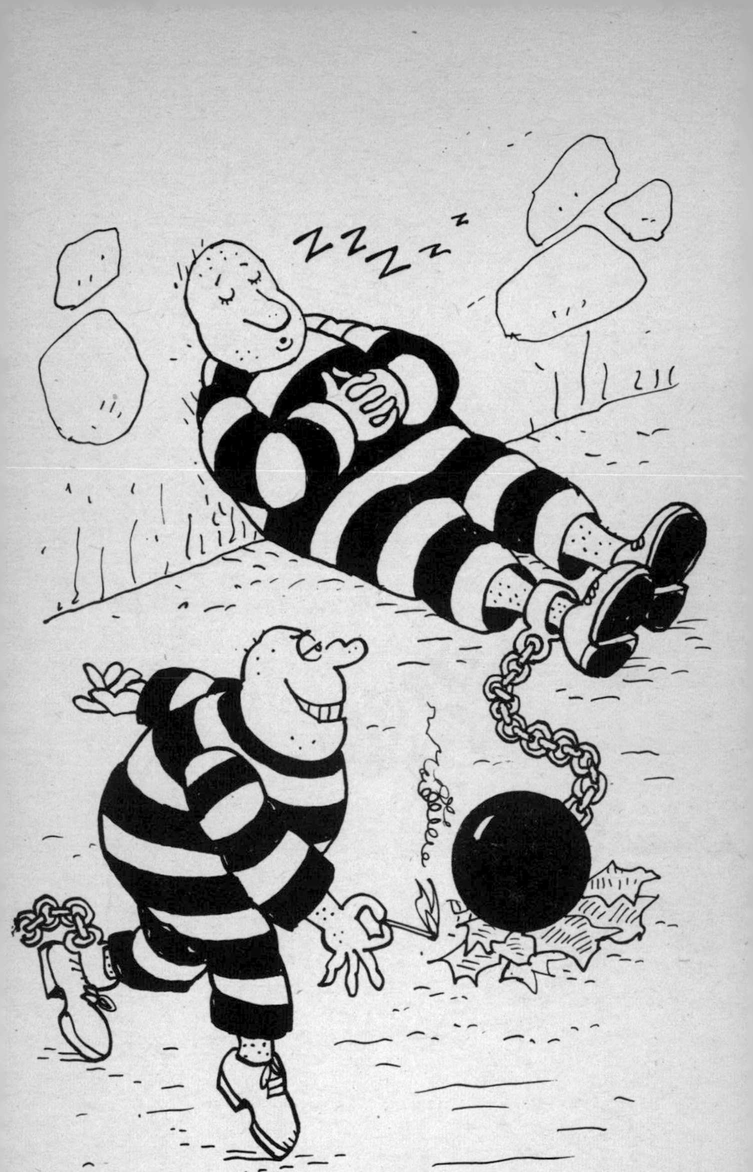
ZZZzz

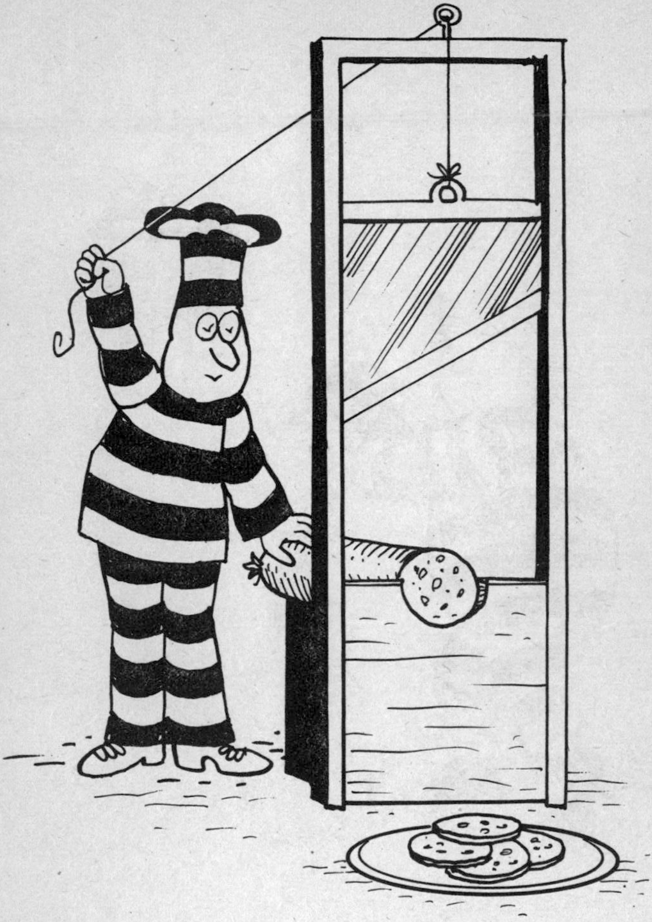

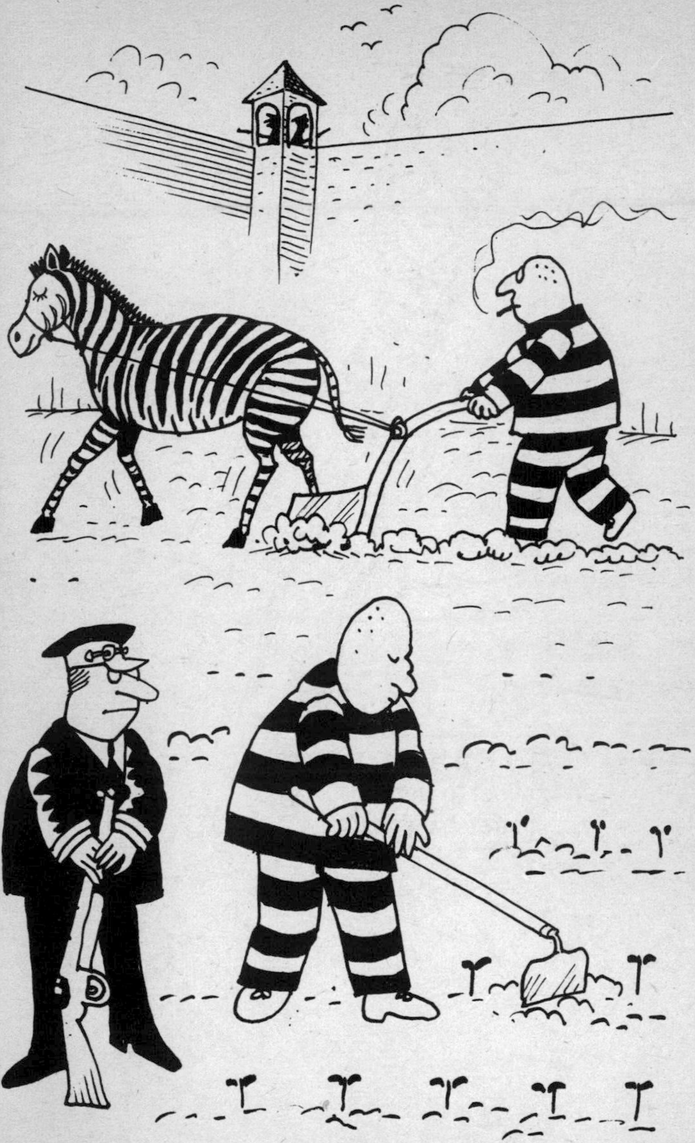

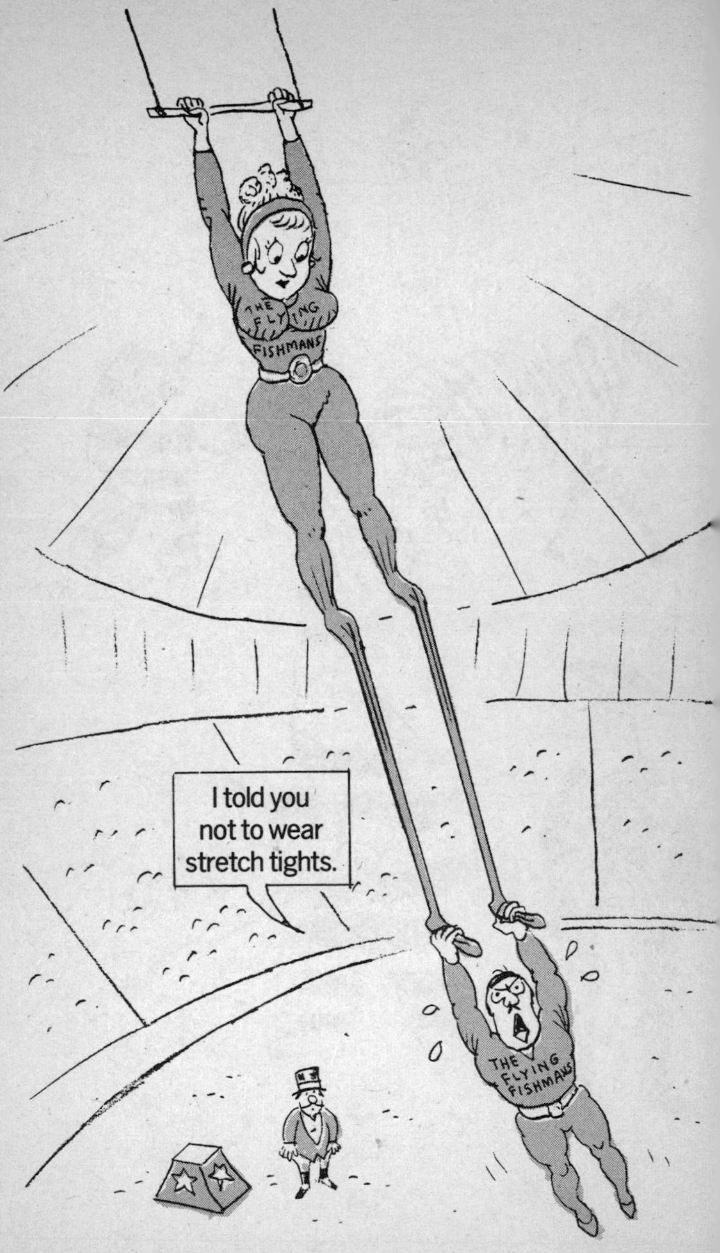
THE FLYING FISHMANS
I told you not to wear stretch tights.
THE FLYING FISHMANS

CRUMMY DUMMY

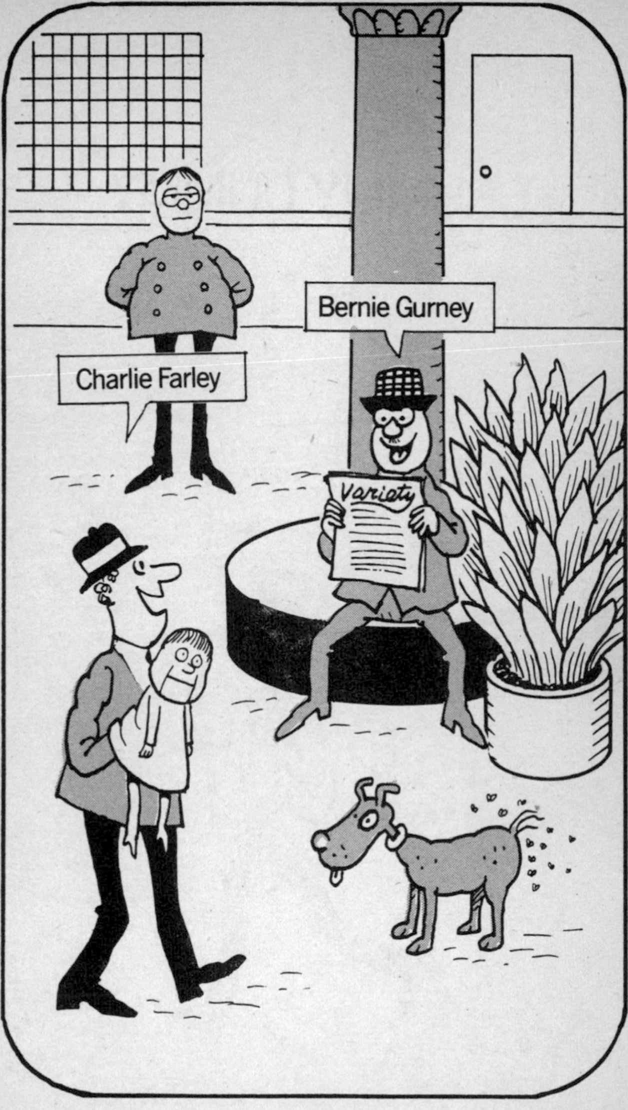
Charlie Farley
Bernie Gurney
Variety

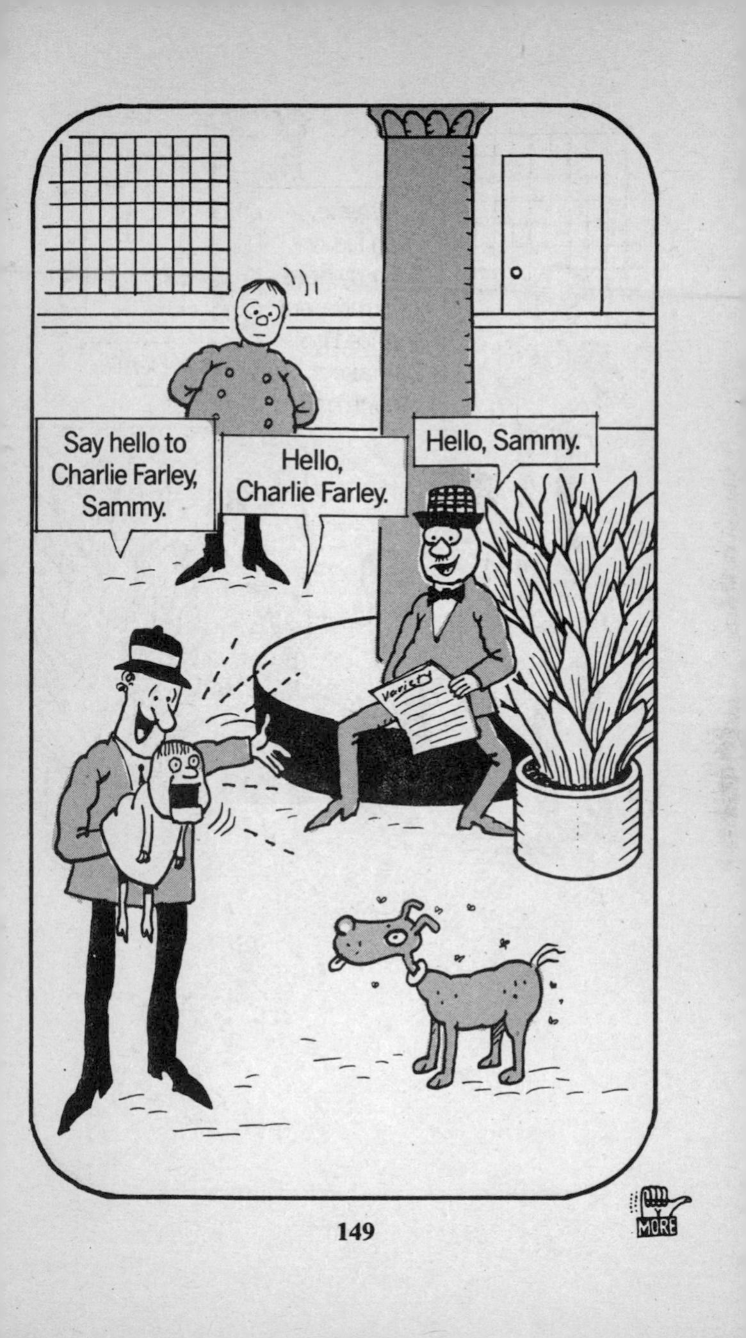

Say hello to Charlie Farley, Sammy.
Hello, Charlie Farley.
Hello, Sammy.
Variety

MORE

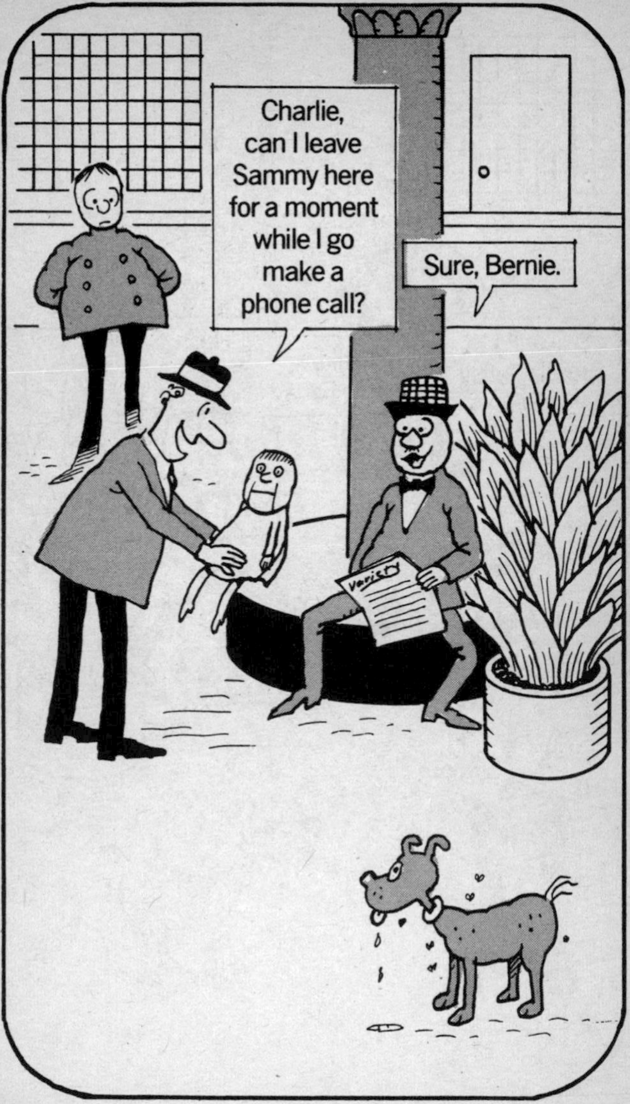
Charlie, can I leave Sammy here for a moment while I go make a phone call?
Sure, Bernie.

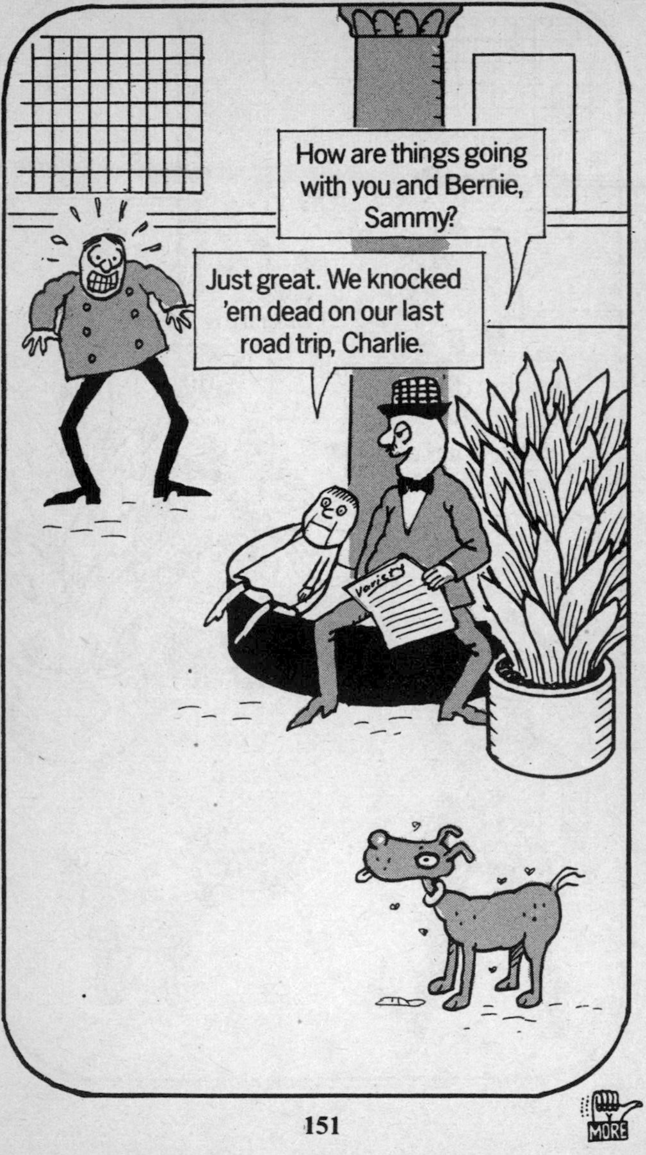
How are things going with you and Bernie, Sammy?
Just great. We knocked 'em dead on our last road trip, Charlie.
Variety
MORE

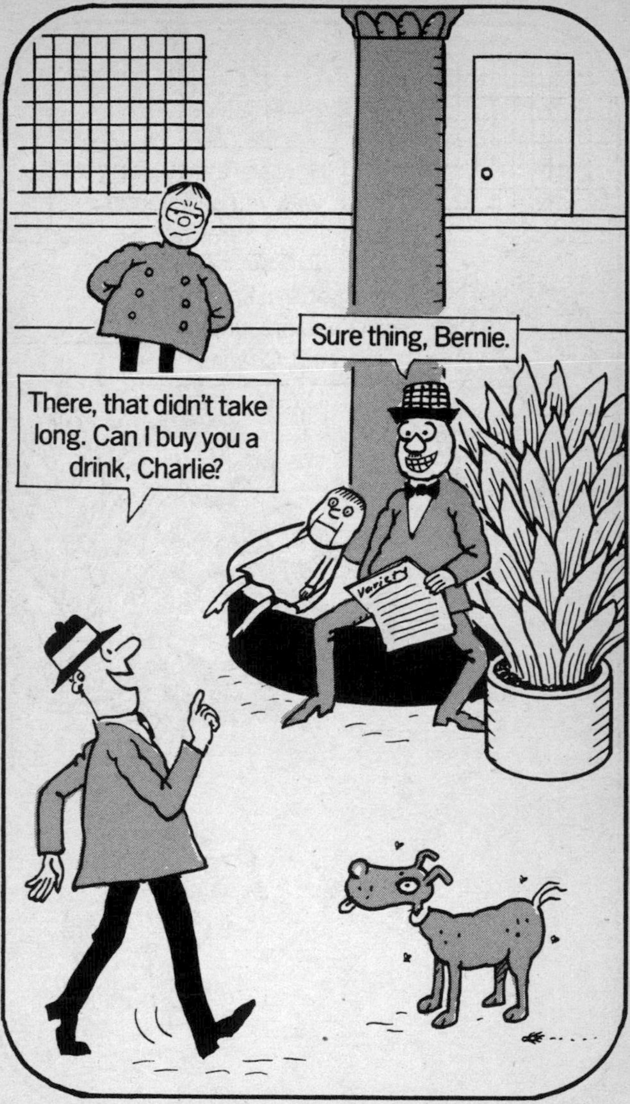
Sure thing, Bernie.
There, that didn't take long. Can I buy you a drink, Charlie?

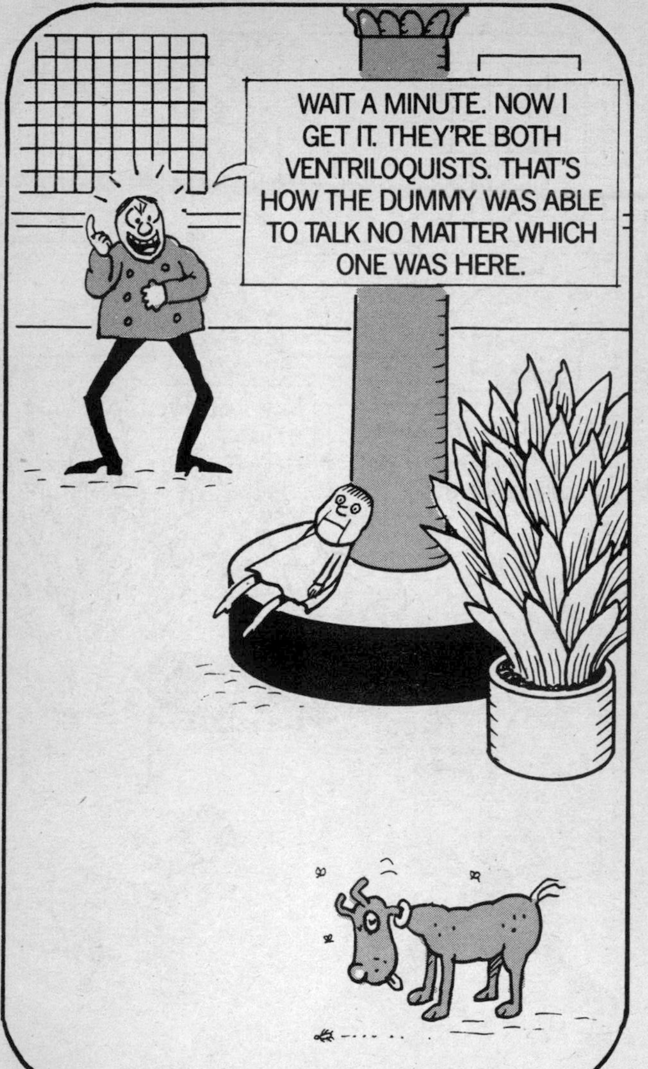
WAIT A MINUTE. NOW I GET IT. THEY'RE BOTH VENTRILOQUISTS. THAT'S HOW THE DUMMY WAS ABLE TO TALK NO MATTER WHICH ONE WAS HERE.
MORE

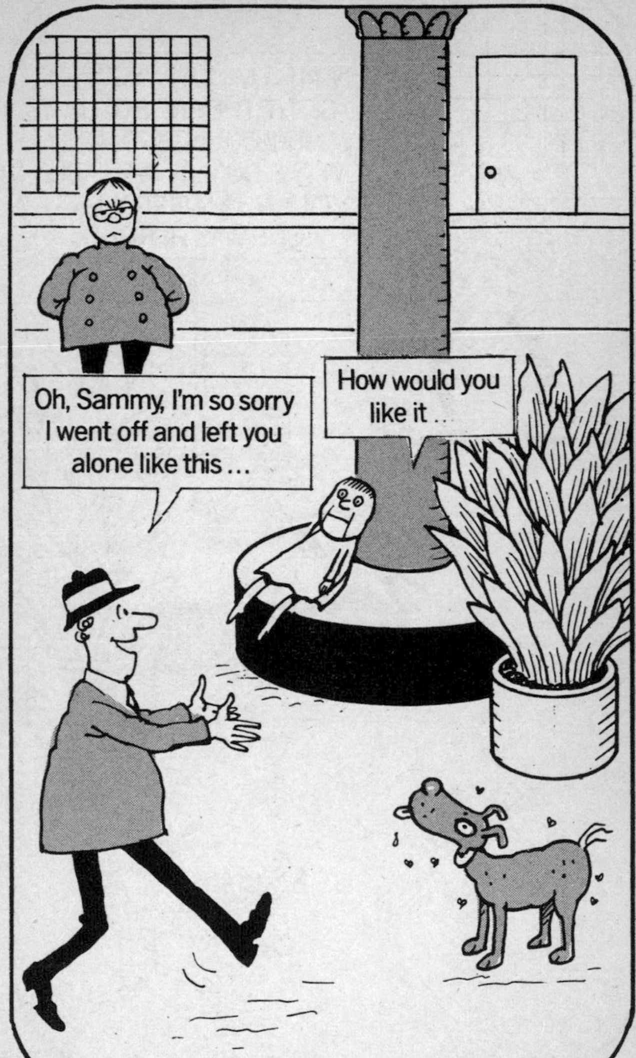
Oh, Sammy, I'm so sorry I went off and left you alone like this ...
How would you like it ...

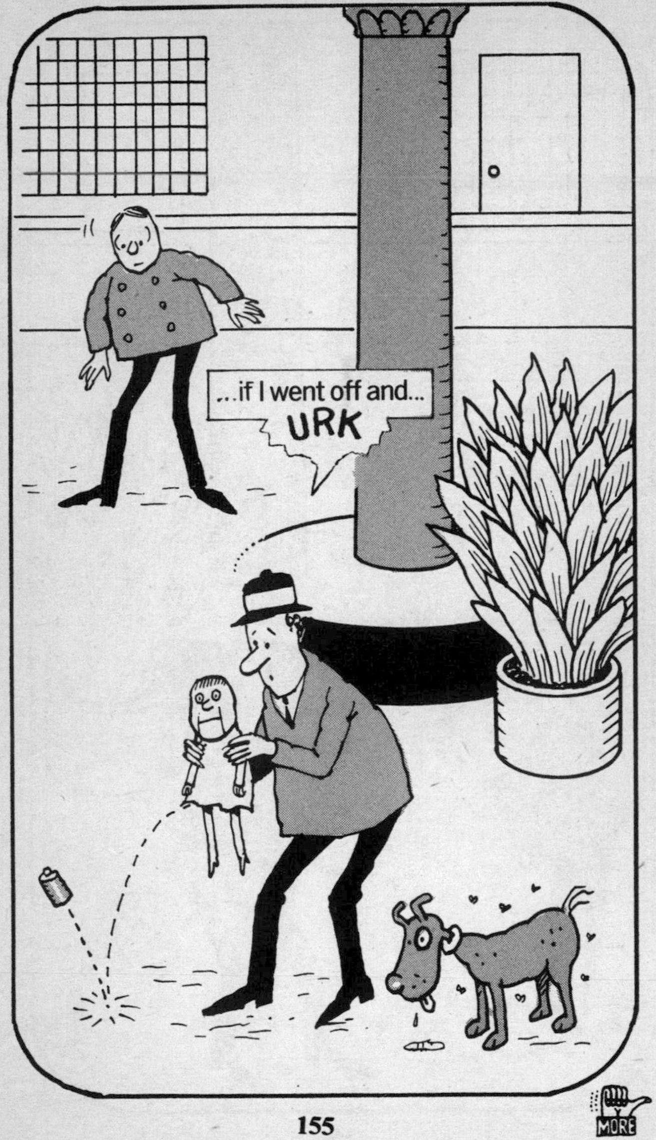
...if I went off and...
URK

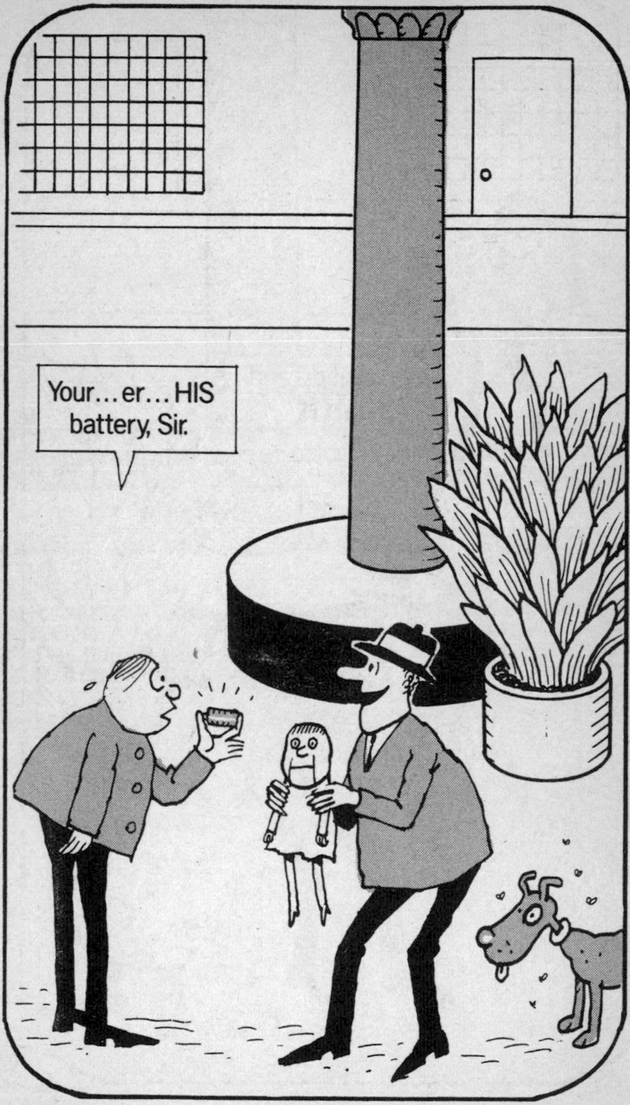
Your... er... HIS battery, Sir.

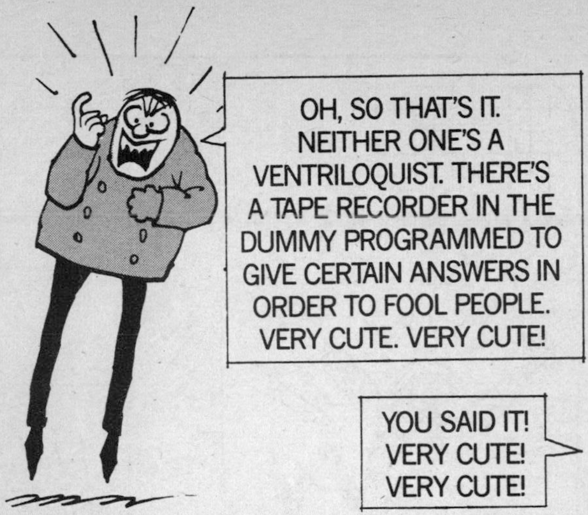
OH, SO THAT'S IT. NEITHER ONE'S A VENTRILOQUIST. THERE'S A TAPE RECORDER IN THE DUMMY PROGRAMMED TO GIVE CERTAIN ANSWERS IN ORDER TO FOOL PEOPLE. VERY CUTE. VERY CUTE!
YOU SAID IT! VERY CUTE! VERY CUTE!

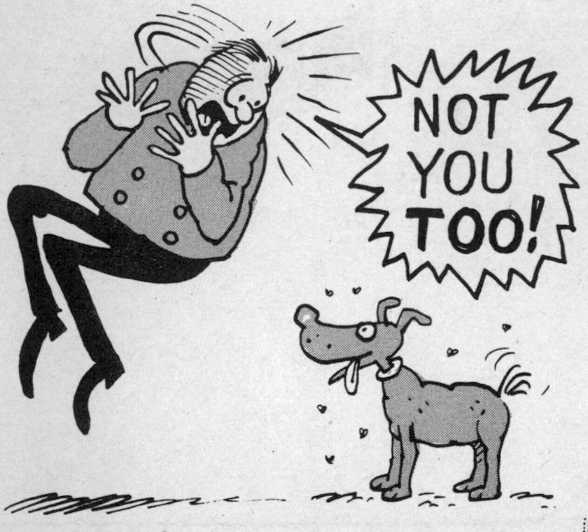
NOT YOU TOO!

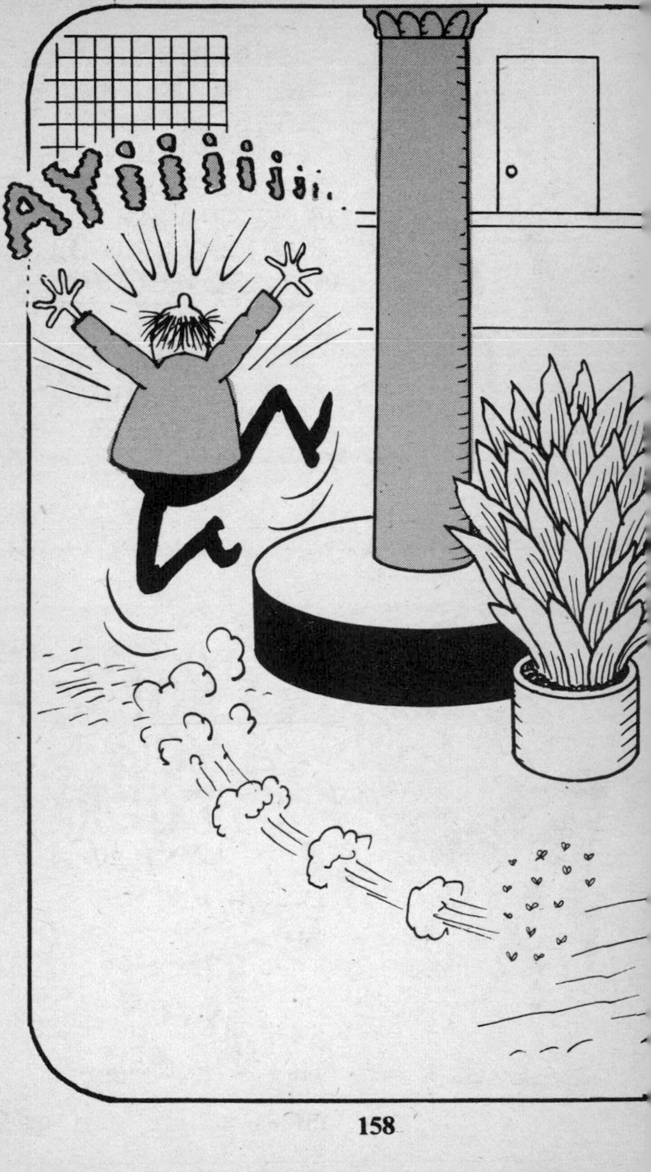
AYiiiiiji.

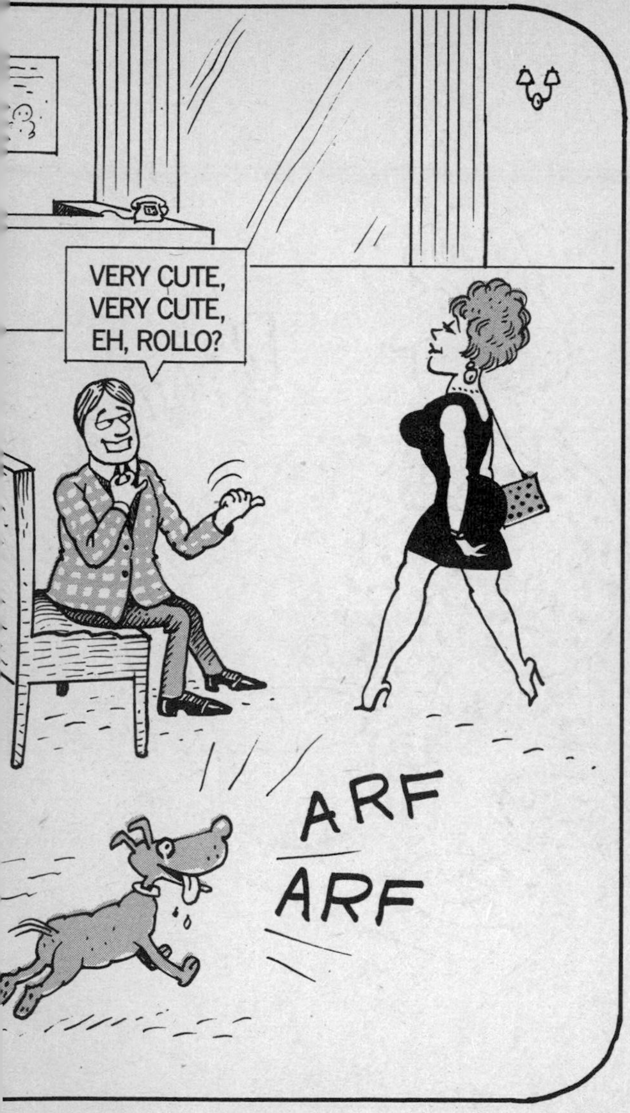
VERY CUTE,
VERY CUTE,
EH, ROLLO?
ARF
ARF

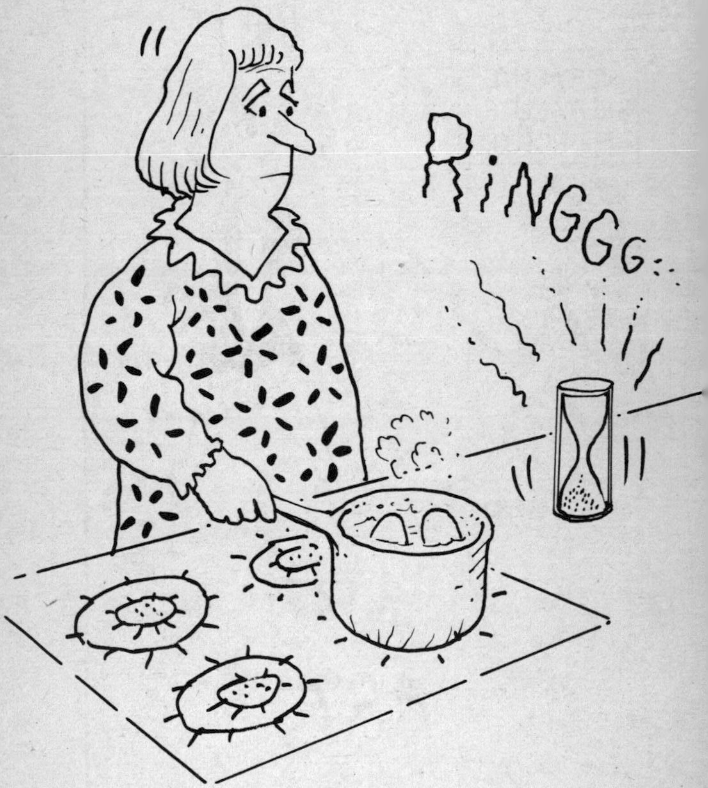
RiNGGG

SICK PIC

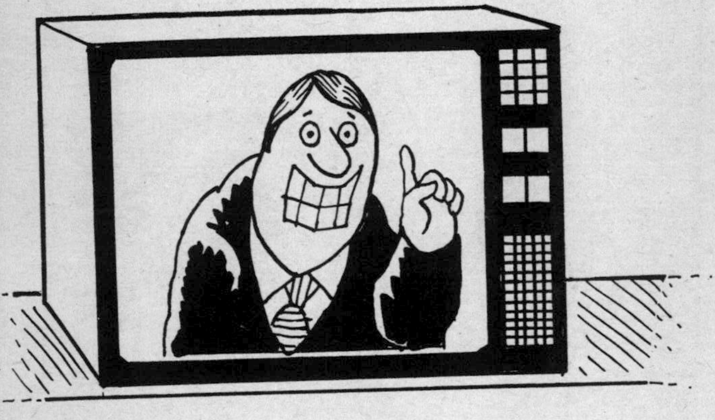

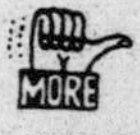
MORE

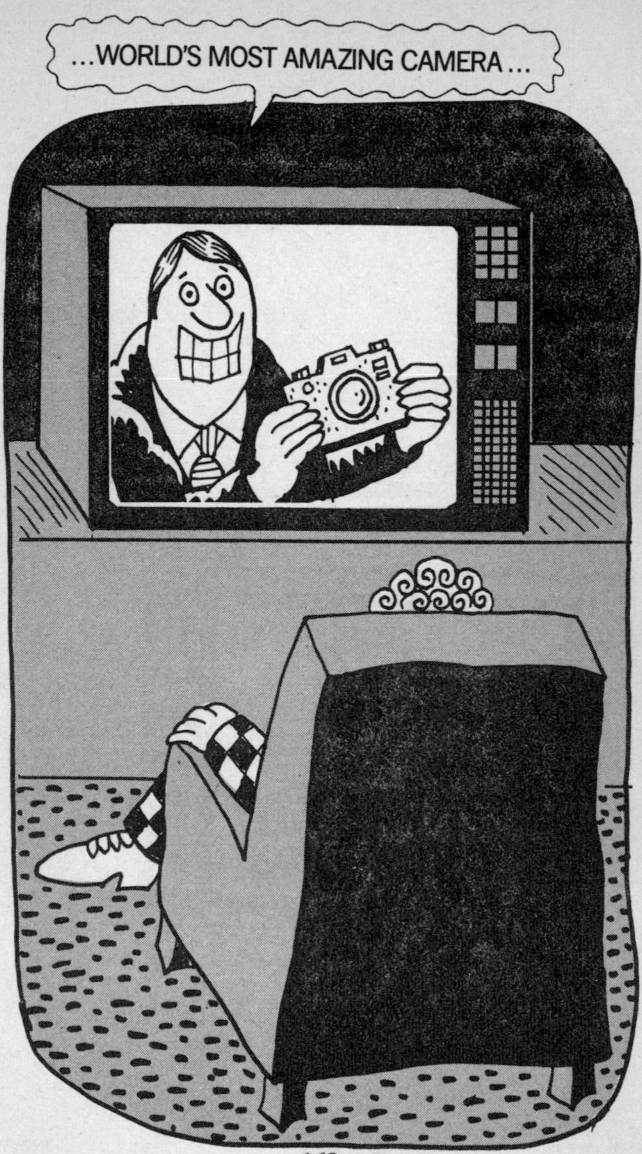
...WORLD'S MOST AMAZING CAMERA...

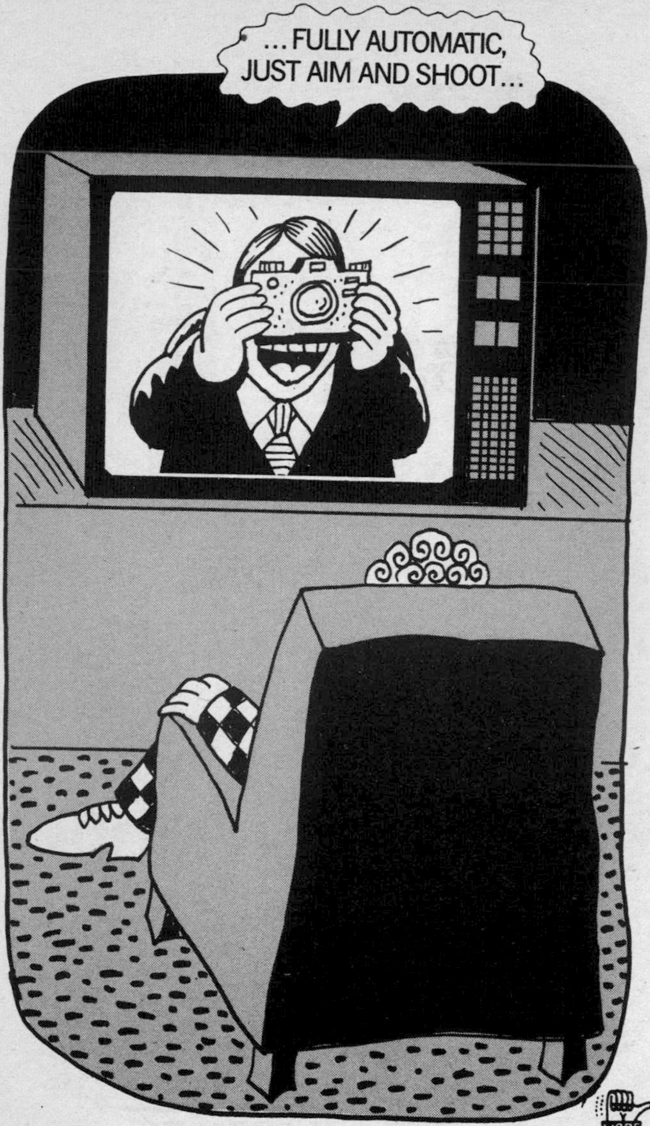
...FULLY AUTOMATIC, JUST AIM AND SHOOT...
MORE

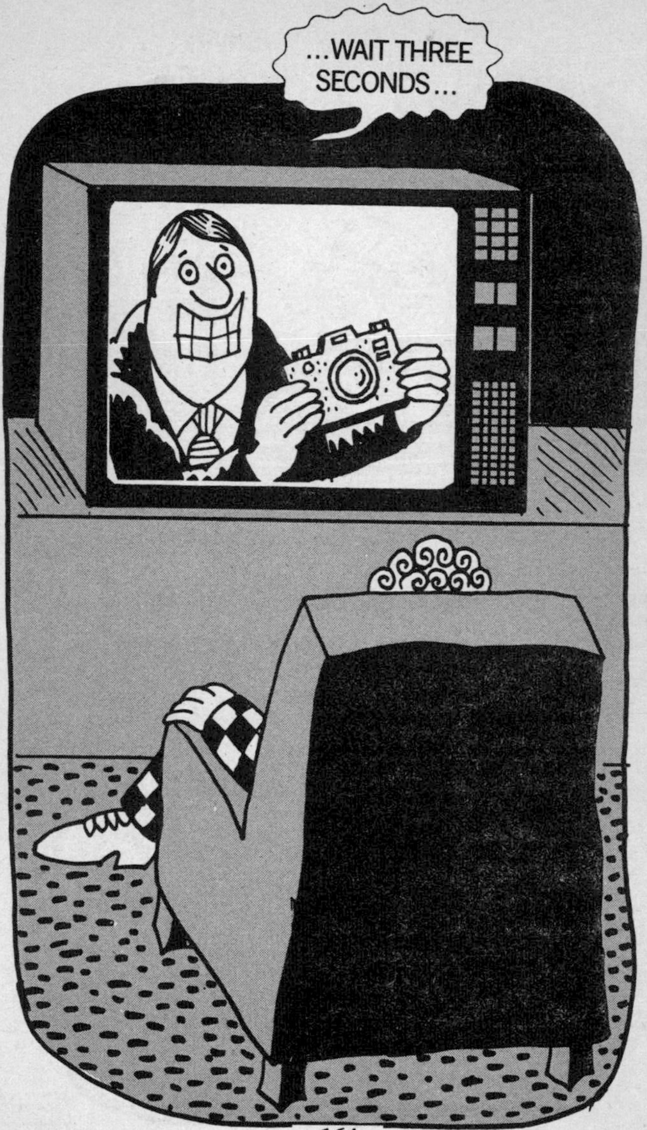
...WAIT THREE SECONDS...

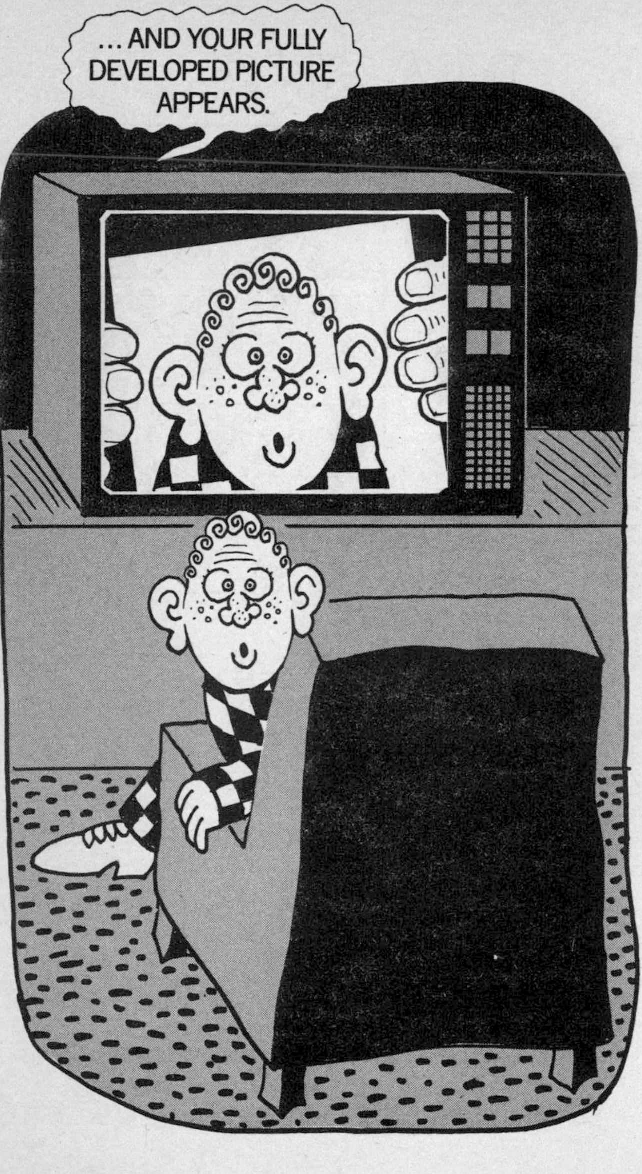
... AND YOUR FULLY DEVELOPED PICTURE APPEARS.

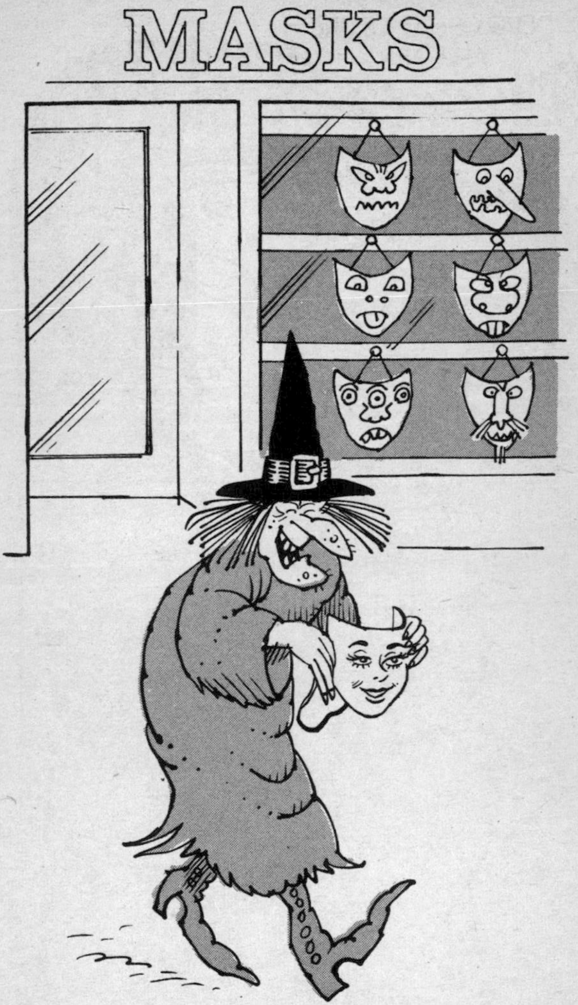
MASKS

PRINCESS WINCES

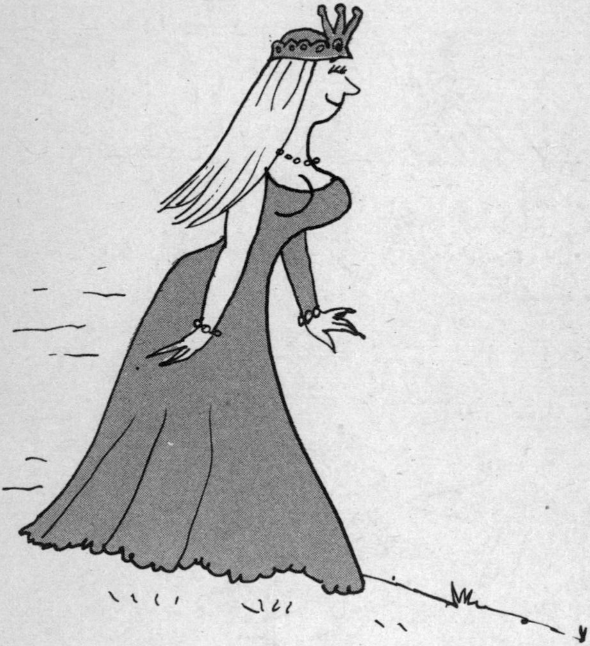

MORE

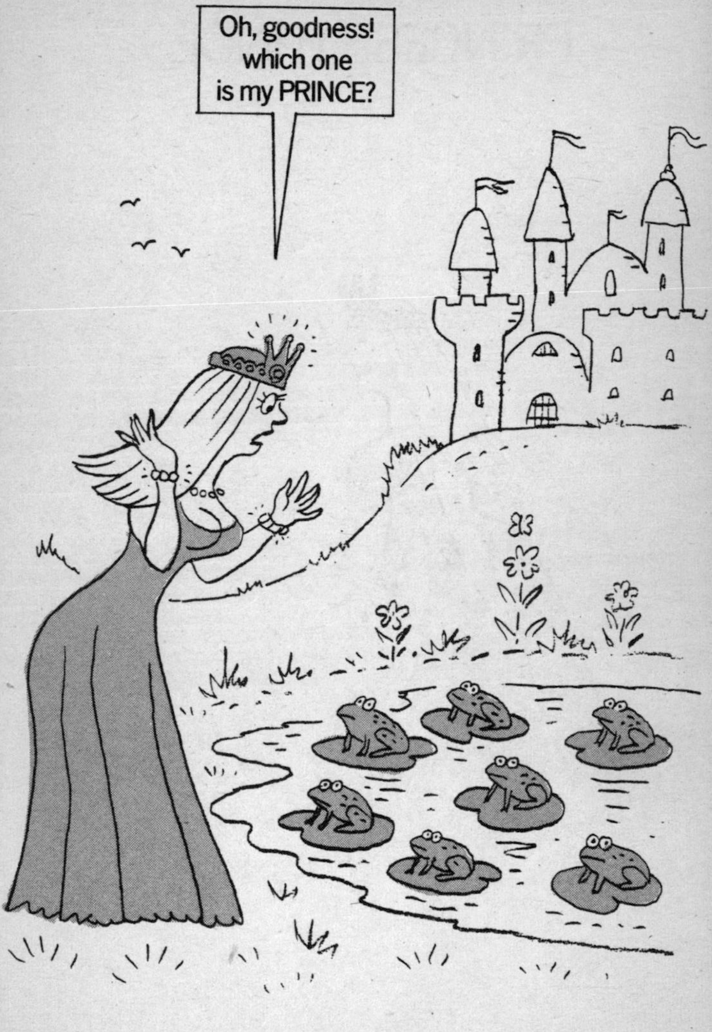
Oh, goodness!
which one
is my PRINCE?

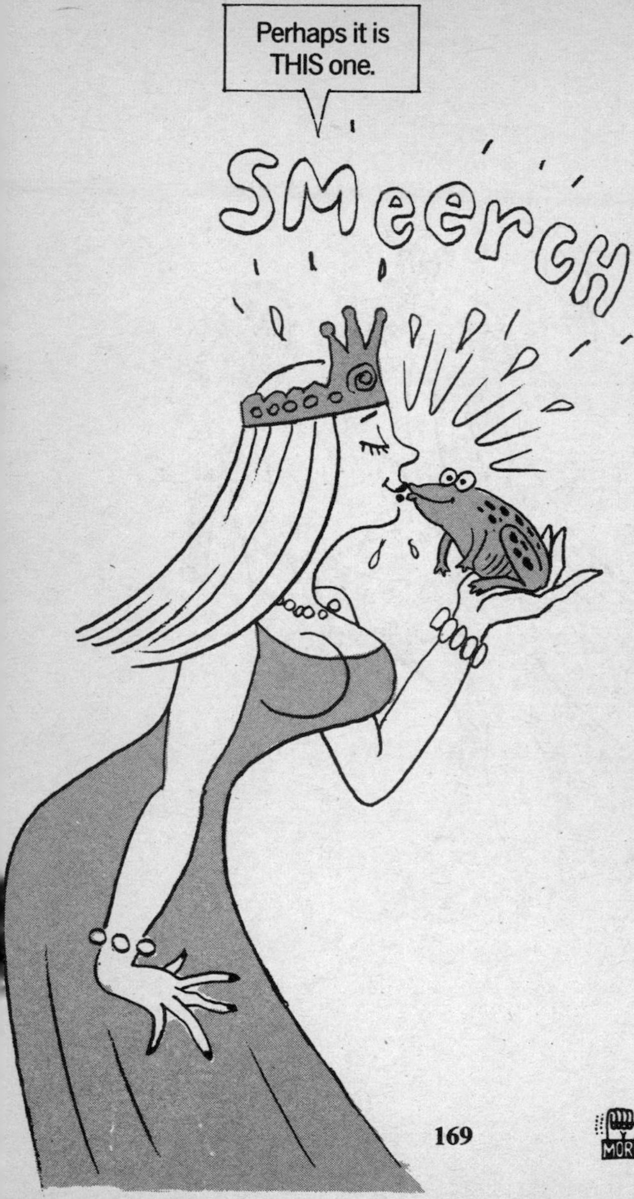
Perhaps it is THIS one.
SMeerCH

MORE

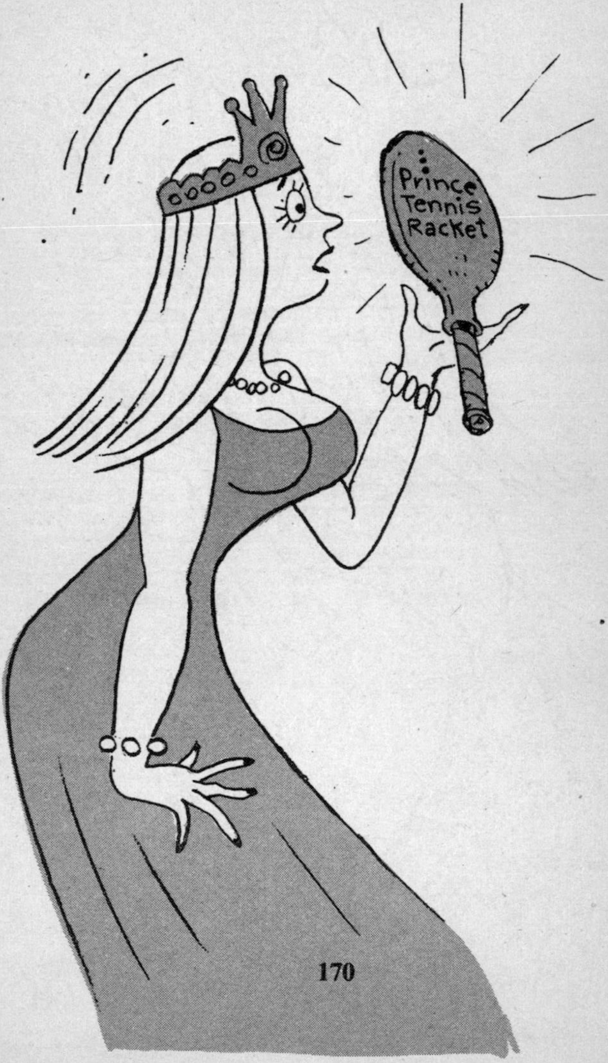
Prince
Tennis
Racket

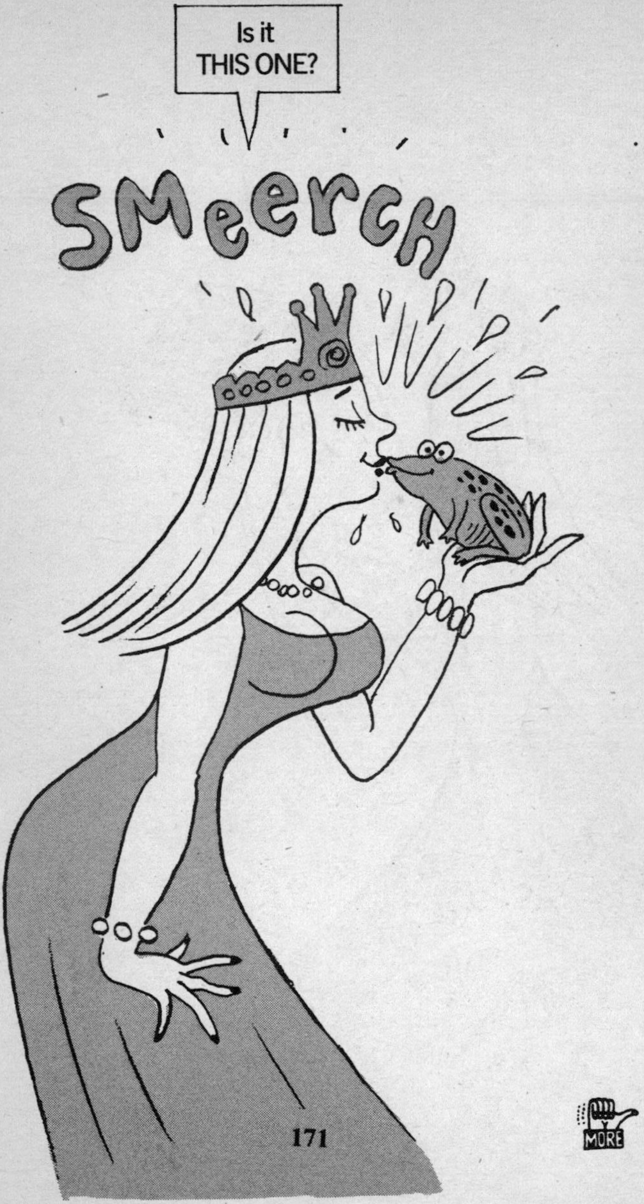
Is it
THIS ONE?
SMEERCH
MORE

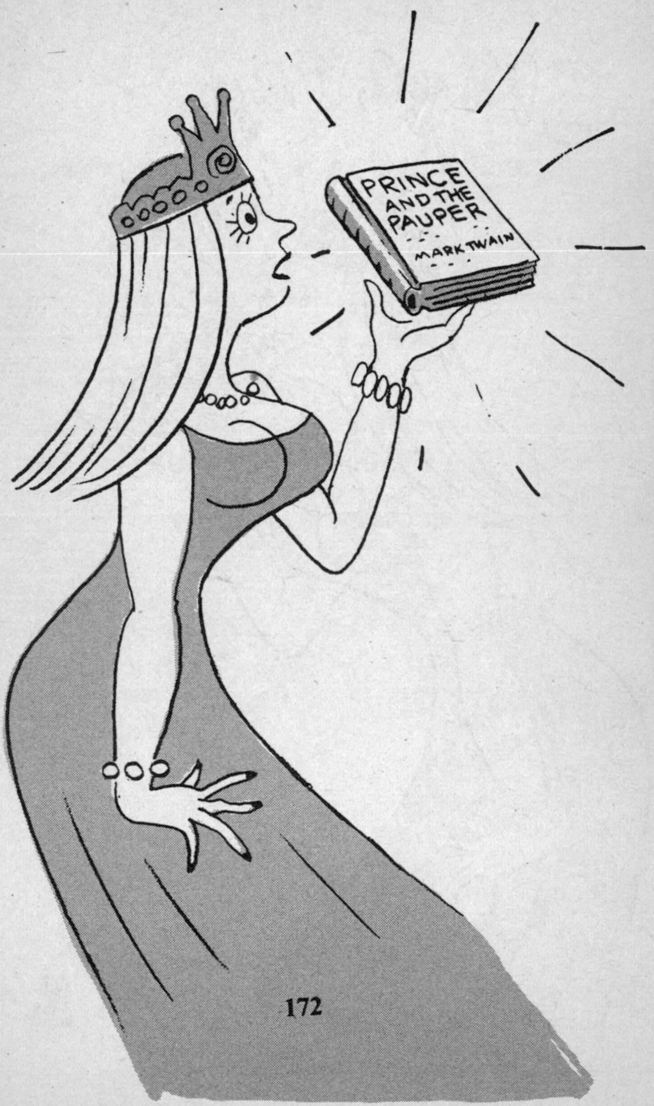
PRINCE
AND THE
PAUPER
MARK TWAIN

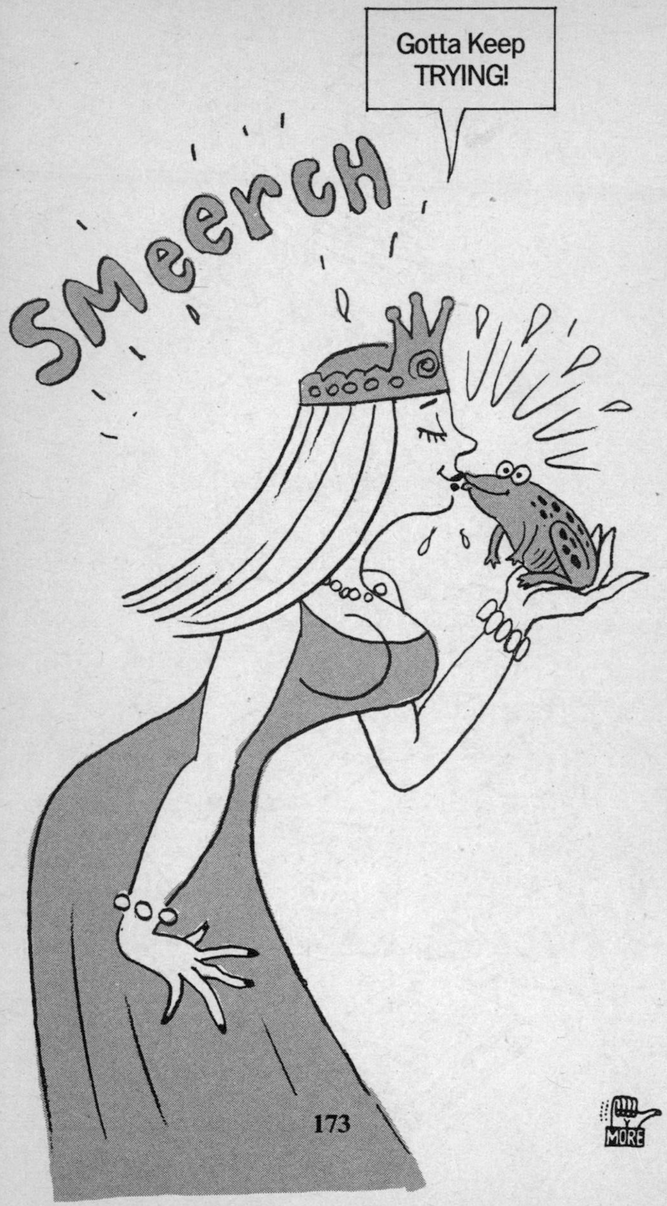
SMEERCH
Gotta Keep TRYING!
MORE

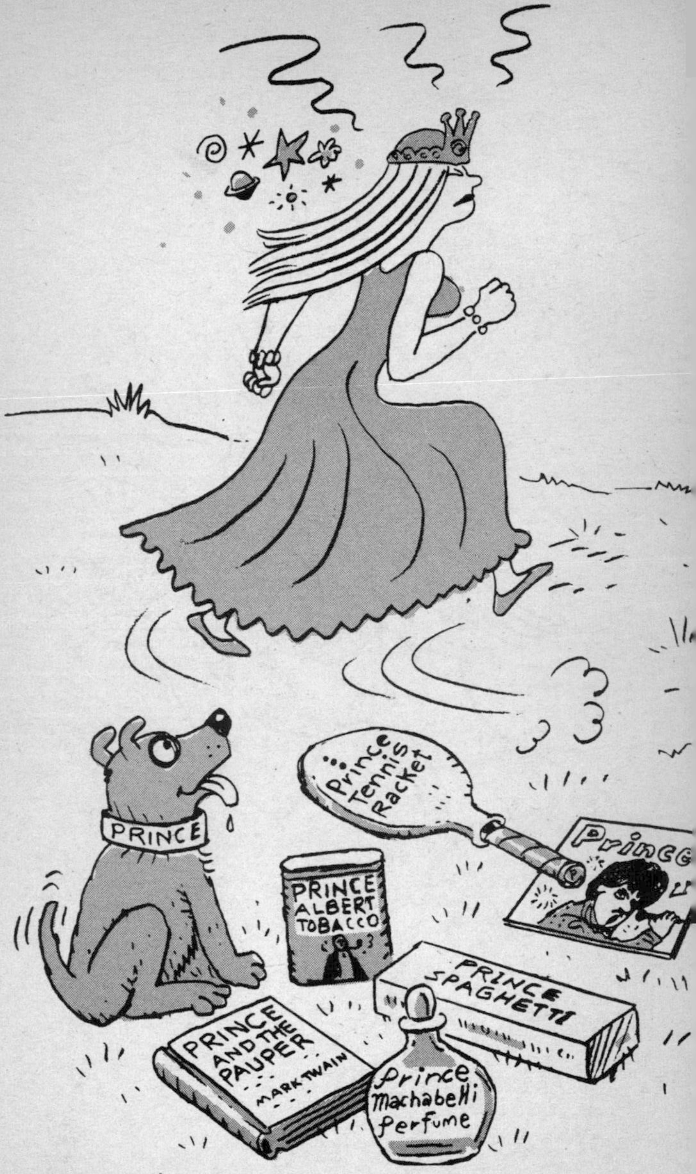

Prince Tennis Racket
PRINCE
PRINCE ALBERT TOBACCO
PRINCE SPAGHETTI
PRINCE AND THE PAUPER
MARK TWAIN
Prince machabelli perfume

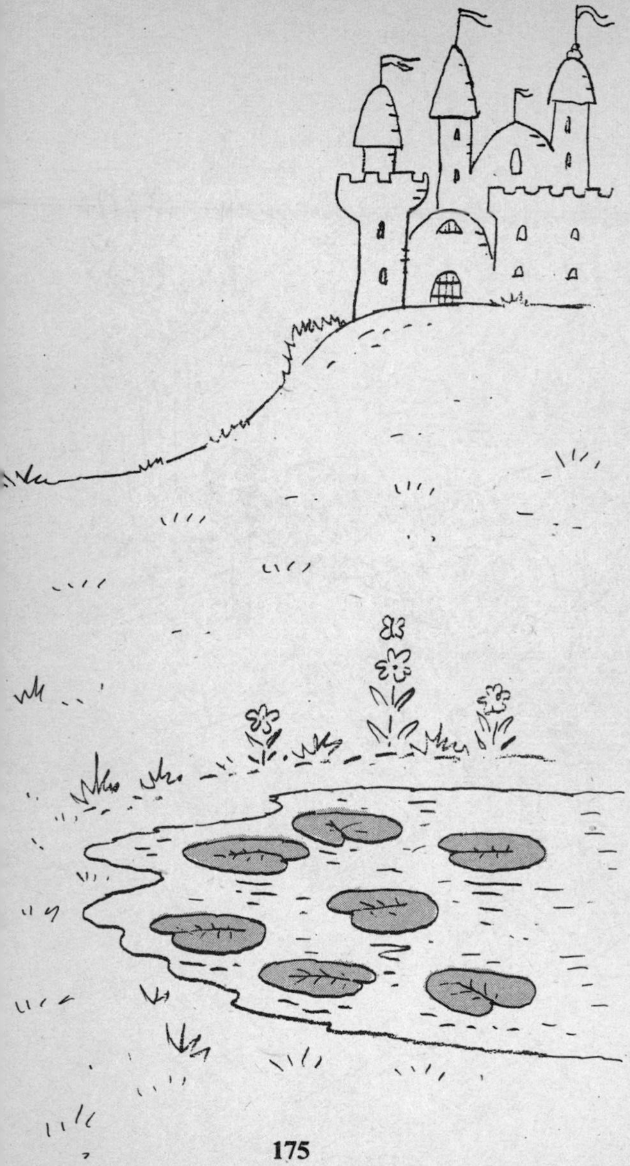

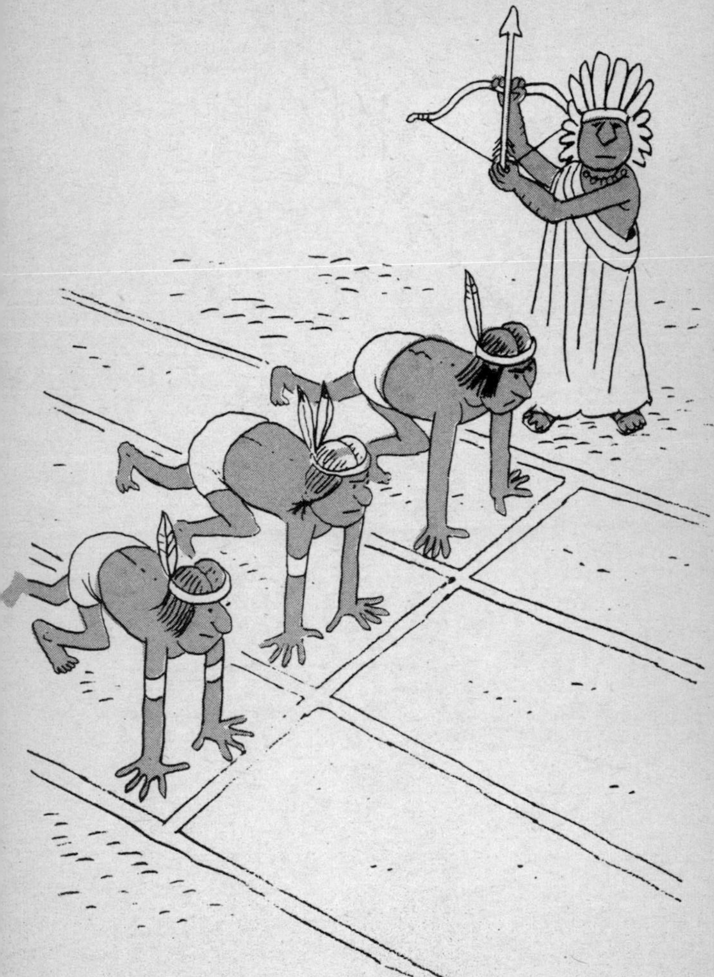

WEST JEST

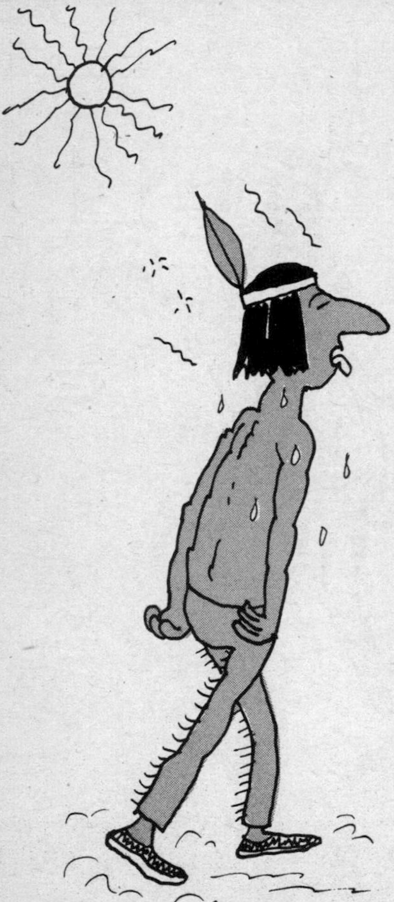

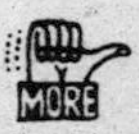
MORE

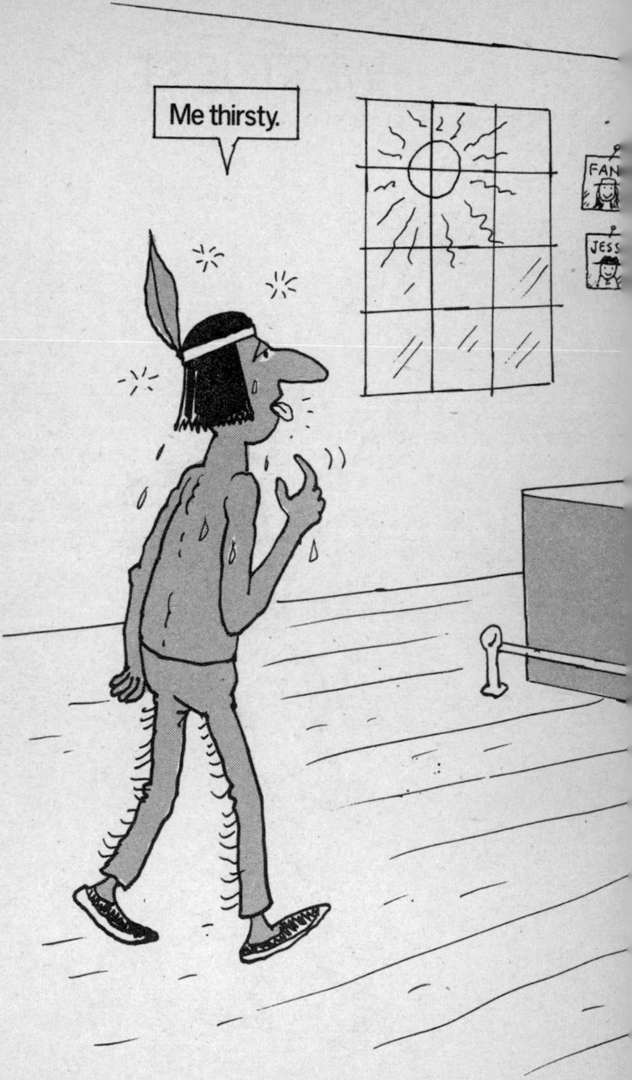
Me thirsty.

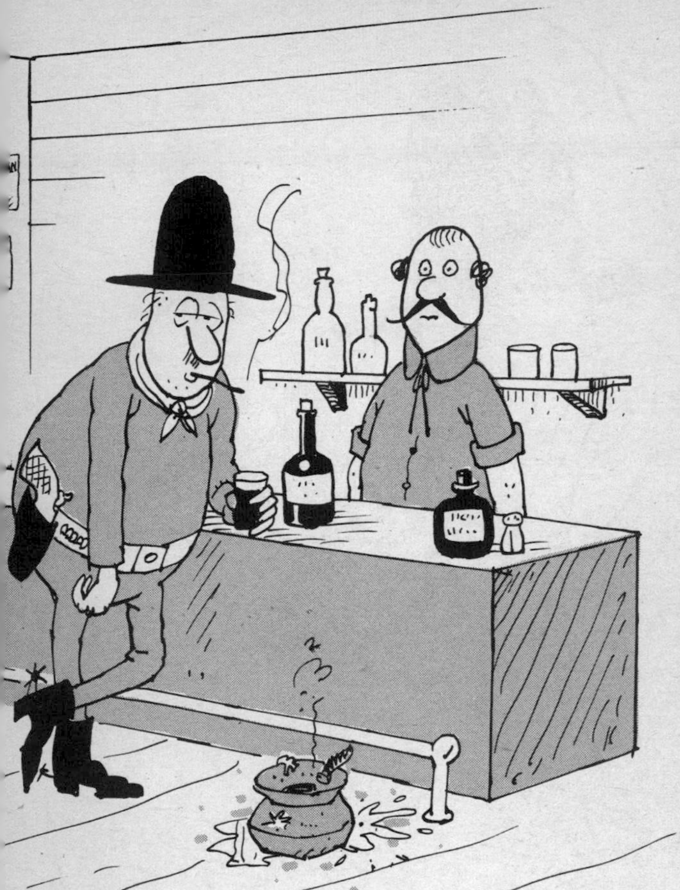

MORE

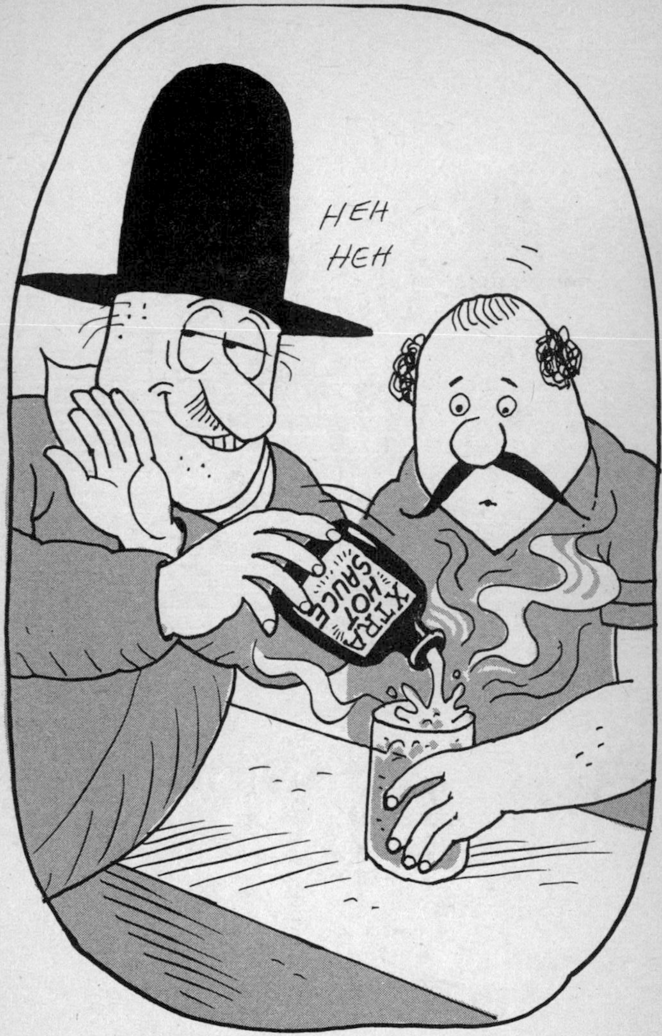
HEH
HEH
XTRA HOT SAUCE

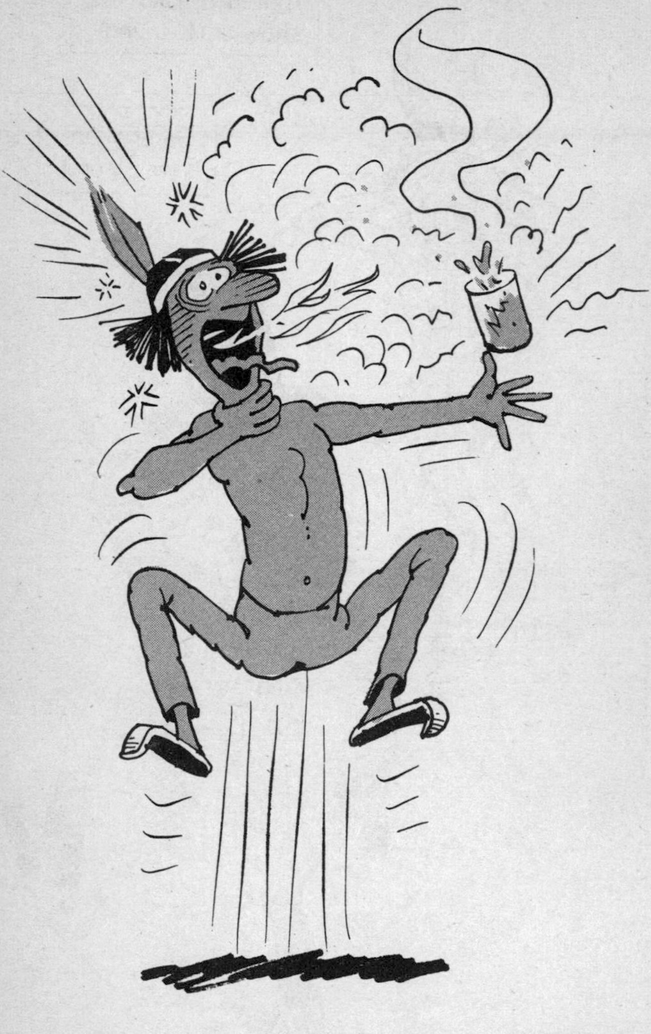

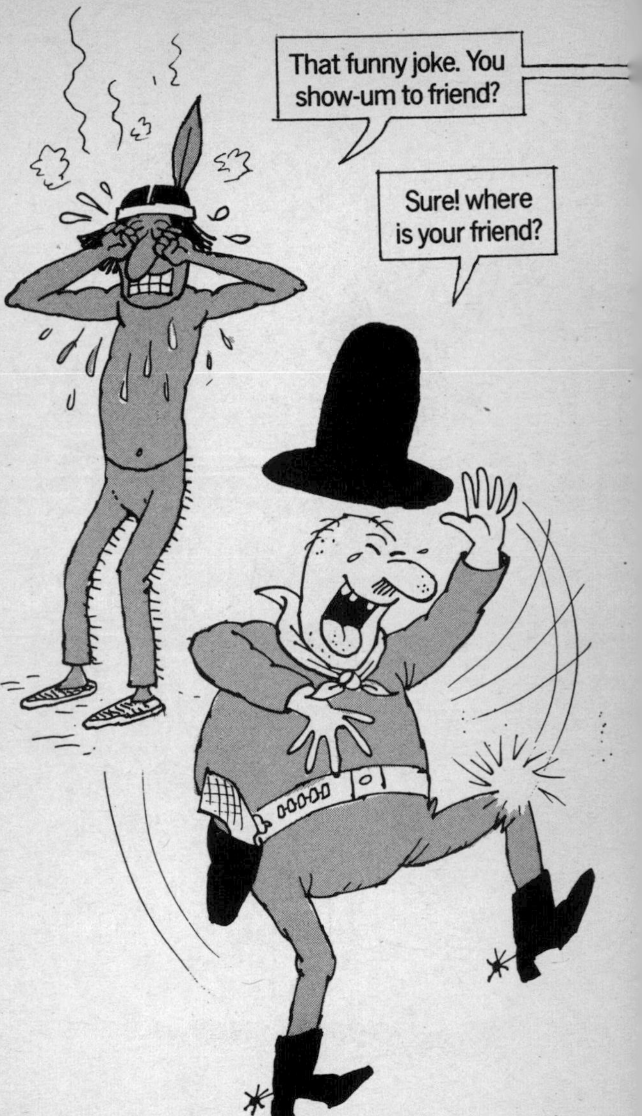
That funny joke. You show-um to friend?
Sure! where is your friend?
O-O-O-O-O

Outside.

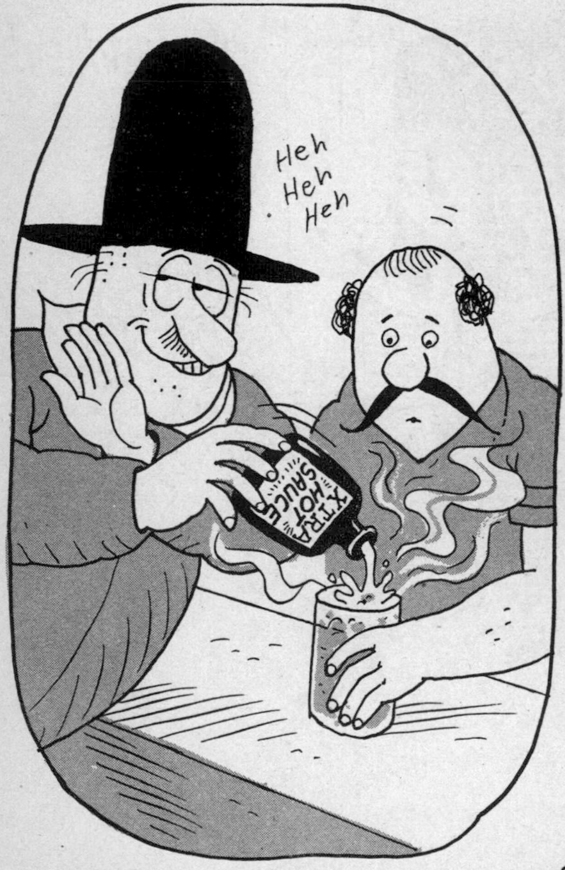
Heh
Heh
Heh
X-TRA HOT SAUCE

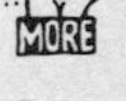
MORE

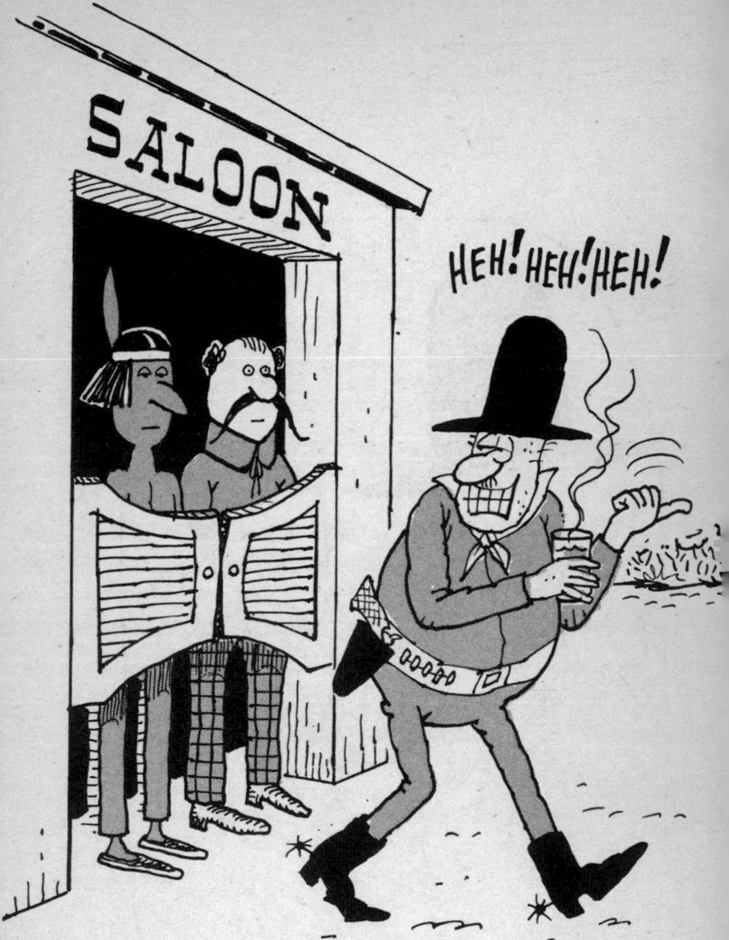
SALOON
HEH! HEH! HEH!

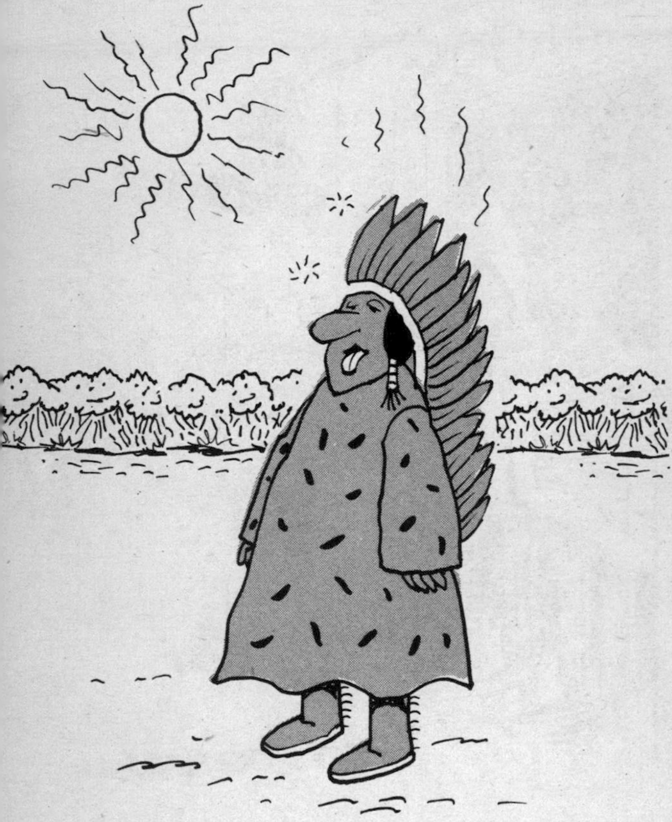

MORE

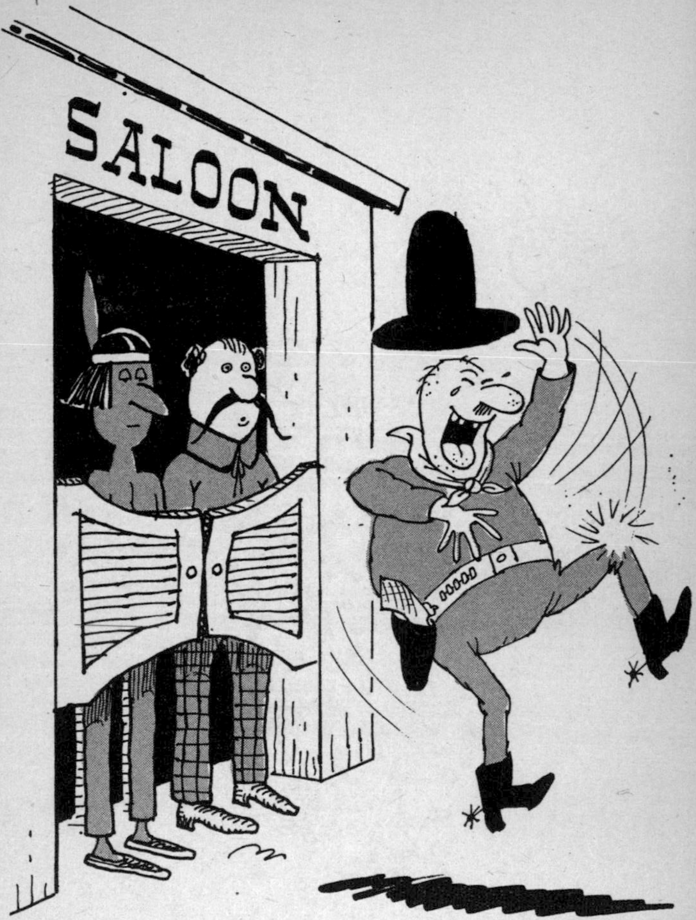
SALOON

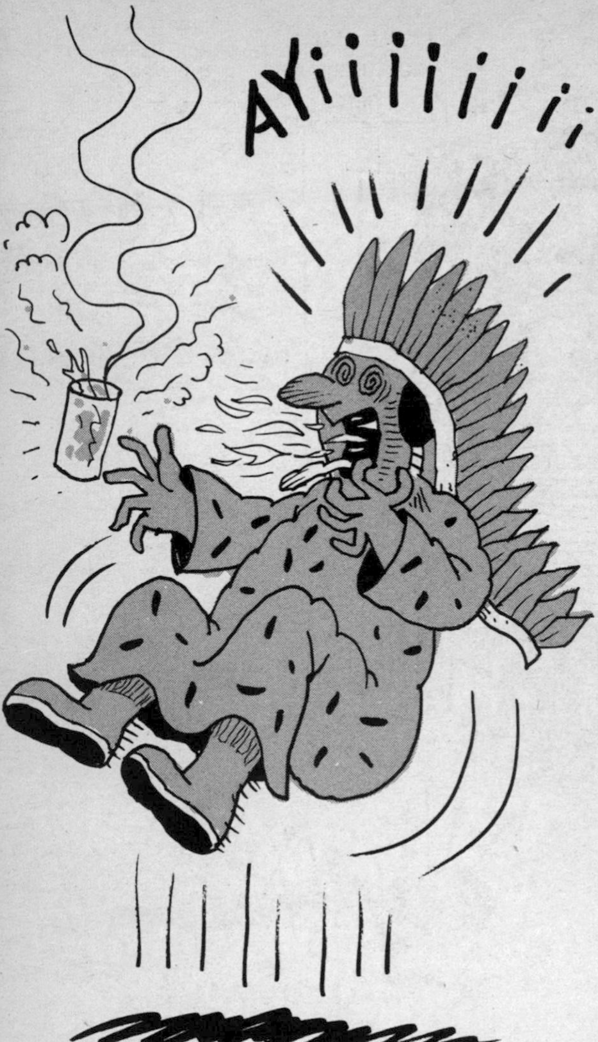
AYiiiiiiii

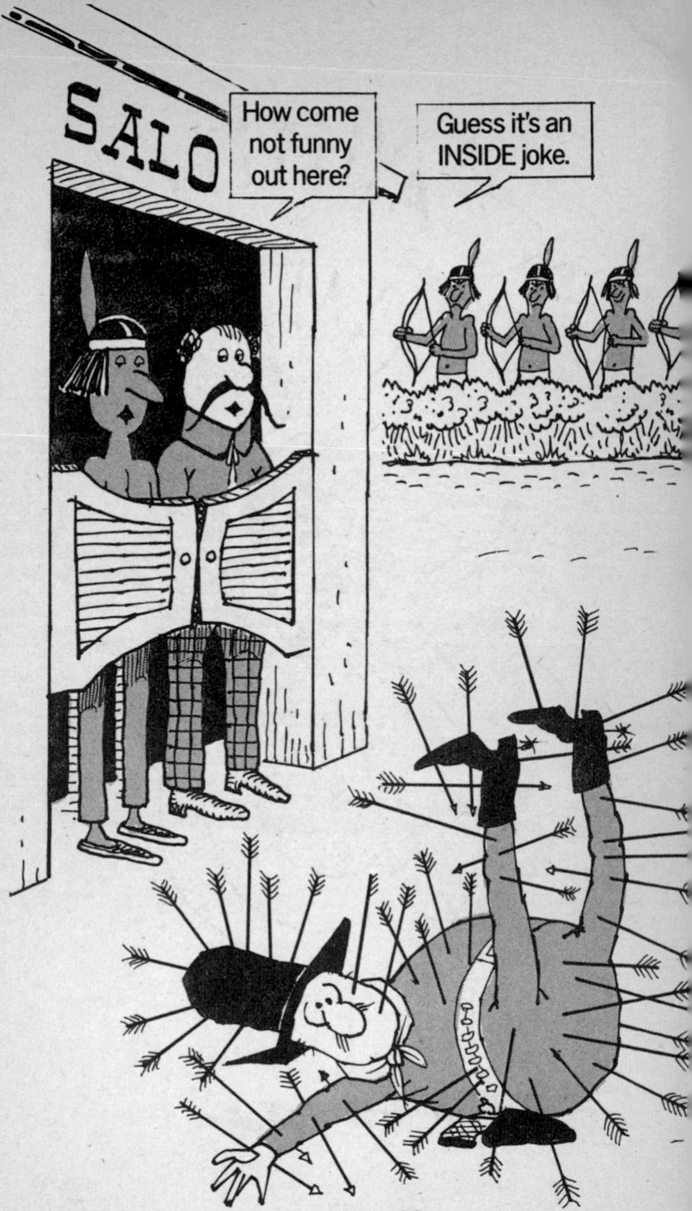
SALO
How come not funny out here?
Guess it's an INSIDE joke.

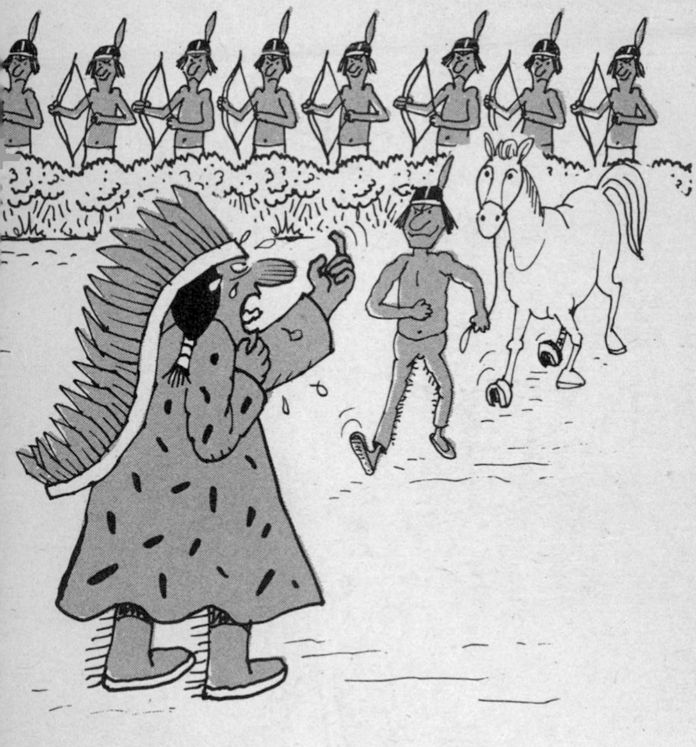

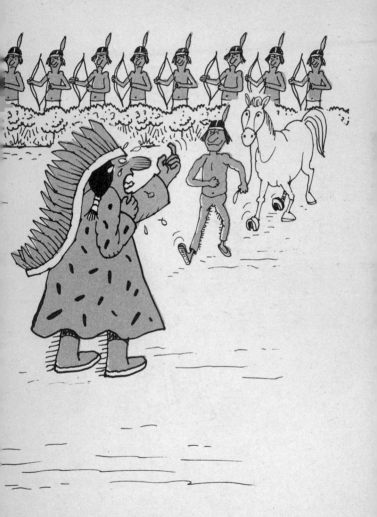

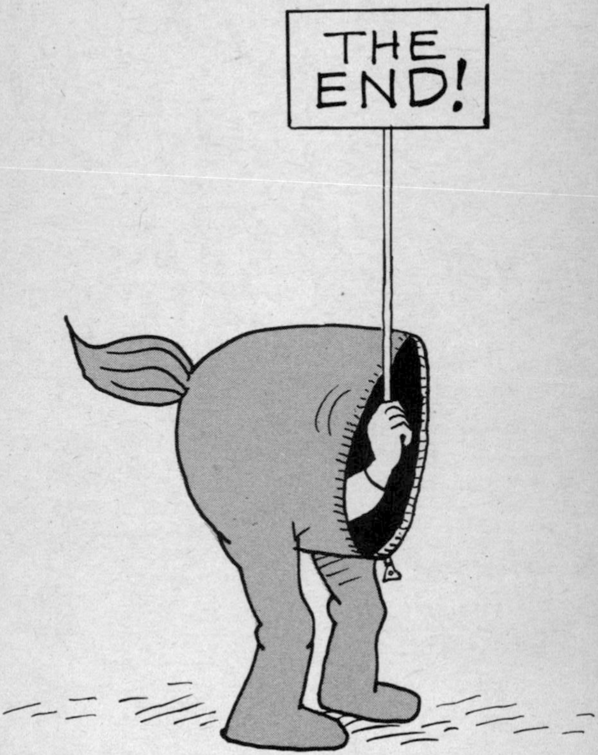
THE
END!

Other books

by Mad's (yecch!)

Al Jaffee

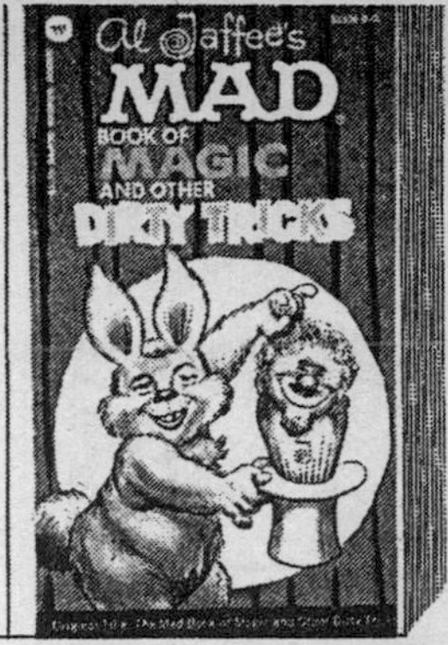
Al Jaffee's
MAD
BOOK OF
MAGIC
AND OTHER
DIRTY TRICKS

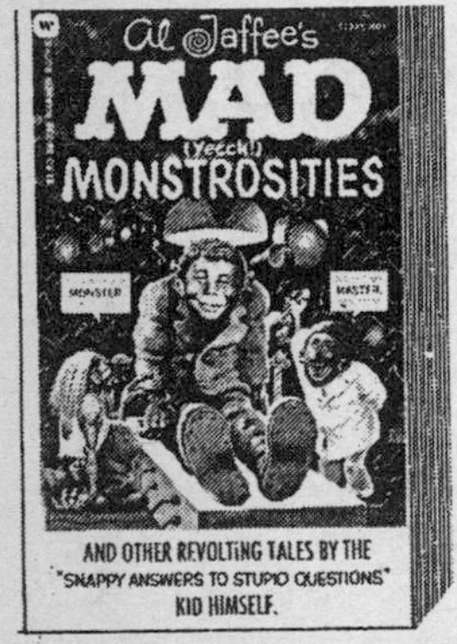
Al Jaffee's
MAD
(Yecch!)
MONSTROSITIES
MONSTER
MASTER
AND OTHER REVOLTING TALES BY THE
"SNAPPY ANSWERS TO STUPID QUESTIONS"
KID HIMSELF.

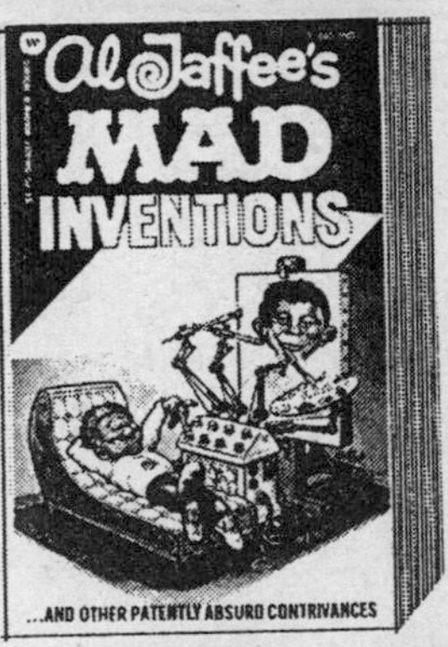
Al Jaffee's
MAD
INVENTIONS
...AND OTHER PATENTLY ABSURD CONTRIVANCES

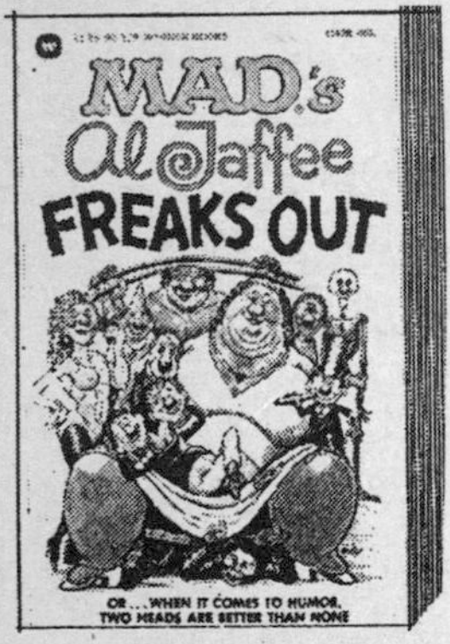
MAD's
Al Jaffee
FREAKS OUT
OR... WHEN IT COMES TO HUMOR,
TWO HEADS ARE BETTER THAN NONE

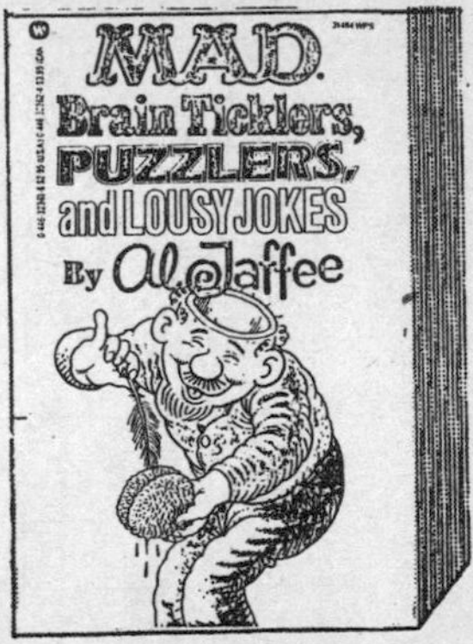
MAD
Brain Ticklers,
PUZZLERS,
and LOUSY JOKES
By Al Jaffee

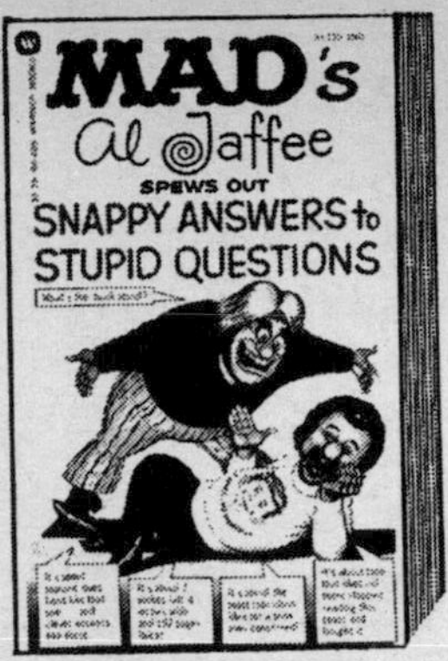
MAD's
Al Jaffee
SPEWS OUT
SNAPPY ANSWERS to
STUPID QUESTIONS

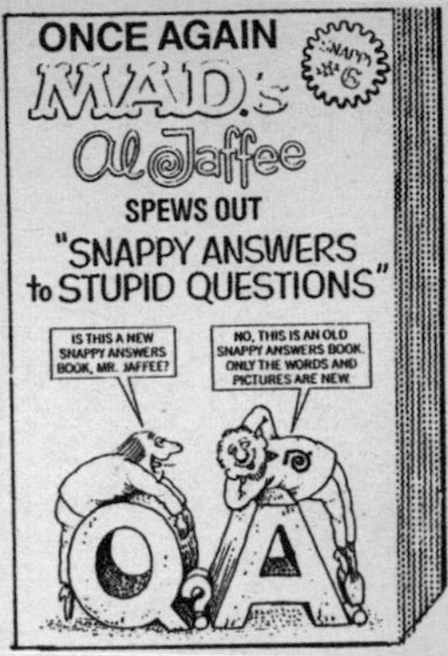
ONCE AGAIN
MAD's
Al Jaffee
SPEWS OUT
"SNAPPY ANSWERS
to STUPID QUESTIONS"
IS THIS A NEW SNAPPY ANSWERS BOOK, MR. JAFFEE?
NO, THIS IS AN OLD SNAPPY ANSWERS BOOK. ONLY THE WORDS AND PICTURES ARE NEW.

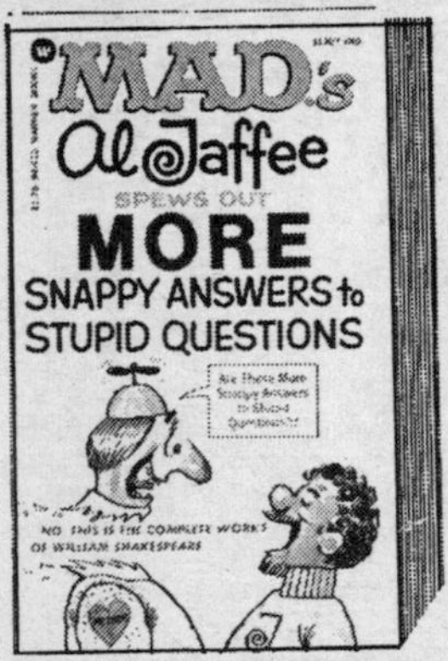
MAD's
Al Jaffee
SPEWS OUT
MORE
SNAPPY ANSWERS to
STUPID QUESTIONS
NO, THIS IS THE COMPLETE WORKS OF WILLIAM SHAKESPEARE

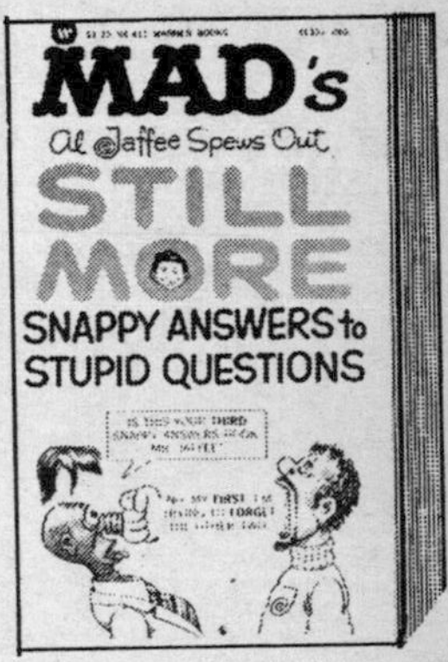
MAD's
Al Jaffee Spews Out
STILL
MORE
SNAPPY ANSWERS to
STUPID QUESTIONS

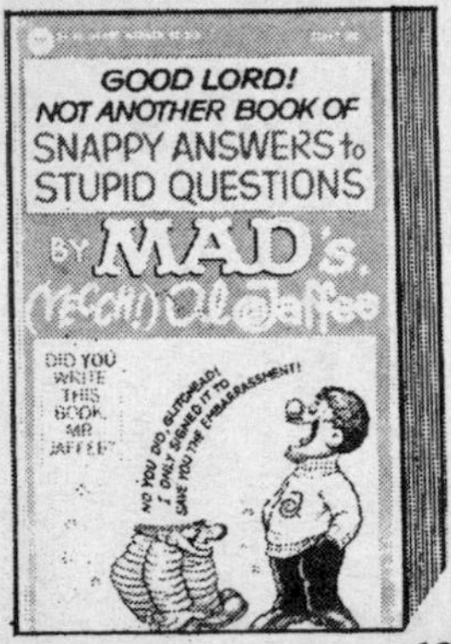
GOOD LORD!
NOT ANOTHER BOOK OF
SNAPPY ANSWERS to
STUPID QUESTIONS
BY MAD's,
(YECCH!) Al Jaffee
DID YOU WRITE THIS BOOK, MR. JAFFEE?
NO YOU DID, GLITCHHEAD! I ONLY SIGNED IT TO SAVE YOU THE EMBARRASSMENT!

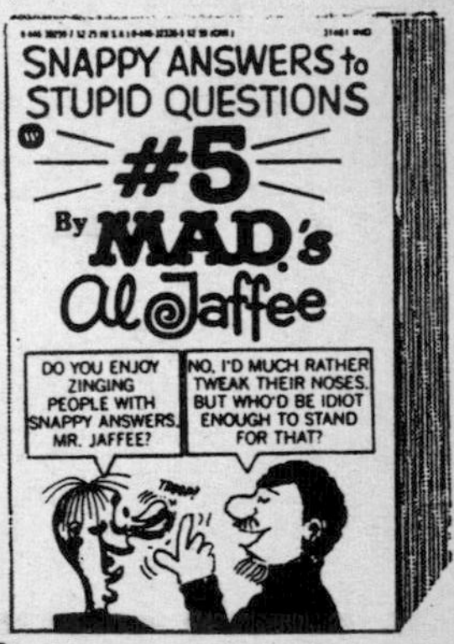
SNAPPY ANSWERS to
STUPID QUESTIONS
#5
By MAD's
Al Jaffee
DO YOU ENJOY ZINGING PEOPLE WITH SNAPPY ANSWERS, MR. JAFFEE?
NO, I'D MUCH RATHER TWEAK THEIR NOSES. BUT WHO'D BE IDIOT ENOUGH TO STAND FOR THAT?